# Behind Everest

*For my husband, the love of my life and father
to our three amazing children.
'We see the same stars.'*

# Behind Everest

## Ruth Mallory's Story –
### First British Expeditions

## Kate Nicholson

PEN & SWORD
HISTORY

First published in Great Britain in 2024 by
Pen & Sword History
An imprint of Pen & Sword Books Limited
Yorkshire – Philadelphia

ISBN 978 1 03611 543 2

Typeset by Mac Style
Printed in the UK by CPI Group (UK) Ltd, Croydon, CR0 4YY.

Pen & Sword Books Limited incorporates the imprints of After
the Battle, Atlas, Archaeology, Aviation, Discovery, Family History,
Fiction, History, Maritime, Military, Military Classics, Politics,
Select, Transport, True Crime, Air World, Frontline Publishing, Leo
Cooper, Remember When, Seaforth Publishing, The Praetorian Press,
Wharncliffe Local History, Wharncliffe Transport, Wharncliffe True
Crime and White Owl.

For a complete list of Pen & Sword titles please contact:

PEN & SWORD BOOKS LIMITED
47 Church Street, Barnsley, South Yorkshire, S70 2AS, England
E-mail: enquiries@pen-and-sword.co.uk
Website: www.pen-and-sword.co.uk
or
PEN AND SWORD BOOKS
1950 Lawrence Rd, Havertown, PA 19083, USA
E-mail: uspen-and-sword@casematepublishers.com
Website: www.penandswordbooks.com

To Ruth:

I remember a passionate lark, from fields at home
Launched in the fern-spread cradle of summer air,
That filled, as no bird but the proud lark dare
With life of liquid sound the whole heaven's dome.
But this lone mystic of Italian hills,
With wings beating at the doors of Paradise,
Not only charms my wakeful ear, but fills
With fire of the one true vision, my smouldering eyes.

Now I am lost in listening, and the streams
Of pure music suspended at a great height
Drop even to me, then borne through quivering light
Float o'er unmeasured space, until it seems
That the same lark winging the universal blue
Wakes the same trembling ecstasy in you.

George Mallory,
Easter Sunday, 1914

'Dearest One, you must know that the spur to do my best is you and you again. I want more than anything to prove worthy of you.'

'I can't tell you how [Everest] possesses me.'

George Mallory to Ruth Mallory

# Contents

# From Everest's Historians

'[Ruth] is in the shadow when she should share the light. She lost [George] towards death four times; once to war and three times to the mountain. To know only George's side of things, to see only through his eyes and those of the men who accompanied him, is to see an incomplete Everest, a partial myth, and to further confirm the heroic-tragic male mountaineering/exploration paradigm.'

Robert MacFarlane
Author of *Mountains of the Mind*

'The key to George Mallory is his beloved wife Ruth, and yet until now Ruth has remained a great mystery. Kate Nicholson's biography is both vital and long overdue ...'

Wade Davis
Author of *Into the Silence*

'You have unearthed some wonderful, compelling material. I was deeply impressed with all you have found out and you have brought life and meaning to a powerful and important character ...'

Peter Gillman
Author of *Wildest Dream*

'a photograph of George Mallory naked in the Himalayan foothills with his rucksack on his back – I do not think one could ever tire of these images.'

Sara Wheeler
Author of *Terra Incognita*

# Acknowledgements

Thank you to Audrey Salkeld (author of many books on George Mallory including *Mystery of Mallory and Irvine*) for her scholarship and generosity; to Peter and Leni Gillman (*Wildest Dream*), Wade Davis (*Into the Silence*) and Robert MacFarlane (*Mountains of the Mind*) for their enduring expert support and belief in this project over many years. Thank you to Sir Christopher Greenwood, Master of Magdalene College for his thoughts on the League of Nations in the context of the interwar period, which included 1921–1924, the Everest years.

Thank you to everyone whom I interviewed when I first started researching this book in 2006 when the last of those who had known Ruth and George Mallory were still alive. It was an enormous honour. For first-hand information about attitudes to women climbers in the earlier years of the century, and traditional climbing kit and techniques, I was privileged to speak to Denise Evans and Gwen Moffat, two of the longest serving members of the women-only Pinnacle Club, then both in their ninetieth year. Denise Evans was the widow of Charles Evans, John Hunt's deputy on the first successful summit of Everest, the 1953 expedition with Edmund Hillary and Tenzing Norgay. Gwen Moffatt (born in 1924 the year George Mallory died) is still an honorary member of the Pinnacle Club and the British Mountaineering Council.

Thank you to all my climbing guides in Wales, Cornwall and the Lake District for memorable days of vertical adventure. I am very grateful to Pinnacle Club archivist Margaret Clennett for finding Ruth's application form and for checking climbing texts. Thank you to all the members of the Pinnacle Club for an unforgettable stay in their club hut and to an introduction to slate climbing in Snowdonia. I am especially grateful to Laura, Justine and Katharine for having been allowed into Ruth's homes: The Holt, Westbrook and Eagles' Nest, all privately owned houses.

This book would not have been possible without interviews with Ruth's relatives and generous access to family material. I am extremely grateful to John Mallory and to his daughter and son-in-law Virginia and Frank Arnott; Ruth Mallory's nephew Paul Morgan; Franz Knefel's wife Marianne Nevel; Mark Arnold-Forster's wife Val and their children; David Pye's sons Tristram and

William; Ruth's friend Hilda Haig-Brown; Geoffrey's son Jocelin Winthrop Young; Andrew Huxley; Geoffrey Keynes's daughter-in-law, Anne; Mary Ann's friend and executor, Joanna Gordon; Kathleen (Scott) Kennet's second son Wayland Kennet and Emily Shackleton's second cousin, Jonathan Shackleton.

Thank you to the amazing archivists at Magdalene College, Cambridge University, Balliol College, Oxford University, the Royal Geographic Society, the Harry Ransom Center, the Scott Polar Research Centre, the Godalming Museum, the Alpine Club and the librarians at Banff Centre for Arts, Canada. I am so grateful for such generous guides and guardians. Thank you to everyone who has allowed me to use quotes and images contained in this book. All letters supplied by Magdalene College are transcribed by permission of the Master and Fellows of Magdalene College, Cambridge. The rare double portrait of George and Ruth at The Holt, from the Francis Fortescue Urquhart Album, has been supplied and reproduced with the kind permission of the Master and Fellows of Balliol College, Oxford University. Thanks also to John Mallory, Marianne Nevel, Frank Arnott, the Alpine Club, the Pinnacle Club and the private collectors, who wish to remain anonymous, who have been so kind as to allow me use of their photographs in this book. Thank you to Joanna Gordon, on behalf of the estate of Mary Ann O'Malley, for allowing me to use all quotes from Mary Ann's unpublished biography of George and her notes from 1924. (Mary Ann became a best-selling novelist writing under the pseudonym, Ann Bridge.) I am also sincerely grateful to the Harry Ransom Center, The University of Texas at Austin, where Mary Ann's papers are archived. Thank you also to The National Archives, Kew. And finally thank you to all my tutors at the Banff Centre for Arts and Creativity – the home of the Banff Mountain Film and Book Festival – for their belief in the importance of this project, their expertise and encouragement.

Thank you to the whole Pen & Sword team, particularly to Lori Jones for her time and expertise and to Amy Jordan for her support from the beginning.

I have endeavoured to contact all copyright holders, and provide proper credits for all material included in this book that is not my own. However, if I have omitted a full credit to any copyrighter holder this is a genuine oversight and I would kindly ask that you make yourself known to the publisher so that this may be corrected in any reprint or future edition. I have thoroughly researched all events and dates, but should there be any inaccuracies please contact the publisher so that these may also be rectified in any subsequent edition.

The phrase 'check your privilege' is a constant pulse for me, as for many biographers. Peggy McIntosh describes it perfectly in the context of *Behind Everest* when she says that '… privilege is like an invisible weightless knapsack of special provisions, maps, passports, codebooks, visas, clothes, tools …' I have tried to be aware of the weight of responsibility in that invisible knapsack whilst attempting to make this book about the universal response to risk. I hope it resonates for some readers. 'My life has a superb cast,' reads a notice on the wall behind me, 'but I can't work out the plot.' Deep and heartfelt gratitude to my sensational cast.

Finally, to Melanie Walton for her inspiration – the leading lady who left the stage well before any of us were ready to live without her. Mel was an example of the best a human being can be. She left behind a secret trail of yellow post-its on which she had scribbled aphorisms in blue biro. I have just turned up one that she must have stuck in my address book on one of her last visits with her family Jim, Sonny and Milo: 'Remember what Mervyn Peake said, "To live at all is miracle enough".'

# Foreword

My father, David Pye, was one of George and Ruth Mallory's closest friends and became George's first biographer in 1927. In the early 1920s my father was still a bachelor. So back then, on George's first expedition to Everest in 1921, George relied on my father to look out for Ruth and to report back in letters posted to Everest Base Camp. Later, my parents, both climbers, got engaged at the Pen-y-Pass Hotel while on a Geoffrey Winthrop Young climbing party. You will hear a great deal of Pen-y-Pass in this book.

I have agreed to write this foreword for two reasons. The first is a letter to Mallory from my father dated July 1921 which I received from Kate Nicholson in January 2024. [See Chapter Fifteen.] It describes a Sunday lunch at The Holt in Godalming with Ruth. As he outlines the scene to George, my father paints a word picture with detail, anecdote, warmth and humour. It beautifully evokes the friendship between these closest of friends and reveals a precious insight into my father's character. He died after a long illness when I was still a student and although I had always loved and idolised him, I had not had the time to get to know him properly as a man of culture and intellect that I always knew him to have been. Readers may appreciate why I have found this letter so precious and moving to read.

The second reason that I have agreed to write this foreword is that after the telegram announcing George's death in 1924, it is revealing that my father didn't write a letter of condolence but went straight around to see Ruth. [See Chapter Twenty-Six.] Each day after her bereavement he collected her to go for a long walk, and all the while he was dealing with his own grief at losing his best friend.

It is odd to learn more about one's own parents when one is in one's eighties but that is what books like these are about. That generation, our parents, or for some readers, grandparents, were on the whole extraordinary people living ordinary lives with grace, resilience, and with a real sense of adventure.

Although I don't remember Ruth (I was only three when she died) I grew up in that world. She was my sister's godmother and I was christened at Westbrook, Ruth's family home in Godalming. This book has repeopled the past with characters like Geoffrey Winthrop Young with his peg leg and the

Mallory children, particularly Clare who I visited in Berkeley with my own family during 1976 when I was teaching in California.

Although the Everest story is 'the' story, this is the story behind it. It is about the impact on those left behind. It is often told like a legend, but it is a real account of people who included my parents. It is the human story that fascinates, that still fascinates and will continue to do so.

William Pye,
2024

# Preface

Christiana Ruth Leigh-Mallory (née Turner) 'Ruth Mallory' is the lady who has been 'inaudible', and perhaps invisible, obscured behind a man and his mountain. Robert MacFarlane, author of *Mountains of the Mind* asserts that George's love affair with Everest was 'a deeply selfish love affair, [that] Mallory could and should have broken off, but which instead destroyed the lives of his wife and his children – as well as his own ...' *Behind Everest* is an attempt to examine MacFarlane's 'love triangle' not from the summit of the triangle down, but from a new and different angle. As George's friend Virginia Woolf put it: 'It is the action of the human heart & not of muscle or fate that we watch.'

A biography of Ruth is the biography of 'the human heart' because Everest is not just Everest, it is an archetype, a figure of speech. Everyone has *their* Everest. It is not just about 'climbing your mountain'. We all live with loved-ones who take risks of some kind or another. This is an extreme version of life, it is what happens at the far edge of normal experience.

This story is about our attitude to risk, to danger. It is about falling; different ways of falling and different kinds of metaphorical rope that can arrest a fall or break under the strain. Part One focuses on a fall witnessed by David Pye in 1914, where George Mallory 'forcibly pushed' his new wife Ruth off a mountain.

In Part Two, George pushes Ruth to a metaphorical edge as she is put under extreme pressure to agree to him joining three successive Everest expeditions. In Part Three, both Ruth and George are falling. Ruth is trying not to fall into the trap of believing that George never intended to return from Everest. She is trying not to give in to total despondency, grief and loss of agency having become beholden to her father. She is trying to ignore rumours that George never planned to use his ticket home.

Part Three examines how George is falling on Everest through a trail of artifacts that provide clues to what happened on 8 June 1924. In the maelstrom, there is a hand-knitted woollen mitten, number 9 oxygen cylinder and an ice axe with three nicks in its wooden handle (later found to be Andrew 'Sandy' Irvine's).

Both the Mallorys face danger, but only when they are climbing together are they facing the same danger. This book examines the balance between not just physical danger, but the danger of expectation; the danger of prejudice; the danger of ambition, and that complicated real and present danger: summit fever.

Climbing Everest was a risk undertaken through personal choice unlike the danger faced by the millions who had just died in what would become known as the First World War. But it was a choice influenced by the momentum of that war, duty to the British Empire and the expectations of heroic self-sacrifice. Despite this, in many ways, Ruth and George were part of a generation who were truly modern; their sensibility forged before the war and not just by it. They questioned everything: gender roles, parenting, religion, class, education, nationhood, sexuality, art and architecture, fashion (clothes or no clothes) and more, so that both emerge as strangely modern and relatable.

Part of the reason that Ruth's story has not been told in full before is that her letters to George in the Everest years are, with one exception, missing. (I discuss what may have happened to them in Part Four.) But the Everest letters (written between 1921 and 1924) are not the only letters Ruth wrote. Ruth wrote daily to George during the First World War. Other Everest historians have been looking at them for an insight into George's character rather than Ruth's. I am interested in them insofar as they provide an insight into her, which means that many of the quotes in this book have never been published before. In these letters, we can hear a voice that is honest and unequivocal. Ruth's voice in the 'love triangle', which Robert MacFarlane refers to in the opening quote, must become 'audible' if it is to lead us through the story that we are about to hear.

I am interested in Ruth's story because my husband climbed Everest by the same route that Mallory reconnoitred from the north. The main tension for me, as it was then and still is now for anyone who has skin in the game, is 'will they come back'. Many don't. Everest is strewn with bodies. Like George, my husband was a schoolmaster. Our children were the same ages that the Mallorys' three children were, in 1921, on the first of George's three expeditions to Everest. When George and my husband left home they left a crawling baby, when they returned the baby could walk. Except that the third time George left his family for Everest he did not come back.

During the time that my husband was away, the time that the final outcome was yet to be decided, Ruth Mallory held my hand across a century. That is the best way I can describe it. When he came back she stuck around. Oddly, that was perhaps when I needed her most. I think that I must have experienced some kind of post-stress reaction. Life was not straightforward when my husband was away. Our middle child was ill. But I think, now, that it is time to pass Ruth on to other people who need her inspiration, her 'crystal wisdom' and her hand in theirs.

To find Ruth, I have interrogated the sources, picked up odd phrases and granite boulders (more difficult). I have walked around her homes for what I am now dismayed to realise is two fifths of my life. But I have spent happy days piecing together unpublished handwritten manuscripts, journals, climbing scrapbooks and family photograph albums. I have trawled through archives of her letters (which are self-edited) and spoken to Ruth's relatives and friends (which are not).

To construct Ruth's story, I have used narrative non-fiction techniques delivering 'scenes' as historical reconstructions to put the reader into the middle of her life and into 'the room where it happened'. I have interleaved these with a more conventional biography, close reading and re-reading of key turning points in her life. Each chapter presents the reader with the key sources that I studied. This is not a glazed mirrored high-rise building with all the services hidden under a smooth skin. I think of it like the Lloyds headquarters in London or the Pompidou Centre in Paris – all the workings are on the outside. I am trying to wave the piece of evidence in front of you, to show you the workings; its heft (in the case of the boulder) and its texture (the hand that wrote that letter) and then try to give it context and meaning as a way into understanding Ruth's attitude to risk, danger and life.

Ruth was there at the beginning of a revolution in attitudes to women's climbing. She was one of the pioneers. Ruth did not see George's expeditions from an armchair, but from a mountain. To understand her, I have learned to climb.

Ruth was a 'natural' climber. She learned to climb before there were such things as purpose built climbing walls, auto-belays, nylon ropes, helmets and harnesses. I have reclimbed some of her precise climbing routes. I have pushed my toes into the cracks she must have used as footholds, hooked the tips of my fingers into her handholds feeling the texture of the rock. I have felt the exposure of those rock faces, the muscle tension of holding positions, the thrill, the danger and the story in those climbs: their beginning, middle and end.

George was happiest on a rock face and happier still on a rock face with Ruth. Theirs was a vertical romance: flirting with danger. Throughout the First World

War, Ruth and George climbed all over the British Isles whenever George had leave from the fighting. Ruth lived in fear of the random bullet that might kill her husband, the father of their children. Until Armistice in 1918, she climbed as though every climb might be their last together. Somehow in seven years – sixteen months of which George was away fighting – Ruth learned to lead climbs herself.

But Ruth was tied to a man who was roped to that mountain. As Robert MacFarlane says:

> Eventually and terribly, [George] Mallory's yearning for mountains would prove stronger than his love for his wife and family. Three centuries earlier he would have been cast into Bedlam for his obsession with Everest. In 1924, his death on the mountain cast a nation into mourning and Mallory into myth.

This, then, is the woman behind that myth. The woman 'behind Everest'.

# Magdalene Centenary Project

*Behind Everest* is published in the centenary year of George Leigh-Mallory's death on Everest on 8 June 1924. Ruth's letters to George are all archived at George's alma mater, Magdalene College, Cambridge University. The Magdalene Centenary project to make 440 of Ruth Mallory's letters available online, is underway as *Behind Everest* goes to press. It has been a privilege to preview the work in process. Archivists Katy Green and Kate Stockwell are still 'frantically' scanning and metadata-ing each letter to allow access at the touch of a button.

There are perhaps two advantages to the analogue versions that I have worked with. The first is touch. There is something of the portal sensation to sitting at a desk in the oak panelled Pepys Library, holding a letter that Ruth touched – the texture of a history with the scent of the past. The other advantage is 'the chance meeting'.

One day in the university summer holiday, I arrived at Magdalene College to work in the archive and became lost in the forest of scaffolding of a renovation project. Seeing a man wandering about in deck shoes, I asked him for directions. Once I was sitting at my archive desk, it dawned on me that my guide had been none other than Sir Christopher Greenwood GBE CMG KC, Master of Magdalene College and a former British judge at the International Court of Justice. Since international arbitration is central to Ruth's story, I am very grateful for that chance meeting and for Chris's generosity and expertise.

# Notes on Sources

**Magdalene College Archives, Cambridge University: Mallory Papers**
The Mallory Papers, including letters between Ruth and George, and to them, are all at Magdalene College Archives. (Group F Mallory Papers Files 1-VII, received January 1968 and March 1986 from John Mallory.)

**Alpine Club Archives**
The Alpine Club Archives in London holds Geoffrey Winthrop Young's Pen-y-Pass photograph albums, Harold Porter's journal and minutes of Mount Everest Committee meetings. Pen y Pass Albums – Geoffrey Winthrop Young – C140. Climbing Diaries Volume 1 1905–1925 – HEL Porter – D63. Mount Everest Committee Papers – P37.

**Royal Geographical Society Archives**
The Royal Geographical Society Archives in London holds Geoffrey Winthrop Young's collection (EE/3/5 RGS), including Ruth's letters to Young (EE/3/5/18-24) and Ruth Mallory to Arthur Hinks (EE/3/4/22). G. Mallory correspondence (Box 3 EE/3/1). Arthur Hinks to John Noel (EE/31/4/13).

**Harry Ransom Center, The University of Texas at Austin**
The Harry Ransom Center, The University of Texas at Austin in the United States of America holds Ann Bridge (Mary Ann O'Malley) Papers. (5C EW Box 19, Folder 8 and George Mallory Papers 5C EW Box 19, Folder 2.)

**Other Archives and Collections**
Private collections, family collections and interviews are referenced in the Appendices.

# Introduction
## '... pushed her forcibly over the edge!'

'There is a line made by climbing and a line made by falling. There is the flawed line of my body. The parallel lines two bodies make. The line of someone walking into the distance. Someone else moving close. The line of want, the line of touch, of merging.'

Helen Mort,
*A Line Above the Sky:*
*A Story of Mountains and Motherhood,*
Ebury Press, an imprint of Ebury Publishing,
Penguin Random House, London, 2022

## Snowdonia, North Wales – December 1914

It is a clear night in Snowdonia. The Milky Way makes a glittering line above the sky. It is perfectly lined up with the white valley rising to Llanberis Pass. Behind the Pen-y-Gwryd Hotel, the land rises steadily up to the rocky teeth of Glyder Fach. To the south-west the surface of Llyn Llydaw is like the crater of a frozen volcano. In the moonlight, the miners' track traces a contour of shadow outlining its northern bank. Above it all, the pyramidal peak of Snowdon shoulders a few wisps of snowy cloud.

The door to the Pen-y-Gwryd opens sending a shaft of light out of the classical pillared portico, down the stone steps. Two silhouetted men emerge onto the forecourt in shirt sleeves. A plume of smoke rises vertically up from the hotel's chimney into the clear night air. Is this the end of the gale or the eye of the storm? In the stables, the hotelier's coach horses whinny and stamp hollow hooves. The men walk back up the steps and shut the door behind them leaving the mountains to the stars.

Inside the lobby of that famous hostelry, steeped in British mountaineering history, Ruth sits beside the fire. A paraffin lamp is on the table beside her, with the brass dial on the neck turned up to allow a bright flame. Light flickers off the gold chain encircling the plait around her head. In her right hand, she holds a pair of heavy scissors. She makes a small incision at the top of her hand bag and works down towards the bottom. Turning the leather in her hand she proceeds across the base and on until she lifts a square of leather off the bag and sets it on the wooden table in front of her.

At her feet a stout walking boot lies on its side revealing a sole criss-crossed with nails. There is the lingering smell of burned leather where the upper part has a scorched hole. By mistake she placed it too near the fire to dry out after a day on the hills. With her fingers she pushes the square of leather inside the boot until it forms a patch under the crack. Ruth slides a thick palmer onto her right hand and picks up the needle. She has always wanted to work with leather and there is a familiarity here that she has not yet mastered with climbing. Until her marriage to George, at the end of July 1914, she had never climbed anything but an apple tree. In the last five months, she has been on a near vertical learning curve. But George is a hard master. He has high standards.

Ruth turns the boot on her lap. The action of sewing, even leather, soothes her. Sewing takes her back to the comforting presence of her late mother sewing fine art pieces to exhibit at the New Gallery in London's Regent Street. If Ruth raises her head from her sewing she can see a piece of faded red Irish frieze nailed to the wall. The frieze was torn from a dress belonging to climber Edith Stopford who was climbing the Roof route up Y Lliwedd when she ripped a foot off the bottom of her skirt to be free for a foothold. Before it was retrieved as a trophy for the hotel, it lay through long seasons on the East Buttress as a touch of colour and a protest against 'a perishing fashion'. Back then ladies had to approach the climb in corsets and long skirts with plus fours underneath. When they reached the intended crag, they disappeared behind a rock and removed the corset, taking care to replace it on their return lest they should be considered 'fast' by the locals.

While Ruth repairs her boot, the two men – George and his climbing companion and friend David Pye – discuss plans for the following day. They spread a map to trace a route over the Crib-y-Ddysgl ridge to the summit of Snowdon. They might climb the Parson's Nose to get there. Is Ruth game? George quotes a letter he once received from his friend the writer Lytton Strachey: 'Can anything be more bitter than to be doomed to a life of literature and hot-water bottles, when one's a Pirate at heart.'

Ruth is a climbing novice but she is also a pirate. She is fit, strong and she walks so fast that her sisters complain they have to run beside to keep up. Ruth is struck by George's notion of climbing as a form of dancing; somewhere between sport and art. There is such grace and beauty in the way that George moves across a rock face, it's like 'watching water flowing uphill'.

Now in the early days of their marriage, Ruth is not only his wife but his climbing pupil. The barometer on the wall by the porch is falling when the hotelier gives out candles to light the stairs to bed.

* * *

The next day Ruth is hunched against the shrieking wind. They have climbed the Parson's Nose and now they are following the horseshoe ridge round towards the path leading up to the summit of Snowdon. To her left is the snow slope down to the frozen lake, Llyn Llydaw. In the mist and driving snow, the slope between where she is standing and that lake looks precipitously steep, terrifying. Ruth's eyelashes are frosted, she is cold, deeply cold. A thick climbing rope leads forward to George and back to David. It is tied around her, pressing her tweed jacket against her waist. Inside her boots, her frozen toes feel uneven. Last night's mend? Ruth tips the crown of her head into the wind and, eyes smarting in the stinging snow, tries to see to place her feet in George's footsteps.

When they reach Bwlch Glas, the dip in the ridge above Llyn Llydaw, the whirlwind intensifies still further so that it's difficult to keep their footing. Ruth angles her face away from the wind, pauses and gulps air into her lungs between every couple of steps. George turns and comes towards her. It looks as if he wants to tell her something.

Ruth stands with her legs apart, bracing against the blast of freezing air. George puts his face against her hair. She can feel his warm breath against the side of her face, the top of her neck. His closeness is intimate but she can't hear what he is saying. He moves back and looks intently into her face to see if she has understood. She shakes her head. He gives up and gestures at Ruth, pointing down the horribly steep looking slope. Then he mimes diving over it. A deadly game of charades. She hesitates. In that moment of hesitation there is a stillness. Ruth tries to reconcile George's instruction to throw herself over the edge, with her instinct is to cling on. Can ropes really be trusted to 'catch' a person in mid-air or to arrest a fall, a slip?

Bracing herself now against the force of the gale screaming up over the ridge, Ruth checks the twisted rope around her waist through her woollen gloves. She can smell the mineral scent of snow-sleet dry in her nostrils. Her eyes are screwed up trying to read George's expression; to deduce his intentions from the small part of his face that is visible between his muffler and his hat. Ruth has risked being roped to this man both on and off the mountain. Surely, he cannot mean that he wants her to dive off the ridge down that precipice?

Suddenly, George's expression changes. He takes her by the shoulders and pushes her over the edge. She is turning, falling through space.

# Part I

# Before Everest

'Are you a climber?'

I'm standing in a garden in Pretoria, South Africa with a man who has done a lot of climbing, but has avoided high altitude peaks. It's a reasonable question. Am I? I'm not sure. In 1995, I climbed 19,347 feet Cotopaxi in Ecuador as a sort of tourist-climber.

'That's quite high to go just as a tourist,' he says, 'what was it like?'

'Crevasses, crampons, ropes, ice axes, climbing in the dark.' I don't tell him that although I was working in Quito, Ecuador's capital at an altitude of 9,350 feet, I had only done about half an hour's technical training for the climb on the scree slope outside Cotopaxi's Refugio. I also don't tell him that at the summit I experienced overwhelming ennui. (I am never bored.) I told my guide that, if it was all the same with him, I would just have a little nap. There *was* a photograph of me on the summit looking as if I would rather be watching paint dry. Fortunately, we made a speedy descent and I made a speedier apology. It was my first experience of altitude sickness.

In *Travels Amongst the Great Andes of the Equator* by Edward Whymper, published by John Murray in 1892, he describes Cotopaxi as 'the perfect volcano'. Whymper was drawn to Ecuador because Chimborazo (20,548 feet), Cotopaxi's then unconquered near neighbour, was thought to be the highest mountain in the world. At the time there was some discussion over whether height should be measured from sea level, or from the centre of the earth to account for the equatorial bulge.

Looking at the 'perfect volcano' framed in the window of Whymper's bedroom at Hacienda San Agustin del Callo, I had to agree. It is a blunt equilateral triangle with icing on the top. Like me Whymper ascended from the north, but unlike me, he really did sleep on the summit of that mountain. He did so, deliberately, as part of a study into the causes and effects of altitude sickness. The first edition of his Andes book includes pages and pages of data at the front. It is as if he was trying to prove to the critics of mountain climbing per se that he was not just a summit bagger, but a responsible man of science: an explorer. He was awarded the Royal Geographical Society's Patron's Medal, the highest honour for his work, but most of his peers still believed his science was an excuse for climbing rather than a reason.

Back then, as Robert MacFarlane lays out so eloquently in *Mountains of the Mind: A History of a Fascination*, published by Granta Books in 2003, climbing mountains was considered by many to be a kind of madness. Queen Victoria tried to ban it. There were so many fatalities. She didn't need summits in the British Empire; she needed men to 'found colonies and settle them' and she wanted productive land.

In MacFarlane's chapter 'The Pursuit of Fear', he quotes Leslie Stephen (a man who is introduced properly later). Stephen liked to imagine himself not just as an Alpinist, but as a polar explorer. 'Struggling in the winter towards a hut,' Stephen wrote, 'one is but playing at danger, but for the moment one can sympathise with the Arctic [or Antarctic] adventurer pushing towards the pole'. The mountains were a place to reimagine yourself, or as Stephen christened the European Alps 'a playground' – in which grown men could play at danger. 'Nevertheless,' concludes MacFarlane, a mountaineer himself, 'it didn't matter how you imagined yourself or the mountains: the landscape could still kill you.'

This is a book about Ruth but she never puts her opinion on Everest into words. Even George struggles. 'I can't tell you,' he reveals to Ruth, 'how it possesses me'. Later, he calls it 'that infernal mountain'.

In a paragraph taken from notes for a lecture script that George gave at the Broadhurst Theatre in New York in 1923, we can hear him. We can also hear Ruth. This rhetorical style – the question and the expected answer – allows us an insight into their conversations. George used Ruth both as a practice audience for his lectures and as a sounding board for life. I imagine George, standing with his back to the fire in his study at The Holt, asking Ruth whether she thought this paragraph 'would go'. It was the expression she would recognise from rock climbing. It meant, 'would be climbable'. In this context, he needed to know whether she thought it would grab an audience's attention. (Since Ruth didn't accompany George to New York, he may later have tried it out on Stella Cobden-Sanderson who was already there.) But for now, at The Holt in 1923, halfway through Ruth's story, imagine her there in one of the shabby armchairs with her blue eyes fixed on her husband. The question in her head: 'would it go?'

'Does the Mount Everest expedition serve useful ends?' George begins and then pauses.

It may. The geologists want a stone from the top. The physiologists will be interested to know more about the limits of human endurance in a rarefied atmosphere. But I confess it is not as a potential victim of physiological experiment that I regard my own part in the expedition. And cutting out all scientific objects, do we still want Mount Everest to be climbed?

Here, I imagine a pause for Ruth's silent response.

'Well,' finishes George, 'if I were to tell you anything else, I hope you would howl me down at once …'

That is what George hopes. Will we? Did they? Would she?

# Chapter One

# Falling

David Pye,
pp.74–75,
*George Leigh Mallory: A Memoir*,
Oxford University Press, Oxford, 1927

Returning now to that moment in Snowdonia in December 1914, Ruth is still mid-air. She has just been pushed off the ridge in Snowdonia by her husband of a few months. That vertical vignette is written up by David Pye in his slippers with his fire crackling in the grate of his bachelor rooms at Trinity College Cambridge. By then David also has access to *Mountain Craft* by Geoffrey Winthrop Young, published by Methuen & Co. Ltd. in 1920. Geoffrey is George's climbing mentor. On page 25, Geoffrey advises leaders like George about what to do if they encounter what he calls 'hysterical obstinacy' in their climbing party.

> The hysteria takes the form of a refusal to move up or down, and, without any violent symptoms, remains impervious to reason or direct remonstrance … I have seen a guide use a startling slap on the cheek, in an extreme, case with good effect; or a jerk on the rope that forces the victim to scramble to recover his own footing, [which] may break the spell.

Was Ruth being 'hysterically obstinate' in refusing to dive off Bwlch Glas or just sensible? Was she scared or was she dumbfounded that George would suggest jumping when they could climb down with control?

For George danger held a deadly glamour. He told Ruth that climbing would lose its allure without the 'spice of danger'. But, for me, this particular scene, where George pushes Ruth off a mountain, addresses different kinds of risk, different species of danger. To start with, there is the gamble of who we choose to spend our lives with.

This story migrated from David's write-up into two pages of the biography he would write of George in 1927. In that biography, Ruth is, as Robert MacFarlane states, almost inaudible. David never quotes her directly. The nearest he gets is to say that 'she told me':

She had always, she told me, been one of those who could never be at the foot of a hill without longing to be at the top.

This gives us an insight into how Ruth later saw Everest. On some level, she must have empathised with George's 'longing to be at the top'. But David never tells us what 'she told me' about being pushed off that mountain in Wales by her husband of five months. Instead he sticks to Ruth-the-rock-climber. He explains that Ruth was 'a first rate and devoted rock-climber' with 'the spirit of the mountaineer'. What exactly happened after George pushed Ruth off that mountain? Whatever happened it must have happened within a few seconds.

Firstly, David watches George take Ruth by the shoulders. Does George push her shoulders from behind? Does she fall face forwards so that she is able to put her hands out to have some control over the landing? Or is George facing her? Does he push her over backwards so that she has to flail her arms to turn in the direction of the fall? David doesn't say, but he is obviously shocked. Later when he fixes this scene for posterity, he uses an exclamation mark. 'Taking his wife by the shoulders, Mallory simply pushed her forcibly over the edge!'

Why does David use the word 'forcibly'? Forcibly does not sound like a gentle push. Nor does it sound as if Ruth was compliant. In the next sentence David says, 'I meanwhile, guessing what he was up to, stood down on the windward side to hold her rope.' David is obliged to guess. So when David sees George take Ruth by the shoulders, he moves upwind and braces himself to take the strain on the rope.

David knows that it will only be the counterweight of his body against hers that could stop her falling as he does not have time to secure himself with a piton or other climbing gear. Ruth is about 5 foot and 6 inches, and slim. She must only have been airborne for a moment. But Ruth is wary of ropes.

In a decade from this scene, George will select a light weight 9 millimetre cotton rope with a red tracer thread to take on his final push to the summit of Everest. The tracer has a lower stretch capability than the rope itself. If that thread is broken the rope has been under too much stress and should be discarded. It is a risk reducing measure. Geoffrey might almost be talking about Ruth when on page 75 of *Mountain Craft* he states:

Even when a rope shows no appreciable wear, it may have been subjected to some sudden severe strain which has robbed it of its virtue. The virtue of a rope lies in its resilience, its spring and give, not in its toughness or thickness.

Ruth only stops falling when the rope between her and David holds. The rope between her and George should never have had to take the strain because they were roped at regular intervals and George was nearer to Ruth than David. 'Next he [George] jumped down beside her.' Does George wait until she has secured herself on the slope or is she still scrabbling for purchase on the steep snow? At some point David joins them. The ridge shields them from gale-force wind screaming over their heads – 'and soon we were all gasping in comparative peace while the wind still roared.'

Can you hear Ruth's reaction or are her words whipped away? Instead of telling us what Ruth said, did or felt afterwards, without breaking paragraph, David immediately gives us another anecdote. It seems that the incident was just one of many in the Christmas holiday fortnight at the Pen-y-Gwryd Hotel, where George was testing Ruth. Immediately after pushing his wife off a mountain, George tells David to lead, to go in front of Ruth on the rope so that George can keep his wife, 'his pupil under his corrective eye'.

Later, roped as a three with David in front and George behind, Ruth suddenly jumps forward. Perhaps she is jumping between two rocks, two footholds? The rope from her waist to George tightens. George is obviously shocked. It nearly pulls him out of his steps. It nearly pulls him off the mountain. 'Damn you, dear,' says George, 'you mustn't do that'.

When George pushes Ruth her reaction is not recorded. When Ruth pulls George his reaction is. David is writing George's biography not Ruth's, but David's verbatim quote is interesting. Rather like converting the worth of money into 'today's money', a century ago 'damn' was as strong as it got in front of a lady. That 'damn' was a more powerful swear word by 100 years-fold.

Did Ruth swear when George pushed her? 'I did say a lusty damn' she will admit to him in the future, on 28 May 1916. If Ruth swore back in 1914, David would have edited it out of the official record as inappropriately unladylike. Perhaps her reaction was less coherent or less distilled than a single 'damn'; more like a scream or a cartoon speech ballooned 'arggg'.

The more I try to unravel this scene and its 'damn' follow up, the more Ruth eludes me. But there are somethings that we do know. Ruth was human. When humans are pushed off mountains, when humans fall, there is a flash of adrenaline through the body. When humans are brought up short by a rope around their waists, the rope presses into the soft tissue, it makes itself felt. Sometimes when it tightens from above, when the person on the other end is above the person falling, it squeezes the ribs and pushes the air up out of the lungs. Winded lungs, a cold sweat, the heart pistoning, the brain racing so that the moment seems to slow down.

This moment will have a direct parallel on Everest in a decade's time, on 8 June 1924. The 9 millimetre rope around George's corpse, found on Everest in 1999, has a frayed end. Unlike the rope tied around Ruth's waist in Snowdonia in 1914, the one around George's waist broke. Before it broke, it tightened suddenly from above; inflicting significant bruising and damaging his ribs. For bruising like the marks found around George's torso to form, the body must have been alive for at least twenty minutes to one hour after the injury occurred. This becomes important, perhaps even central, to the story ahead. But for now, George is found on a slope of about the same incline as that down which he pushed Ruth. From barometric readings at the 1924 Everest expedition's Camp I, it is highly likely that George fell in a snow storm 'of hurricane strength'. The circumstances are strangely similar, but for the small matter of Snowdon having a height of 3,560 feet and Everest, well.

But this is not yet about Everest. This is not about George. This is about Ruth. It is about a specific moment in Snowdonia, which David describes as 'pure mountain melodrama'. 'Melodrama' rather than tragedy. The lines between the genre are blurred. Edward Whymper's *Scrambles Amongst the Alps*, published by John Murray in 1871, is a foundation text for George, and sets the theme for the first part of their marriage. It is George's 'bible', but I want Ruth to introduce it, to see the story not from the top of the triangle, but from her angle. For now, all we need to understand is that in this 'bible' there are etchings of the climbers in mid-air. Whymper, the author, illustrator and expedition leader has captured the moment that his teammates leave the security of the rock face, the moment their rope breaks. At the time Whymper is having nightmares. Every night he dreams that his four friends are sliding across his bedroom floor, arms outstretched, bodies intact, a surprised expression on their faces. By etching it, he can rewind to before the rope breaks, and play it forward to the moment they disappear. But in the 'bible' he has etched the very moment that they hang suspended in mid-air. He was trying to understand, to explain to the court and the court of public opinion but mostly perhaps to himself.

By slowing the melodramatic moment that Ruth is pushed off Bwlch Glas right down, by etching it, by cross hatching it in words, we might catch her expression, imagine what she feels, hear her reaction. If we can catch her mid-air, perhaps we can finally begin to understand Ruth.

# Chapter Two

# 'Twice Born'

Mary Ann O'Malley,
Unpublished manuscript
of biography of George Mallory,
1924–1925,
archived in the Harry Ransom Center,
The University of Texas at Austin, USA

Mary Ann O'Malley, a friend of George Mallory's, has just noticed a letter that has landed on her doormat. Six foot tall and pregnant, she stoops carefully to pick it up. Jane Austen, Mary Ann's favourite novelist, often brought characters into her stories via a letter. Who will Mary Ann find in this one? In a decade's time this letter will be quoted on page 85 of Mary Ann's 'story' of George. It is the first written mention of Ruth.

At the moment Mary Ann receives the letter in May 1914, she does not know Ruth. On opening it, she will meet her for the first time as 'my niece, Ruth Turner'. Mary Ann prides herself on uncovering a biography. She will quickly find out that Ruth Turner is the unmarried middle daughter of Arts and Crafts royalty. Ruth's father is the eccentric dandy architect Hugh Thackeray Turner, and her late mother, the celebrated fine art embroiderer Mary 'May' Elizabeth Turner.

As friends and disciples of renowned activist and designer William Morris, both Ruth's parents exhibited at the first annual Arts and Crafts exhibition in London in 1888. The family live in some style at Westbrook, Godalming; a country house designed by Thackeray Turner himself in the Arts and Crafts style. It is possible that Gertrude Jekyll, May's great friend, shucked off her infamous gardening boots and embroidered her suffragette banners in the morning room at Westbrook, while Ruth's mother created her Opus Anglicanum. May was the more accomplished needle artist, but when it came to designing the garden at Westbrook, Gertrude's signature is everywhere. The garden was, and is, a work of art.

In 1914, seven years after May Turner's death, Mary Ann is opening the envelope addressed to Mrs O. O'Malley. The letter inside is signed by Rosamond

Wills. Ruth was 15 when her mother May died of pneumonia in February 1907 at the age of 53. Since then, Rosamond has become almost a surrogate mother to Ruth. But she is not as artistic or enterprising as her late sister May.

Mary Ann may already know that May Turner and William Morris's daughter May Morris set up the Women's Guild. It was formed on 18 January 1907 in the studio of muralist painter Mary Sargant Florence. The Women's Guild was established as a vital alternative to the two men only guilds: the Art Workers' Guild (founded in 1884) and the Guild and School of Handicraft (founded in 1888). The Women's Guild had approximately sixty members; one of whom was Emma Jane Catherine Cobden-Unwin (sister of Julia Sarah Anne 'Annie' Cobden-Sanderson, a friend of Ruth's parents). The eleventh Arts and Crafts exhibition, at the Royal Academy of Arts, Burlington House, London will be held two years after Mary Ann receives Rosamond's letter. Ruth will exhibit her art with the Women's Guild at that exhibition.

But for now, in 1914, Mary Ann O'Malley turns to the first page of the letter that she has just taken out of the envelope: 'My niece, Ruth Turner, is engaged to be married,' writes Rosamond:

> ... she is one of the 'twice-born': a soul of the most crystal wisdom, simplicity and goodness – pure gold all through. She is going to marry a young Charterhouse master, George Mallory – I hope he is good enough for her, but it is hardly possible.

Mary Ann has been dreading this letter. The year before, she had not given up hope that she might be 'going to marry a young Charterhouse master, George Mallory' herself.

George is the son of Herbert Leigh-Mallory who is rector of Mobberley, Cheshire and will later become vicar of St John's, Birkenhead. After Winchester College and then Magdalene College, Cambridge University, George began working as a teacher at Charterhouse School. This allows him a modest income and long school holidays in which to pursue his passion for rock climbing. George met Mary Ann climbing with her brother in Zermatt in 1909. George subsequently introduced her to Geoffrey Winthrop Young's exclusive climbing meets which gather at the Pen-y-Pass Hotel in Snowdonia at the head of Llanberis Pass.

As Mary Ann reads the letter, she can picture George, tall, dark haired and painfully handsome. His peers, men and women alike, swoon at the mention of 'Sir Galahad' as Bloomsbury artist Duncan Grant nicknamed George. Lytton Strachey wrote to Virginia Woolf's sister Vanessa Bell: 'My hand trembles, my heart palpitates ... he's six foot high, with the body of an athlete by Praxiteles and a face – oh incredible.' But George was uneasy in female company and told Mary Ann that she was the first girl that didn't make him feel 'like a mouse'.

At the time she receives Rosamond's letter in May 1914, Mary Ann is newly married but still chronically heartsore. She would still far rather be the subject than the recipient of Rosamond's letter. When, much later, David Pye asks her: 'How much were you in love with George?' Mary Ann will reply honestly and record her reply on page 52 of her notes titled 'November 1925': 'I was prepared to be to any extent – in fact I suppose I was.'

Rosamond, who does not know this, first met Mary Ann through the Ladies' Alpine Club, founded in 1907. Rosamond is the wife of another climber, Dr William Alfred Wills. Her father-in-law Sir Alfred Wills was a High Court judge and president of the Alpine Club. His ascent of the Wetterhorn above Grindelwald in the Bernese Alps in 1854 heralded what is now known as 'the golden age of Alpinism'. Wills became president in 1863; seven years after Mount Everest was discovered to be the highest mountain in the world.

When Rosamond writes her letter to Mary Ann, the Ladies' Alpine Club is just 7 years old. It was founded as an alternative to the long-established Alpine Club, which refused to accept women members on account of their supposed physical and moral deficiencies in the matter of mountain climbing. Based in London's Marylebone, the LAC organises a monthly lecture and a dinner. Each member can invite a guest. Just over one year before Mary Ann received Rosamond's letter, she invited George. He regretted that he could not accompany Mary Ann to the dinner because he had already accepted an invitation from another member, a Mabel Capper. He was sorry, but she must see that etiquette demanded etc. At the time Mary Ann was deeply hurt by what she saw as George's rejection. When subsequently, he declined to come climbing with her in Scotland, she quickly accepted the first marriage proposal that came her way.

A year later, married and five months pregnant, Mary Ann stands by her escritoire, trying to read both the text and the subtext in Rosamond's letter. This man, 'George Mallory', Rosamond writes, is a teacher and a 'young' one at that. There is, of course, no money in teaching. Rosamond knows that Mary Ann has not married money. Her husband, Owen, has a junior role in the Foreign Office but things are tight and neither of them have family money to fall back on. By contrast, Mary Ann is aware that Rosamond's father, Ruth's maternal grandfather Thomas Wilde Powell, was a successful businessman and well known philanthropist. Ruth Turner, whoever she is, must be beyond financial worries.

Mary Ann might have understood Rosamond's reference to Ruth as 'twice-born' as a typical colonialism that peppered polite conversation at this time when the sun never set on the British Empire. In Buddhism, the main religion in Tibet, 'twice-born' meant a physical birth, followed by a spiritual one. What would Rosamond and Mary Ann have known of Tibet? Whatever they knew of that 'Forbidden Kingdom', they would both have associated it with the name, Sir Francis Younghusband.

At the time of Rosamond's letter to Mary Ann in 1914, Francis Younghusband is on track to be elected president of the Royal Geographic Society, headquartered in London on Kensington Gore. Younghusband intends to use his tenure to conquer Mount Everest. He wants to put a British subject on the very top of the world. Any expedition – which will require a campaign-style caravan of luggage, porters and yaks – will favour access to the mountain over the plains of Tibet rather than the mountains of Nepal.

Younghusband is central to Ruth's story. With a preposterous stiff grey moustache covering half his face, he is the quintessential colonial adventurer. Educated at Clifton College, Bristol, Younghusband has fellow pupil Henry Newbolt's jingoistic poem *Vitaï Lampada*, as his mantra. He sees himself as a key player in the British Empire which urges all Englishmen to 'play up, play up and play the game'.

Back in 1903, Younghusband was tasked with entering Tibet by then Viceroy of India, Lord Curzon of Kedleston. Tibet lies between Russia, China and British India. Curzon was concerned about the Russians rather than the murky suzerainty claims of the Chinese. Younghusband translated Curzon's instruction to 'enter' Tibet into 'invade' and forced a bloody surrender with the loss of many Tibetans. Younghusband's growing obsession with Mount Everest has carried forward from that invasion, to his presidential seat at Kensington Gore. Some say Everest is impossible to climb, but Younghusband just stiffens his moustache. Urging the Fellows to 'play up', he determines to get rid of 'the ridiculous notion of the smallness of man in comparison to the mountains'.

At the Ladies' Alpine Club there is less British Empire posturing. The Matterhorn is climbed by Lucy Walker in 1871, six years after its first ascent by Edward Whymper. (Some say that exposure to the dangers of mountaineering is unnatural for women, but Walker claims that she never felt that her was life in peril in the Alps.) Victorian climber Alfred Mummery concluded that a peak goes through three stages: an inaccessible peak, the most difficult ascent in the Alps and finally an 'easy day out for a lady'. After Lucy Walker's stroll, American geographer and explorer Fanny Bullock Workman is photographed with her 'votes for women' banner unfurled astride glaciers in the Karakorum.

At the Royal Geographic Society, Younghusband and Curzon complain that the Fanny Bullock Workmans of this world are 'bounders' and all other female explorers, 'globetrotters'. Meanwhile, at the Ladies' Alpine Club, a five minute walk east along the bottom of Hyde Park, they like to tell the story of some cousin with Alpine experience who took a party of ladies to climb Tryfan in Snowdonia. He insisted on testing every boulder before the ladies stepped on it. He was so thorough that the ladies got tired of waiting. Eventually they carried on up the mountain leaving him to test alone.

When Mary Ann receives Rosamond letter in May 1914, all she learns is that Ruth Turner, whoever she may be, is 'a soul of the most crystal wisdom, simplicity and goodness – pure gold all through.' Rosamond makes no mention of Ruth's physical appearance, Mary Ann just has to imagine that. And neither Rosamond nor Mary Ann ever write down how Ruth and George fell in love. Perhaps they never knew?

It was sometime in 1913, somewhere in or near Godalming. But was it when they acted alongside each other at an amateur performance of Alfred Tennyson's *The Princess* in a country house drama? (Ruth was a hopeless actor; she was too honest – but perhaps George was charmed by the ingénue?) Or was it at arts journalist Arthur Clutton-Brock's dinner party, where George remembered the sound of Ruth crunching grape pips between her teeth? (Such an intimate memory, the dinner conversation slipping into the background as George focuses on what is happening inside Ruth's mouth.)

However it happened, both Miss Turner and Mr Mallory were so deeply impressed by each other that their default characters were momentarily derailed. Ruth (who generally saw the best in others) decided that Mr Mallory was so good looking he was bound to be 'spoiled'. She never elaborated. George (who posed as a sophisticate) told his mother: 'she's as good as gold, and brave and true and sweet. What more can I say!'

Whether they were acting or eating in those first electric moments, George subsequently invited the three Turner sisters – in descending order Marjorie 'Marby', Ruth and Mildred – to attend some Shakespeare readings at Charterhouse. At about this time, he wrote to his old friend Mary Ann, not specifically about meeting Ruth, but obliquely about a transformation in his attitude to marriage:

> Of course, I can only profess to believe that maidens & bachelors have the best of life: but I don't mind admitting to you privately that I consider them only half women & men.

The spires of the Charterhouse school chapel can be seen from the gardens of the Turner family home at Westbrook. Ruth's father, Hugh Thackeray Turner invited George to come over to play billiards. When George subsequently received an invitation to join the Turner family in Venice over the Easter holidays, he accepted fully aware of the danger he was letting himself in for: 'a man and his three unmarried daughters!' he wrote to a friend. 'Have you ever heard the like?'

Five years before Ruth and George met, E.M. Forster's 1908 novel *A Room with a View* was a best seller. In that novel, the character of George Emmerson kisses Lucy Honeychurch for the first time in a meadow above Florence. In a curious non-fiction equivalent, George (who knew Forster through Geoffrey Winthrop Young's brother Hilton) 'finds' Ruth Turner, in a meadow above Asolo. In fiction, George's father had to explain what Forster describes as 'the holiness of direct desire' to the object of his affection. But for, twice-born Miss Turner, explanation was unnecessary. She already knew.

\* \* \*

Mary Ann takes her seat at her escritoire taking care to leave room for her pregnant belly. She fills her fountain pen. (She longs to become a bestselling novelist like Forster but for the moment, writing letters is the nearest she gets to 'writing'.) She writes the date, May 1914. As she composes her reply to Rosamond, she realises that if she is to remain friends with George she must play her cards right. Mary Ann's writing leans forward rushing along the line. She replies tartly (or as she will later claim in her manuscript of George's biography, 'with exquisite pleasure') that George happens to be a friend of hers and is one of the 'rarest spirits of his generation and it sounded on the whole as though she [this 'Ruth Turner'] might be nearly good enough for him!' Mary Ann reads back over the letter and underlines 'she' and then for good measure 'him' and adds an exclamation mark.

If this were a game of Bridge, of which Mary Ann is extremely fond, Rosamond has played her 'twice born' 'Queen' and Mary Ann has raised her 'rarest spirit' 'King'. Whoever Ruth Turner is Mary Ann will not have George, the love of her life, diminished with words like 'young', 'good enough' and 'hardly possible' whatever else she has to suffer.

\* \* \*

What does this exchange, this biography and counter biography of Ruth and George in May 1914, tell us? What does it tell us specifically about how Ruth might have reacted to being pushed off that mountain six months later? Sharply like heartsore Mary Ann? With indignation like her aunt Rosamond? With angelic grace like a 'twice-born' paragon? For all Rosamond's defensive eulogy of Ruth and Mary Ann's blustering defence of George, Mary Ann concludes

on page 86, above a tortured, cross hatched paragraph with many line crossings
out, that

A total stranger, meeting both for the first time at some climbing centre
has has told me … the actual shock of delight & astonishment which
[Ruth and George] produced – 'They seemed too good he wrote to be true.'

# Chapter Three

# Engagement 'with a little danger in it'

Three page letter
from Ruth Mallory to George Mallory,
Lough Gartan, County Donegal,
24 May 1914,
Magdalene College Archives,
Cambridge University, Cambridge

It is late spring and Ruth is on a family fishing holiday. She is staying near Lough Gartan, County Donegal. Sitting outside on 'rather boggy ground' she writes to her fiancé, George Mallory. She writes first in ink and then, when the ink smudges, she changes to pencil. She is writing on a large lined block of paper, perhaps a pad from her old school room at Westbrook.

Like other governess educated girls, Ruth and her two sisters sat in their home schoolrooms reciting: 'the earth is an oblate sphere'. From their Wills climber relations, the three Turner girls probably know more than most about Mount Everest, the highest point on its oblate surface. In her mid-teens, Ruth attended Prior's Field, a girls' school just across the Wey Valley. Julia Huxley, the school's founder and headmistress pursued an experimental curriculum that prioritised creativity, culture and personal development over pure academics.

Even now in her early twenties, Ruth still writes like a school girl. She leaves a tail out at the beginning of each word as if she has only just learned joined up. Her spelling is atrocious. She tells George that he must take it as one of the 'worses [sic] in the for better for worse of their marriage vows'. Ruth is in the first heady days of her engagement. She writes long daily letters to George; posting them at the local Post Office each afternoon and collecting his to her. Sundays are an endurance test for both of them as there is no post. 'Oh!' writes George, 'my arms are aching dear for you – to draw you swiftly and firmly close to me.' Hundreds of words later, George says:

> I can see, my dearest Ruth, that you have a dangerously unselfish disposition, but you shan't spend your life doing little jobs for me; I hope that I shan't be horribly selfish – and that you sometimes will be.

In spite of Thackeray Turner's initial invitation to Venice, Ruth's father now seems to be having second thoughts about Mr Mallory's potential as a son-in-law. It is term time and George is at Charterhouse but Thackeray Turner insists that Ruth accompany him on this fishing trip to Ireland. On May Day, just three weeks previously when George asked Ruth's father for his daughter's hand in marriage, he asked how George planned to keep her. 'Oh I couldn't possibly marry a girl,' replied George, 'with her own income.' 'You couldn't possibly marry a girl,' retorted Ruth's father, 'without'.

This is still Ruth being discussed by others. Her aunt Rosamond describes her as 'my niece', and Thackeray Turner and George refer to her as 'a girl with her own income'. But in a letter dated 24 May 1914, we are about to hear Ruth's voice. The letter is in response to a conversation about climbing, which we have not heard. George has been trying to explain to Ruth exactly what mountain climbing means to him. He wants his betrothed to understand what he calls simply 'it' and 'me' before she can really make a judgement.

'At present dear I am glad that you don't fish,' Ruth states in her letter to George. 'I expect some day I shall only wish you did something with a little danger in it.'

Perhaps George has told her that climbing has 'a little danger' in it. Not too much for a prudent experienced mountaineer like him, but undeniably, more than fishing. Ruth does not seem to hear him. For Ruth the word 'danger' has been contracted to 'a little'. It is teasing. It is chivalric, aligned with fifteenth-century writer Thomas Malory's *Le Morte d'Arthur*. Ruth is telling George that the lady expects some day that she would like her knight to do something 'with a little danger in it' to prove his devotion.

In the passion of her betrothal, Ruth identifies with William Morris's Arthurian revivalism. She is familiar with Morris's tapestry 'Le Morte d'Arthur' based on Thomas Malory's story. Morris's philosophy of the Arts and Crafts movement is woven into the fabric of Ruth's life. Malory's legends are the texts of Ruth's childhood.

But for all George's pale and knightly loitering, Ruth is aware that a man must have 'a past'. At the time of their marriage, she is 22 and he is 28, but George has asked Ruth to marry him and she does not sense any danger from his previous relationships. Ruth is nearer to the present. She is weighing up fishing and rock faces. Ruth has already told George that their family holiday in County Donegal is 'frightfully fishy' and that she is glad that he does not fish.

Before Ruth left for Ireland, George slipped a modest diamond onto her finger and a book into her pocket. The title of the book is Edward Whymper's *Scrambles Amongst the Alps*. Ruth understands it as a cipher to his, now second, passion: climbing. She agrees to read *Scrambles Amongst the Alps*, and he asks her to send Arthur Clutton-Brock's new biography of William Morris so that he may learn her creed in return.

Over the long holiday days, Ruth takes a break from rowing her father up and down after fish, and works her way through *Scrambles Amongst the Alps*, but she is a slow reader. To start with she tells George that she thinks Edward Whymper makes 'light of the dangers'. Is this the chivalric climber's attitude: the stoicism, the bravery, the lightly worn courage?

Two years later, on 25 March 1916, she confides in George that she remembers a climbing story her headmistress's husband once recounted.

> Mr [Leonard] Huxley told us of a perfectly horrible climbing accident, the people were saved but almost by a miracle of good climbing on the part of one member of the party. One was a woman with children at home.

In March 1916, Ruth still remembers that one of the climbers was 'a woman with children at home'. The story must have seared itself into her teenage mind. But back in 1914, in the 'little danger' letter, Ruth reacts to one she has just received from George in which he warns her not to depend on him too much.

> You tell me not to depend too much upon you, I will try and bare [*sic*] it in mind but you know I think women are born with a kind of passionate desire to do so, mixed up in a strange way with a great deal of independence. I want to be your comrade and to share with you the joys and the sorrows and to be as strong and brave as you are.

Can one depend upon someone who wants to do something 'with a little danger in it'? Does Ruth assume that George will change? In 1914, the theme of Ruth's letter is mostly focused on 'fish' and 'danger' two words that swim along the lines of her writing pad just a ruled line apart. She writes the 'danger' sentence after one about the weather. The danger is still abstract and disembodied; it is suspended in lightly comic theory in the final paragraph. The 'I expect some day'-future will look after itself. There may be a time in that future, she tells George almost to humour him, that she might want him to do something with a little danger in it, but not now; not in May 1914.

To empathise with George's passion, Ruth persuades her sisters to climb a mountain. They walk along the side of Lough Gartan, right up into the heart of the hills, where 'it got wilder & wilder'. They reach a track leading up to Dooish, 'our big mountain' at 1,115 feet. When the track runs out they high step over tussocky bog. There is a hail storm on the way up. 'The wind was awful', but by the time they get to the summit the storm has passed, and to the north and west they can see the sea. They can also see another mountain, which is much less benign than Dooish. Ruth tells George that 'it looks a thrilling … the sides are very steep and look rocky and loose and it has a very sharp ridge along the top.'

When they finally get home at 'a quarter past seven', Ruth is pleased to find that she is

> not nearly as tired as I should have expected in fact not tired all over at all. I don't think that is so bad as we certainly did not have more than an hour's rest in a ten hour walk.

And then the real reason for her adventure. George has suggested a honeymoon in the Alps. Ruth is testing herself to see whether she is physically fit enough for such a honeymoon. 'I am afraid when its climbing in Switzerland you will find me a drag.'

Her reference to Switzerland is safely in one letter, her reference to danger in another. The two are in separate envelopes, separated by paper and not yet connected with the Leonard Huxley story, which she will only recall in two years' time. Will her May 1914 theory about doing something 'with a little danger in it' have an influence on how she reacts to being pushed off a mountain in December, in six months' time?

\*   \*   \*

The fishing holiday is nearly over; Ruth has been arranging George's love letters in date order: 'a lovely occupation'. She has not quite finished *Scrambles Amongst the Alps*. She has reached Chapter 33. She knows she must finish it. One evening, she sets down her embroidery and begins reading. Her sisters, her father and her uncle Hawes are all around her in the living room of the peat-smoke scented fishing lodge. But for Ruth it is 3.00 pm on 14 July 1865 on the Matterhorn and Edward Whymper has just planted the British flag on the summit. They are about to descend to the safety of Zermatt when: 'I heard one startled exclamation from [Michel Auguste] Croz,' writes Whymper,

> then saw him and Mr Hadow flying downwards; in another moment Hudson was dragged from his steps, and Lord Douglas immediately after him. All this was the work of a moment. Immediately we heard Croz's exclamation, Old Peter [the guide] and I planted ourselves as firmly as the rocks would permit: the rope was taut between us and the jerk came on us both as one man. We held; but the rope broke midway between [Peter] Taugwalder and Lord Douglas. For a few seconds, we saw our

unfortunate companions sliding downwards on their backs, and spreading out their hands, endeavouring to save themselves. They passed from our sight uninjured, disappeared one by one, and fell from precipice to precipice on to the *Matterhorngletscher* [Matterhorn Glacier] below, a distance of nearly 4,000 feet. From the moment the rope broke, it was impossible to help them.

Ruth stops reading. Why has George given her this book? Is this what happens when a 'little danger' is taken to its logical conclusion? Is this level of risk taking somehow essential to him?

'I have finished the alpine book with the awful accident,' she tells George at the top of page 2 on her next letter. What can she tell George about how she feels about his 'bible'? (She cannot lie. Ruth's scrupulous honesty makes her 'the terror of her friends'.) What must it have been like for the families of Hadow, Douglas, Croz and Hudson when they were given the news? After weeks spent reading *Scrambles Amongst the Alps*, all she can honestly say to George about his 'bible' is that her first reaction is concern 'for those left behind'. That is it. After two short sentences she moves on as if she cannot trust herself to say more.

What aspect about 'those left behind' concerns her most? Two years later, on 8 June 1916, Ruth will bring up the subject again, this time 'those left behind' in fiction. In her father's library she has found a signed copy of a first edition of *Vanity Fair* written by his cousin William Makepeace Thackeray. 'I came to the part where they were in Belgium with Wellington just before the battle of Waterloo ...' Ruth will tell George. It is Chapter 30, 'The Girl I Left Behind Me'. From behind the lines, the soldiers' wives in *Vanity Fair* can hear the danger, the booming of the cannon, they can smell the cordite and see the riderless horses galloping away, but they are powerless. They can do nothing.

Six months after reading *Scrambles Amongst the Alps* in Ireland as Miss Turner, Ruth is Mrs Leigh-Mallory and she is falling off a mountain. She is falling, not because the rope has broken, as it had in Whymper's case, but because she has been pushed. Ruth's son remembered that his mother had exceptional recall, perhaps a photographic memory. In that moment of falling off the ridge above Llyn Llydaw in December 1914, was there a sense of Whymper's text scrolling upwards past her – words, stones, white pages, snow?

As Miss Turner in Ireland earlier that year in May 1914, Ruth must have realised that she had committed herself to George. Emotionally, she was already tied, roped to him. She had heard that 'little' word 'danger' and dismissed it. She had heard his warning not to rely upon him and waved it away. She had read his bible and absorbed the knowledge that this was his idea of romance. But it was still just theory. Back then as his fiancée, Ruth had never climbed.

She had never been married. She did not know exactly what it meant to be on a rope with another human. She did not know that it is possible for climbers to fall in tandem, as many believe George Mallory and his future climbing partner Sandy Irvine may have done in June 1924. A decade before, in 1914, Ruth did not know that it is possible to fall and in falling, to drag each other off the mountain.

# Chapter Four

# Honeymooning and '....'

Letter from Geoffrey Winthrop Young
to George Mallory,
May 1914,
Magdalene College Archives,
Cambridge University, Cambridge

As Ruth recovers from the shock of reading *Scrambles Amongst the Alps* in Ireland, Geoffrey Winthrop Young, George's best friend, receives a letter. It is a request from George for advice on his proposed Alpine honeymoon. George is not worried about the climbing; he assessed Ruth's physique in that first blushing glance. He confirmed his assessment in Italy at Easter. (George has an erotic image of Ruth wading thigh deep in an Italian stream picking butter yellow kingcups, which will repeat for the rest of his life.) But, for the moment, he is unsure how his virginal fiancée will stand up to sex. The rumour amongst his male friends, many of them homosexual, is that sex for a woman is enervating.

Unlikely as it seems, George has already asked his mother for advice on what he refers to delicately as 'the physical state of girls immediately after marriage'. His mother, the vicar's wife, is 'most particular in such matters' and advises her son that 'it was a period when women ought to take more exercise than usual.' But George who has never really trusted his mother's wisdom seeks corroboration from a doctor, who has 'no qualms for Ruth ... if she takes a full day's rest after an expedition.'

On first reading George's letter, Geoffrey is appalled. He cannot believe that George can even suggest a honeymoon in the Alps. The Joneses – Humphrey Owen and Muriel Gwendolen, their friends from Pen-y-Pass – were killed in an accident while honeymooning in Switzerland, climbing the Aiguille Rouge de Peuterey on 15 August 1912 in Italy. Now he is determined to bring George to reason. Firstly, there is the issue of sex, of 'throwing oneself into another's being'.

Ruth scribbling letters to George on the bank of a lough in Ireland has no idea that she is being discussed as if she were a brood mare. But then George finds himself part of the discussion. Whether or not he is a virgin, Geoffrey tells George that as a newly married man he will be so consumed with physical passion for Ruth that he will be dangerously distracted, unable to maintain the 'single eye of the mountaineer'. That 'single eye' is essential for the safety of everyone on the rope. In June 1914, Geoffrey writes to George,

Now look here ... [Humphrey Owen's] wife was physically and emotionally overdone those days, *not* by big climbs. He had to take the more care for her; both of them were steeped in the double romance of themselves and the mountains. And the accident came of his over-care for her, his distraction from the single eyes of the mountaineer, that he *must* have and that he *cannot* retain if he is throwing himself into someone else's being ... Now – forgive my going on , but I feel this sincerely ...

Will that do it? Geoffrey is not sure. He decides to lay it on thicker:

I feel ... sincerely – your weakness ... is that you do let yourself get carried away on occasions in the mountains ... I think that it is your failing, the consequence of your combination of extraordinary physical brilliance in climbing and of power of mental absorption in it, that you do not, or at least have not held back from allowing yourself to sweep weaker brethren, carried away by their belief in you, to take risks or exertions that they were not fit for, and which, had the crisis come, neither you nor any man in climbing could have the margin to cover for both ... human relations are more precious than mountains.

Does Ruth know that she is marrying a man whose climbing mentor identifies him as someone who might lead novices like her into danger? Does she know that she is marrying a man who still needs to learn to prioritise people over albeit majestic and inanimate objects? If she knew that George would push her off the ridge in Snowdonia would Geoffrey's words be a warning? 'sweep weaker brethren ... carried away by their belief in you ...' Was the December gale 'a crisis' or just a minor inconvenience. Was forcibly pushing a form of sweeping or carrying away?

George and Ruth marry on 29 July 1914 at St Peter and St Paul's church in Godalming. George's father Reverend Herbert Leigh-Mallory officiates. Geoffrey is their best man. George has taken Geoffrey's honeymoon advice literally but now, danger of sex or Alpine honeymooning has been dwarfed by an existential threat. Their wedding lands on the day after Austria-Hungary declares war on Serbia precipitating what would become known as the First

World War. No one knows what will happen, but many believe the war will be over by Christmas.

George does not take Ruth straight from tying the knot in church to roping up at the bottom of a Swiss Alp. Instead he opts for a very horizontal holiday on a beach near the New Forest, on the south coast of England. Both are naturists. Until now, George has only had a glimpse of thigh in that kingcupped Italian stream but Ruth agrees that to bathe properly, one must bathe in the nude. Ruth's ruthless honestly extends to her attitude to her body so that it is George who is the more self-conscious. In Ruth's family bodily functions are discussed with startling frankness. George is more mannered. In a Bloomsbury Group moment, while being photographed naked by artist Duncan Grant, George claimed to be 'interested in the nude in me'. For Ruth its more about practicality. At home at Westbrook Ruth sometimes takes her clothes off in the garden when it rains 'because it is easier to dry skin than clothes'.

For the newly married Ruth and George, their honeymoon is a chance to bathe naked in the sea, camp under the stars, cook out in the open and sing songs round a camp fire. Pitching a tent on the beach they are at sea level on a flat surface with literally nowhere to fall even if they want to. The 'little danger' has been reduced to a pin prick, but even a pin prick could be dangerous in their bubble of romance.

The family's anecdotal evidence relates that the honeymoon went swimmingly until the sight of holidaying campers aroused suspicion. In the madness of the first weeks of the war, the idea of honeymooning on a beach seemed preposterous to the hyper-vigilant New Forest locals and the claim to be 'just married', an obvious cover story. (Ruth may even have wondered how to spell her new surname – was it one 'l' like the Arthurian author Thomas Malory, or two?) It was quickly decided that 'Mr and Mrs Mallory' might be signalling to German ships in the channel and Ruth and George were held, briefly, as enemy spies.

Ruth's innocence, her lack of suspicion makes her seem naïve but she is a paradox, innocent and wise: 'twice born' with 'crystal wisdom'. George's romantic idealism and Ruth's down to earth practicality are a match or as Mary Ann describes it on page 86 of her manuscript 'a conjunction of two unique creatures'. And then Mary Ann writes 'of widely differing qualities' and crosses it out. Mary Ann is tacking towards a definition. Her continual crossings out and rewriting of Ruth, contrast with her fluency when writing of George. By the time she was writing 'unique creatures' she had known Ruth well for a decade and yet her crossings out speak to the difficulty of pinning Ruth's character to the page. Mary Ann comes closest on the next page when, after scoring through most of her writing, she arrives at the bottom:

[Ruth, was] a person of ~~the most~~ wisest simplicity ~~& the most~~ transcendent practicalness [*sic*] who ~~treated~~ dealt with all the everyday concerns of life with a just & prompt efficiency & was wont to dispose of ~~George's~~ more weighty problems with a summary & almost ~~by contrast~~ irreverent common sense.

How did Ruth react when George pushed her off the mountain five months after their wedding? Did she see it as a necessary act of 'transcendent practicalness [*sic*]'? The only real option in the gale force circumstances. Or did she wonder at the melodrama of choosing to frighten her? Was George's decision to push Ruth of Bwlch Glas in December 1914, a 'Kiss me Kate'-type wearing down of the wife's resistance to her husband's commands?

# Chapter Five

# Threading the Needle

p.46, Harold Porter's Journal,
5–16 September 1914,
Alpine Club Archives, London

Harold Porter is a school friend of George's from his Winchester College days. He is an experienced climber and one of the gang from the climbing meets that Geoffrey Winthrop Young organises at Pen-y-Pass in Snowdonia. Harold's journal is a private record in which he assesses the potential of individual climbers in the manner of a school report. Ruth is not wearing a uniform, but hairy tweed plus fours. It is the first time she has worn trousers. They are practical but they are also scandalously revealing of the female body. George can trust Harold. Most Lake District locals look politely away.

Harold opens his journal to page 46. Ruth is a complete novice, this will be her maiden climb; the day that she exchanges her embroidery needle for a rock needle. Harold has also arranged to initiate another novice, a friend of his called George Walker. Harold's report on Ruth's climbing will be her next mini-biography.

Harold likes the technical side of climbing, particularly he likes to talk equipment. As an embroiderer, Ruth is familiar with arcane knots. (Her mother taught her a secret knot of the Qing dynasty smuggled out of China by the Silk Road.) Is Harold interested in embroidery? After reading *Scrambles Amongst the Alps* Ruth is certainly motivated to understand climbing rope. Could Harold tell her about rope?

Harold describes the old fashioned flax rope with a left-hand spiral. New manila or hemp – a right-hand spiralled rope is more comfortable to the grip. He tackles 'the knotty question' of how to tie an end man or a middle man on to the loop of rope around the waist. (They do not, yet, have modern climbing harnesses.) For the end man there is the eye spliced in the rope end or the waist rope hitch threaded through a new device, which he calls the 'snap ring', but which he believes on the Continent they call the carabiner.

On the walk to the climb from their lodgings at Rowhead, Harold might tell Ruth about his first encounter with her new mother-in-law, Annie Leigh-Mallory. He and George had just returned from a school trip to the Alps in autumn 1905. They were staying at the vicarage, George's home when they came up with a plan to climb over the roof. George asked Harold to hold the rope while he climbed out of an upstairs window and hoisted himself up. Unfortunately, as George swung his legs upwards he kicked in a windowpane and woke George's mother who rushed into her son's room to find Harold frantically paying out a rope. Harold recalled that

> George sped over the roof to a known route of descent on the far side, leaving to me the embarrassing task of pacifying his agitated parent until his reappearance.

George and Harold had high japes, but now George at least is married and both are trying to be responsible. Ruth, other climbers later observed, 'is a quick learner'; it is time for the second initiation of married life. George wants to see how his new wife will respond to the reality of a rock face; there is a lot riding on this. He has told Harold that he wants her to start with the most sensational of classic climbs: the Napes Needle.

The 'Needle' is a 20-foot high grey rock pinnacle on the southern flank of Great Gable in the Lake District. It is school-boy-sniggeringly phallic from most angles, but for grown-ups like Harold and George, the Napes Needle is a finger to wag at those inexperienced 'bank holiday' climbers. George tells Ruth that 'bank holiday corpses' are giving climbing a bad name. The phrase does not speak danger to her, it amuses her. She will use the phrase 'bank holiday corpses' in a letter to George the following year. But for now, the Napes Needle is not about corpses, it is sex and climbing in one.

George might tell Ruth that climber and teacher Mabel Barker once came here with Millican Dalton, a pioneering, but eccentric 'man of the hills'. As they stood at the base of the Napes Needle the previous year Dalton said:

> 'Skirt detachable?'
> 'Yes,' replied Mabel.
> 'Take it off.'

Mabel obeyed and, she later told George, 'knew the feel of the rope for the first time'. A detachable skirt was important but so, in Mabel's opinion was safety. Mabel liked the climbing stories where, as she put it, 'nobody woke up dead'.

The four 'climbers' – Harold, George and novices Ruth and George Walker – follow the narrow stony path ascending a gradual slope towards Great Gable. The bracken is turning orange. Pungent long-haired mountain goats skitter over the scree, bleating. They ascend a path in single file before the Kern Knotts

Crag and arrive at the base of the Napes Crag with the Napes Needle to the left. George quickly begins to ascend a two-sided chimney on the eastern side of the Napes Needle gap. Ruth watches closely to see where her husband puts his toes and his fingers, how he transfers his weight between one position and another. His moves are fluid, continuous, confident and controlled. Can she hope to emulate that?

Standing next to Ruth, Walker is already having trouble. They are standing at the base of the Napes Needle looking up but he has the hollow feeling that he is at the top looking down. He is looking down with 20 foot of vertical precipice on every side. He is, he admits, scared to the point of incontinence. He insists that it would be in everyone's interests for him to stay put. George (Mallory) and Harold can sometimes bully a reluctant novice up a rock face, but Walker has them in a fix: 'no inducement could persuade him to join us'.

Ruth is in the same position as Walker. She has the same level of experience: none. But unlike him she does not have a choice. She has married a climber. She can either risk her neck or her marriage. The question is not whether she will climb, but whether she will 'thread the Needle'.

There are two principal routes up. Both meet on the shoulder under the summit block that forms the crux of both climbs. The gap is the cleft to the left of the Napes Needle between it and the main crag. Threading the Needle is the traverse of this gap. Ruth approaches the rock. She places her right foot finding a position that will take her weight and she places her hands, hooking her fingers into the grooves in the rough surface. Taking the strain, she heaves herself up and, for the first time as a 'climber', she leaves the ground.

The grey rock in the chimney is dusted with green lichen. There aren't quite enough foot and handholds to be comfortable. Ruth can feel the grainy texture of the rock beneath her fingertips, but her fingers are not strong enough to rely on a hold that is shallow. She wants a hold like a handle. The rain is beginning to spit. Dark dots appear on the grey rock in front of her. She tries to remember to use the big muscles in her legs rather than her weaker arms. After some time Ruth reaches the narrow cleft between the Napes Needle and the Needle Ridge. To 'thread the Needle' she must go through that cleft and down the other side. George assures her that there are more places to put her hands and feet on the other side, but down-climbing with her feet beneath her, it is difficult to see which holds will take her leather booted toes.

Finally, she is in the scree-filled gully below. She crosses to the other side and clambers a short way up to the 'Dress Circle' from which to enjoy the view. The feeling of elation is short lived. This is a brief pause. They have more climbing to do before the heavens open. Pillar Rock, above Ennerdale is another iconic climb and it is calling Harold.

Back in their rooms at Rowhead that evening Ruth changes out of her tweed plus fours into a dress for the dining room. After a good supper George lights his pipe. In the presence of the nearly-incontinent man no one is going to praise Ruth's performance too loudly, but later that night Harold gets out his journal in the privacy of his bedroom. He notes that Ruth has bypassed the novice stage in one elegant move. 'Mrs M., a complete beginner, shewed great confidence and adaptability.' He puts it down to 'her complete trust' in George. The incontinent man's school report will be the equal but opposite of 'Mrs M's'.

In the privacy of their bedroom George confirms that she is no longer a climbing virgin, she has shown herself to be a complete natural, as he always knew she would be. As David Pye later writes gushingly in his biography of George, 'she had in her the spirit of the mountaineer, only waiting to be aroused.'

The next day, an early start for Pillar Rock. 'Muggy and hot. Rocks even perspired freely. We did the New West. Walker being once again a spectator, came down the Old West ...'

They climb all day; returning to Rowhead at 7.30 pm. They take the obligatory post-climbing bathe in the dark. Ruth is learning that climbing is a continuous business. They climb from dawn to dusk. On Scawfell Pinnacle the next day, they go up the West Wall Traverse, so up the Joneses' pinnacle route. On their way home they take the traverse out of Steep Ghyll and the top of Moss Ghyll taking Collie's exit then down Broad Stand before heading home.

That night Harold notes the contrast between his male novice who once again 'fled incontinent', and the female novice: 'Mrs M again did wonderfully.' Home by 5.30 pm. 'Slacked and bathed'.

For Ruth, the Lake District may be literally a honeymoon period in her climbing career. Whilst Walker's performance is disappointing, Harold marvels at the effect of Ruth's 'great trust' in George. He has passed her with flying colours, her school report is spattered with praise in her 'confidence', 'adaptability' and the fact that she climbed 'wonderfully'. Ruth might come to regret her success. Having achieved many of the classic climbs in the Lake District on her first trip, George's ambitions for her escalate. War has, of course, been declared and hostilities commenced, but once it is over the Alps beckon. Now she must train on snow and ice.

As they leave Rowhead for Godalming, Ruth does not know that it is only a matter of weeks until she will be pushed off a mountain of snow and ice in a gale. Will she interpret that push as a 'trust fall'? How far, and how many times will she let herself be pushed not just to the edge but over it?

# Chapter Six

# Childbirth and Vicarious Danger

Letters from George Mallory
to Geoffrey Winthrop Young and David Pye,
Magdalen College Archives,
Cambridge University, Cambridge

Unpublished biography of George Mallory
with quotes from the letters George Mallory wrote
to Mary Ann O'Malley between 1915 and 1917,
The University of Texas at Austin, USA

The next document in Ruth's biography is a letter from George to Mary Ann essaying his reaction to Ruth being in danger. He does not like it. For Ruth the danger is justified, inevitable, natural. It does not sound natural to George as he paces beneath their open bedroom window. It sounds as if she is being murdered.

Ruth spent the first two months of this, her first pregnancy, in a hospice when her morning sickness became so acute that she could not hold anything down. She was still there on 10 March 1915 when George moved into their first married home, The Holt, alone. The house, a wedding present from Thackeray Turner, is just down from Charterhouse on the opposite side of the Wey Valley from Westbrook where Ruth grew up. In Ruth's absence, George proceeded to throw himself into the task of decoration.

Eschewing her usual Morris & Co., Ruth teasingly proposed a mountain theme – instead of chairs they could just have stone boulders 'which would be cheap'. But George had developed a sudden and extravagant zeal for interior decoration. He is egged on by Ruth's uncles. Her uncle Hawes Turner is keeper of The National Gallery, London and her uncle Laurence Turner is a notable stone carver and fine arts plasterer. (Laurence was chosen to carve William Morris's gravestone at Kelmscott.)

George shows Ruth swatches and matching wallpaper as she lies in bed at the hospice trying not to vomit. On Ruth's family friend Gertrude Jekyll's advice, he begins grubbing up gorse in The Holt's steep garden. He wants to create a gap through which they can see down to the bottom, to the glinting River Wey.

The Holt becomes, for the next seven years, a main character in Ruth's story. Perhaps it is worth leaving Ruth writhing in 'childbed' with George pacing beneath her window, while we look around.

'The Holt,' George tells Geoffrey, 'is a charming little place'. Perched on the top of a steep slope it hangs above the valley with the great bulk of Hindhead standing up to the south-east 'a real mountain shape'. Its drawing room and dining room open onto a loggia, a covered terrace with a tiled floor and low brick wall 'to lean your elbow on'. The loggia leads to a steep garden. George confides in Geoffrey that when the sun comes out, he has the urge to rip his clothes off and lie 'naked on our grass bank.' Marriage suits him. It is a 'deliberate adventure', one that he relishes. It is 'what life ought to be like'.

Until she swelled up like a melon, George teased Ruth that she was the perfect 'Watteau', the perfect leisured aristocratic lady as painted by French painter Jean Antonine Watteau. But Ruth is too practical to be a 'Watteau'. She is practical but she is also a talented artist. At Westbrook, their greatest excitement is opening boxes packed with wood shavings, to reveal the fired results of their ceramic painting. Ruth's porcelain designs are so accomplished that they are often exhibited in London.

With Ruth writhing in bed and George rolling naked on the bank, it falls to Mary Ann on page 83 of her handwritten manuscript to describe a visitor's impression:

> the beauty of the house presented a surprising contrast to the rather unpromising exterior; the sober gravity of old furniture, the fresh gaiety of patterned & bright materials, the complicated richness of rugs, the fantasy of porcelain & the satisfactory solidity of good modern oak, were all combined into a whole which was at once harmonious and striking and above all comfortable.

Less wordy, George's Cambridge friend Geoffrey Keynes called it 'a mixture of Morris and Omega'. Mrs Fletcher, the headmaster's wife, declares that George is a 'postie' – a Post Modernist – but that is less about his interior design choices than his fashion sense. George had a penchant for plain black or bright red shirts teamed with preposterous jellybag hats. Between Ruth's William Morris inheritance and Julia Huxley's experimental form of 'aesthetic' education at Prior's Field, she learned that instinct for good design was almost a moral virtue. Mary Ann concludes her tour by declaring that the house, The Holt, is 'a perfect expression of them both'.

In George's view, from his position on the grassy bank beneath their bedroom window, The Holt is almost their first child. By the sounds issuing through the window, it is certainly less painful than the flesh and blood equivalent. The birth of their firstborn is George's first real experience of danger to a loved one; danger completely outside his control. 'I had no idea it could be so awful.' How had women survived this kind of danger? 'What a helpless trial this is,' he wrote to Mary Ann – I can't share the pain'. How had women borne it? Surely, there was a more civilised, less excruciating way of continuing the human race? And the summit of Ruth's achievement? Frances Clare.

Even after Clare's bloody delivery, Ruth suffered with a retained placenta. When her womb did not contract, she experienced a slow haemorrhage with protracted loss of blood. After forty-eight hours of not knowing whether Ruth would live or die: '[Clare] seems a bit superfluous just now', George declared. Of one thing he is absolutely certain: 'If men took their turn at that job, no family would exceed three.'

For all the danger, Ruth feels that the moment Clare is born is transcendent; a threshold moment; a crack in the universe; like dying. But Ruth did not die and for her, the danger inherent in childbirth is worth it. She does not want their family to be limited to three. George wants a son; Ruth wants to give him one. She is prepared, keen even, to embrace that danger again.

Later Ruth tries to describe the first transcendent burst of a mother's love on seeing her child. She's never read anything that has captured the feeling; poets came close 'but they couldn't get it all'. Like the adrenaline that flashes through the body when one is pushed off a mountain, that sensation, that ignition of protective instinct is, Ruth believes, a match for any danger. But George is still reeling months afterwards. Watching danger rather than being in it does not appeal. As a climber this is exactly the vicarious emotion he puts those who love him through every time he climbs.

To encourage George to try for another baby, Ruth reminds him that she always remembers the '….' that made Clare. She doesn't write 'sex'. If she was speaking, would she say it? Ruth is uncompromisingly direct about her body. She writes to George in detail about her period and the tingling sensation she gets in her breasts, she even tells him about her sister's periods. But she writes four dots instead of writing the word sex. The reason for mentioning it at all to George is to remind him of that moment, the very point of conception. She admits to being sexually frustrated when he is away: 'it is trying', she tells him not 'being active with you'. By writing '….' Ruth is deliberately inviting George to picture their night of passion. She wants him to imagine them back into their hotel room in Barrow in the Lake District.

From Ruth's letters, it seems that George invites Ruth to describe her sensual dreams. 'Oh my darling,' she tells him,

how I want to lay my head against you and kiss you. I so often imagine I
can when I go to bed. I imagine I have you in my arms and can kiss your
mouth and thick soft hair and feel how beautiful you are with my hand
and that I can hold you and hold you so ...

Ruth never tells George that she dreams of '....' but she confesses that tells
she hates sleeping in a double bed by herself. She has a high libido, she would
have sex not just once but twice a night. Her reason for encouraging George
to 'try a second time', is that she wants to get pregnant again, preferably with
a son. When she does fall pregnant after he refuses to have sex a second time
in a night, she tells him that if he had given in to her, the baby probably would
not have come.

Ruth is a sensual being. The physical bond between her and George – both
in bed and on the mountain – is essential. Could that fall off the ridge in
Wales in 1914 have been dangerously pleasurable for Ruth? Could it have
been intimate? Could the frisson of danger, the 'spice', have elicited an almost
sexual response? Is danger a form of arousal for both Mallorys? Robert Graves,
a former Charterhouse pupil described the ecstasy that George manifested at
the end of a climb with him in Wales. Is the not-dying, the flirting with danger,
linked to some kind of physical need? But how does George really feel, about
danger where Ruth is concerned. How does he register the sensation of vicarious
danger. What does it do to him?

*   *   *

## Snowdonia – December 1914

A cold winter's day back in 1914, George and Ruth are on the arête climb on
Tryfan. Ahead is the summit wall with ominous bands of overlaps. The eighth
pitch: the last pitch, is by far the hardest.

They start well. Ruth climbs quickly and neatly for the first few pitches.
When she begins to tire halfway George is ready. In describing a similar climb,
on pages 21 and 22 of her handwritten biography of George, Mary Ann allows
us an insight into Ruth's experience:

I can see [George] now, moving about over the rocks like a great cat,
scolding, expositing & encouraging ... It was very defeating to see him
scampering up & down places where [I] could only proceed with the
utmost deliberation. But [I] held on [my] way & by half way up he had
got me, at any rate, into the right frame of mind by which he was so much

encouraged that he unroped [himself] from in front & let me lead. In these circumstances I was occasionally allowed to take the easier of two ways, though never without regretful protest on George's part. Perhaps 50 feet above the slab, however, there comes a bit where there is no easy way – the rock pushes you out a little & though the holds are good you need them & you must use your balance. I tackled it while George watched from above in obvious anxiety – but he let me alone and didn't bother me with advice & when I got it just right, using the sequence of holds that made it safe & not too hard, how great was his pride and satisfaction. To compel someone else to climb a pitch well was like a personal triumph to him.

George can 'keep up a heat' himself, and Ruth is determined not to shiver, but her hands, which are always stretching for holds above her head, are getting numb. It is difficult to rely on them to hold her weight. When she reaches George she shakes the feeling back into her fingers – pain lancing along her veins. It is also difficult to shake feeling back into her frozen feet. She uses 'rubbers' for this kind of climbing but the footholds are slight. She knows that it will be a personal triumph for George if she finishes it well.

By the time they get to the end of the seventh pitch, Ruth is exhausted. Her muscles are tired, she is shaking. This is when climbers get 'sewing machine legs': an incontrollable tremble like the needle of a sewing machine going through fabric. She is also scared: 'she came very near the end of her nervous strength just before crossing the slab …', George will explain to Mary Ann on 7 October 1917. 'Nervous strength'. What is that? Do the Mallorys understand 'nervous strength' to be a form of courage? On 26 December 1916, Ruth will tell George that

> I do so want to become a brave, strong person; and I suppose it may grow better in adverse circumstances than in ones that are always favourable. All the same … I don't want them to go on.

And yet clinging to the rock under the overhang on the arête, Ruth knows that the only way is on. Above her, George is suddenly terrified. Vicarious danger gives him vertigo, a sensation he never suffers from. With Ruth in danger, he feels as if he is standing on the edge of an abyss.

Years later, speculating on what may have happened in George's last moments on Everest David describes the effect of nerves upon a climber: 'It is notorious that the nervous system plays up until it drops. The collapse is complete and absolute … may not the strained cord have snapped?' As George is willing Ruth to find the strength to overcome the overhang on Tryfan a decade earlier in 1914, he confesses that 'I became aware of imaginative leaps abysmally disquieting & intensities of anxiety vertiginously horrible.'

From beneath the overhang looking up, Ruth girds herself. She is determined to use 'adverse circumstances' to become 'a brave strong person', to rise to the challenge that George has set her. All she has to do is get from this underside of the overhang, to George at the top.

After completing the climb, Ruth compares the arête climb to being pushed off that ridge in the gale. In 1927, David concludes, that from what Ruth has told him, 'I do not think she was ever so hardly tested' as that 'severe initiation'. Back then, on that ridge in 1914 it was David rather than George who was the anxious husband, pacing outside the delivery room. Back then it was David who braced himself on the rope as George delivered his wife to her first real experience of the all-consuming physical sensation of danger. Since then Ruth's understanding of 'danger' has recalibrated. The arête climb was mild by comparison to Bwlch Glas. The arête did not involve any time in mid-air.

# Chapter Seven

# War

George Mallory's letters
to Geoffrey Winthrop Young,
letters to and from Ruth Mallory,
letters to his younger sister Avie,
and letters to Mary Ann O'Malley
Magdalene College Archives,
Cambridge University, Cambridge

It is difficult to pick a single significant document in the mountain of nearly 400 letters that Ruth wrote to George during the First World War. I think of those letters, a stack of cardboard archive boxes in Cambridge (and 559 copied sheets in the lever-arched file beside me as I write this). For the reader, the Magdalene Centenary Project to put them online means that they will be a searchable resource. Without trawling through the photocopies, I cannot be certain how many times Ruth uses the word 'danger' in her letters and I am fairly certain that she never counted. But for me those letters are audible. Ruth writes as she speaks. She does not attempt to be literary. In her war letters, Ruth's voice instead of being 'inaudible' is clear, strong and urgent.

Before Ruth became pregnant the first time, she wanted to be posted to France to do whatever she, as a women, could do for the war effort. She'd asked George to find her a position. Ruth will voluntarily put herself in danger for a cause she believes in. At the time, Geoffrey Winthrop Young was working in France: first as a reporter and then with an ambulance unit. On 22 November 1914, George puts a backhanded proposal to Geoffrey. He asks Geoffrey to find Ruth a position but mid-sentence, perhaps remembering the vertigo of vicarious danger, he backtracks. 'she is very strong and competent,' George tells Geoffrey, 'but I don't suppose it is so likely that [you] could find a job for her!'

George as a teacher, is in a reserved profession. Field Marshal Kitchener (Lord Kitchener) – famously known for the 'Your Country Needs You' poster – has given the heads of schools the power to decide who to release and who to keep. Frank Fletcher, the head of Charterhouse, refuses to release George. In the first winter of the war, there is a real possibility that Ruth will be in danger in France whilst George is stuck safely teaching 'blighters' in Godalming.

Instead, with the help of George and Ruth's friend William 'Will' Arnold-Forster, George is offered a job in the contraband section of the Admiralty. He is desperate to take it but his headmaster will not release him. 'Of course, it wouldn't have been risking one's life,' George tells his sister Avie on 22 March 1915, 'but it would have been wearing the King's uniform.'

George met 'Will-the-genius' through Geoffrey. Will was the first person George told about 'finding' Ruth, about that day in a field above Asolo. Perhaps it was Will who encouraged George to act, to propose marriage. For now, in the first years of the war, Will has the job George wants.

Frustrated at missing the Admiralty job, Ruth and George turn their attention to international relations. Their conversations in the evenings after George returns from Charterhouse, are not recorded, but later in letters they will speculate on 'some society …' to prevent a recurrence of 'the old Grab policy which has prevailed' after wars of the past. Ruth believes that 'ideas come during times of action though they need to be worked out in peace'. In three years' time on 8 January 1918, United States President Woodrow Wilson will use the term 'league' instead of the Mallorys' term 'society'. The league: a worldwide intergovernmental league with the principal mission of maintaining world peace, will become known as the League of Nations. It will be the first ever worldwide organisation. If Frank Fletcher had allowed George to take up Will's offer at the Admiralty, George might have had more leverage to secure a job at the League of Nations and Ruth's story might have been different.

After the birth of Clare on 18 September 1915, there is no further written mention of Ruth going to France. Instead she works at a depot in Godalming preparing first aid medical kits to be sent to the Front. She rolls bandages alongside 'work people' as she calls the working class. (An acolyte of William Morris's socialism she insists they call her 'Ruth' rather than Mrs Mallory.) In some quarters Ruth's politics are described as dangerously revolutionary. The only danger that Ruth recognises is the risk of transmitting an infectious disease to baby Clare. Statistics reveal that she was right.

In 1900, 30 per cent of all deaths occurred among children under 5 years old. The three leading causes: pneumonia, tuberculosis and diphtheria, were responsible for a third of all deaths. Although graphs show a steady decline in infant mortality, there is a spike in 1915 due to increased population mobility and the fact that women were working outside the home. But not only does Ruth continue to work at the depot, she holds large meetings at Westbrook, where up to fifty 'educated women' (a borrowed phrase she uses to avoid saying upper-class women) discuss the 'society' or 'league' as a means of securing post-war peace.

Instead of the indulgent 'little danger' in climbing referenced in Ruth's engagement letter to George, it is 'sacrifice' that describes her attitude to danger in the context of war. The moment she braces herself for that sacrifice is recorded in the photograph that is on the front cover of this book. As in the moment where she is suspended in mid-air falling over the ridge in Snowdonia, this can be slowed down and blown up in all its granular black and white detail.

\* \* \*

## Godalming – May 1916

Photographer Adrian Harding walks down Godalming High Street. It is the second spring of the war – bullets and blossom. When he reaches Clark's, the tailors at 38 High Street, he turns left up a side passage emerging into a back yard where there is a small shed. A notice – 'The Barn Studio' – is stuck over the door. This is the place where Godalming's proto-heroes come for their immortality, fixing their image: their 'before'. Harding tries not to think of his portraits bent to body shape in breast pockets, the corners blunted. Those battered photographs so often seem to be returned from the Front in parcels of 'effects'.

Crossing into the opposite side of the dim shed, Harding unpegs the images of the last couple from where they were hung out to dry on a cord strung above a white ceramic butler's sink. When he puts on the big electric lamps, there will be a scent of warmed wooden walls. Although Godalming was the first town in Britain to receive electricity Harding shares his supply with Evans the haberdashers at the front and it can be unreliable. Before switching the lamps he loads the camera in the dim natural light coming through the window behind him. Harding opens the back of the black leather camera case standing on a tripod. He moves the latch to 'O' for open. He pulls the front of the camera away from the back. Checking that he has the spool the right way up he places it in the lower roll holder so that the pin in the spring engages the hole in the film. He closes the back and winds the film on.

The door opens and his clients enter. Mrs Mallory is wearing a dark coat with a square collared white shirt. She does not wear powder. Since securing his commission in the Royal Artillery a few days ago Mr Mallory has obviously stopped shaving his upper lip. Harding instructs his clients to sit on the long stool with their backs to the canvas. He assumes that they want 'Lieutenant Mallory' in the foreground with his wife sitting behind?

Sitting just behind George, the outside of Ruth's left thigh is touching his right. The closeness, the pressure of his body against hers is precious. Since the Charterhouse pupils have begun appearing in the lists of 'missing presumed dead', Ruth knows that George has found his 'fireside an intolerable reproach'. George will be posted to the Royal Artillery's 40th Siege Battery operating north of Armentières in northern France. He will be in charge of No. 4 Gun Detachment. He will be defending freedom and 'ordinary life'. They are a family and have one baby daughter. Ruth wants to give George a son. These are ordinary ambitions. Ruth tells George that 'I always knew that it was absolutely necessary to us that you should [go to war].' But she must tell the 'careful accurate truth'. On 26 December 1917, Ruth corrects herself:

> When I say always, of course I did not realise at the beginning that you must go but I was terribly afraid even in the first days that you would have to or want to …

George does not have to, teaching is a protected profession, but he wants to. Ruth is clear about the distinction. Previously, on 13 December 1915, George assured Avie that '[Ruth] Is perfectly happy, too, and wants to make her part of the sacrifice, which indeed is far the largest …' But George is exaggerating. Although she is willing, Ruth cannot be 'perfectly happy'. Her customary ruthless honesty, is tortured with conditionals. She tells him that that 'if you [get] back alive I should be glad you [have] gone.'

Sitting in Harding's studio, George feels the pressure of Ruth's body on his right. George is relieved to be wearing the king's uniform at last; the rough serge and the brass buttoned epaulettes give him an 'almost childish pleasure'. Heroism is being offered on a plate and he is looking forward to it. George voices his thoughts to Mary Ann,

> I feel so mixed when I think of it – not wanting perfect safety for my <u>own</u> sake … because I prefer adventure & want anyway to share those risks with my friends; but thinking so very differently where Ruth comes in. I'm afraid she'll feel very sore when I'm out there.

The alternatives for him are 'perfect safety' or 'adventure' and 'risk'. Ruth has no such choice. He realises that Ruth will 'feel very sore' with him in danger. Using a climbing metaphor he promises that he will not deliberately invite danger, he will not 'walk under the avalanches'. But to Geoffrey he confides that although he does not want to die for nothing, 'I do not intend to be alive at the end'.

Ruth senses that George is withholding something but in some respects he does not spare her. He tells her that he would feel selfish to try to keep safe for her sake. He must take his place alongside his men. He needs to free to become disinterested about putting himself at risk. He wants to reach a place where he is not afraid of dying.

Part of him is curious. As a climber he knows how far he can push himself up a rock face, but against a flesh and blood adversary how far will his courage take him? Will this war push him to his limit? It is a limit, he realises, that he badly needs to know.

How dangerous will it be for Ruth? How corrosive is a constant state of anxiety, the pulse of unremitting vicarious danger which George describes as 'feeling very sore'? He knows that Ruth will not 'make the most of her anxiety' like his mother seems to. He assures Ruth that he trusts her not to 'wobble in goodness'. She is flattered but she admits that her goodness is partly for his approval so that it is not really 'a good, good'.

In the safety of Harding's studio, neither of them know that in a few weeks Ruth will be walking down Godalming High Street – 20 yards from where they are now sitting – when in a freak accident a car mounts the pavement killing a pedestrian. Similarly, on George's first night at the Observation Post in France, a bullet will pass between George and a man walking a yard in front.

Back in The Barn Studio, Harding adjusts the electric lamp to light up the whisps of Ruth's freshly washed hair. He wants contrast. Walking back round to the camera, he stoops to look at his clients through the view finder. He sees a couple who do not seem to realise that they are as good looking, better perhaps, than any matinee film stars. How can he capture Ruth's sky blue eyes in black and white? He asks her to tip her head forward so that the whole circular iris is visible between her eyelids.

Are they a charmed pair whom danger will bypass? Or will they have to agree with the received wisdom that there is 'no reckoning with death'? There is a steady stoicism in their expression. It is as if they have already reconciled themselves to their 'reckoning' whatever it may be. Harding counts down for the exposure, the shutter clicks. Ruth and George pass into history.

# Chapter Eight

# Children

Letters from Ruth Mallory to George Mallory,
1916–1918,
Magdalene College Archives,
Cambridge University, Cambridge

Ruth realises that bad parenting is 'dangerous'. She uses the word 'dangerous' when telling George that she thinks it will be 'dangerous' for Clare to spend too much time with his mother, her mother-in-law. Ruth's honesty knows no bounds but, as she tells George, she feels it would be wrong to censor her thoughts to him. The 'danger', Ruth identifies here is covered over two letters: 'I heard from your mother this morning,' she informs George on Saturday, 15 July 1916,

> that Trafford [George's younger brother] has gone out to France. Her tone about it annoys me a little, she seems to want to make the most of her anxiety. How horridly critical I am. But I don't realy [*sic*] count it to you, because I think we ought to be able to say things just to one another as if it were to oneself. Only perhaps I ought not to think it.

It is good to hear the 'golden' Ruth being 'horridly critical' occasionally. She is honest to George, she shows him the ugliest as well as the most admirable sides of her innermost self. Despite her criticism she recognises that protracted anxiety (like that which threatened the nerves of soldiers waiting in the trenches) can be dangerous. The constant anxiety of the women at home, those 'left behind', is similarly relentless, but they are not in physical danger. Ruth is determined not to 'make the most of her anxiety'. She is trying to ignore her favourite novel *Vanity Fair* where the character of Amelia prays for her husband's safety whilst he – a character who happens to be called 'George' – lies dead on the battlefield with a bullet through his heart.

Annie Leigh-Mallory is not the kind of mother that Ruth aspires to be. George's parents thought rock climbing was unladylike and likely to damage marriage prospects. George's sisters Avie and Mary are not allowed to climb. Ruth decides that George has turned out the way he has because his mother entirely delegated his upbringing to the nanny. George remembered that the few times his mother ventured into the nursery always precipitated 'a row'. But it was not just George's mother who would be a 'dangerous' influence on Clare, Ruth didn't think much of George's father, either.

The Reverend Leigh-Mallory advised his parishioners on a cure for warts that had worked for him. He told them to take a bag of stones and bury it at the crossroads. They had to take as many stones as they had warts. His disappeared almost immediately. He wasn't joking. 'A person who can believe that,' Ruth tells George, 'can believe anything'.

Ruth's conclusion, that bad parenting can be dangerous will inform two important turning points in her future. At the time Ruth infers to George that it would be dangerous for his parents to be let loose with their daughter, Clare, Ruth has just begun training as a Montessori teacher.

She is painfully aware that she is not classic teacher material and confides in George,

> Owen O'Malley [Mary Ann's husband] says that I am uneducated … The thing I want is to be clever and well educated and I know I'm not and that is what I really mind though I don't suppose I should have minded it much if you had been too stupid to mind it.

Owen's comment fuels Ruth's determination to ensure that their children should not have an 'experimental' education as she had. On 10 January 1917, she decides

> that girls should be as well educated as boys … I do want any girl of ours to be capable of earning her own living decently. Oh I hope Clare will be intelligent. No I know already that she will be that quite well, I hope she will be clever …

The Montessori system does not distinguish between girls and boys – they are offered the same choices in the nursery classroom, the same opportunities to learn. No daughter of Ruth's will be called 'uneducated' if she has anything to do with it.

Nowadays it seems innocuous enough for Ruth to want to train as a teacher but Thackeray Turner believed that a woman of Ruth's social class would lose 'caste' by becoming a professional. To him it seemed that Ruth would be competing with George. He believed that the idea of educating children equally was wrong and that academia was somehow defeminising.

As soon as Ruth floats the idea past her father, he begins to mock her mercilessly, but Ruth deliberately refuses to rise, or to alter her plans. 'I have written to the Secretary of the Montessori Society today to ask about the apparatus', she tells George. Then, ever practical, she wonders whether she couldn't just as easily make the apparatus herself to save money. Ten days later, on 25 October 1918, Ruth has imagined her new future:

> I have great hopes now that I may be able to start a little Montessori class when I get back to The Holt … It is lovely being so full of plans and hopes …

Unlike most upper-middle class women who delegated their children to nannies, Ruth advises George that this career will play to her strengths, 'I really like having the children to look after …' She appreciates that the wonderful Violet 'Vi' Meakin, the nanny, is essential if she is to have the time to train as a teacher. Violet a 'Spanish beauty' of about Ruth's age, has been with them since a few weeks after Clare's birth. Violet lived with her father in North Devon. She was not a nanny by training but when Ruth interviewed her for the role it was trust at first sight. 'We have got a lot to thank Vi for,' Ruth tells George, on 20 December 1918, before raising Violet's salary, 'More than we can ever repay I think … she was so utterly surprised [at the increase in pay] that she had not much to say …'

Ruth's teacher training course in London consists of fifty hours of lectures, fifty hours of teaching using the materials and fifty hours of observation of Montessori classes. Shortly after embarking on the programme Ruth confirms that Montessori is, in her considered opinion 'the thing'. But it is not only the older generation who are sceptical.

George is already shocked to find that the woman he married has turned into such a hands-on 'henny' mother – puffing out her feathers, clucking about. Unlike his own mother Ruth nurses her children for six months before putting them on the bottle. Ruth defends herself robustly telling George that if he didn't realise she would be 'henny' 'there was a big lump of me you didn't know'. But out of his wife's ear shot George confides to Geoffrey that it is 'rather annoying to me' that the children absorbed Ruth's attention for not just nine months of pregnancy 'but more like fifteen'. From his army posting in France, George writes to Ruth asking if they can move both the day and night nurseries out of the way, right up to the third floor of The Holt.

When Ruth first moots the idea of training to become a Montessori teacher, George expresses his concern to Ruth that Clare will be in for a 'dull childhood'. All her toys will be educational toys; all her play will be assessed for its educational potential. But Ruth holds firm arguing that learning will be 'a delightful game [at] any opportunity' and it will never be called a lesson. She believes that the early years of a child's development are critical. Although George may be disparaging, he has begun drawing up a prospectus for a new type of public school for children aged 11 to 18. Over several meetings at The Holt, his teacher-climber friends David and Geoffrey join forces to devise a prospectus.

Ruth's Montessori training can be seen as a major influence. The curriculum for George's ideal school lays particular emphasis on Arts and Craft design. It allocates time for community work outside the school and across all social classes. George and Geoffrey want to pioneer outdoor education, prioritising it over traditional school games. The school (which George envisages a physical school rather than a system of education) is designed to create 'cosmopolitan citizens' rather than perpetuating the traditional system, which stirs up the kind of nationalism that leads to clashes and war.

Ruth agrees with George's idea for developing 'cosmopolitan citizens', but rather than wait for secondary education she wants to begin earlier. Maria Montessori created her international system from modest beginnings at the Casa dei Bambini in Italy. Now it is being rolled out around the world. For her time, Ruth's stance on both Montessori and on equal education for girls is revolutionary. Despite George's initial scepticism, and her father's increasingly cruel teasing, Ruth persists with her Montessori training. She feels that disapproval is a small price to pay for the benefits it will bring to their children and to a peaceful future.

\* \* \*

On 2 August 1915, Ruth tries to describe how she feels about George being in danger:

> You see, I can't write all I think & feel because it is all how much I want you back and my longing for this awful war to be over & my fear for you. And I do not want to give way to it by talking about it too much.

Six days later, she captures the paradox of pride and anxiety that defines her future predicament with 'crystal' precision: 'You know my dear how full my heart is of love for you and that although it means so much anxiety [it] is my greatest joy.' She is proud that he is fighting for freedom. The danger is justified by the selfless, noble motivation. He is doing what is right. 'I don't want to wrap you from all harm and evil,' she tells him, 'I want you to be strong and courageous and rise above it all.'

What does all this tell us about how Ruth would have reacted in December 1914 when she was pushed off that mountain in Wales? Is it possible that Ruth felt that the 'melodrama' at her expense was a 'tease'. Was George's pantomime of diving over the edge the start of some kind of practical joke? Ruth's father teased her relentlessly about her Montessori teacher training, but she persisted. Ruth observed that George's mother could bully her daughters, but Ruth declares herself to be 'unbullyable'. She doesn't 'rise' or react to teasing, instead she consciously 'rises above it all'. She was pushed off a mountain by a man she had married five months before. She picked herself up. She continued. She does not take offence easily, she makes an effort not to indulge her fear. She is resilient and she forges her own path.

# Chapter Nine

# Prejudice and 'Personal Ambitions'

Letter from Ralph Brooke to Mary Brooke,
Magdelene College Archives,
Cambridge University, Cambridge

Letter from Ruth Mallory to George Mallory,
November 1918,
Magdelene College Archives,
Cambridge University, Cambridge

The danger posed by the 'anti-Hun' movement is very real in Britain during the First World War, a time of hatred and hysteria, of persecution of those with German-sounding names. Dachshunds are kicked in the street. Bechstein pianos, once prized, are now dragged out and burned. But Ruth will not even speak ill of the Germans. In her opinion, nationality is simply an accident of birth. Ruth holds her beliefs even when not-hating the enemy is viewed with suspicion. Even when that suspicion is thrown upon King George V and his Saxe-Coburg-Gotha royal family. Kneeling at the altar in St Peter and St Paul's church, in Godalming, Ruth has a mystical sense of comradeship with her German equivalent, the wife of a German soldier. Both of them are praying for 'his' safety 'and yet,' she tells George, 'some must be killed'.

Ruth's principled stance is dangerous. The document that encapsulates this is a letter from George's brother-in-law Ralph Brooke to George's sister Mary. 'Aren't [the d'Arányi sisters] enemy aliens?', Ralph asks his wife. 'I'm glad you didn't have to go to tea with the Huns.'

The 'Huns' that Ralph Brooke refers to are the Hungarian musicians, sisters Jelly d'Arányi and Adila Fachiri (née d'Arányi). Jelly is the more famous of the two. She is Ruth's age, a stunningly beautiful virtuoso violinist. Following sell-out concert tours of the United States and Europe before the war, she and her sister settled in London. After war was declared, Prime Minister Herbert Asquith tried to protect Jelly by leaving the prime ministerial car outside her concerts lest the anti-Hun demonstrators ruin the show. Although Ruth doesn't share Asquith's immunity as prime minister, she too defies the anti-Hun hysteria and invites Jelly to Westbrook for tea. By doing so, she not only embraces the risk of disapproval or denunciation, but something more personal.

Following Clare's birth, Ruth was in bed recovering for nearly a month. Ruth was still in bed when Jelly happened to give a concert at Charterhouse, so George went by himself. After the concert, George confessed to David that when 'Miss d'Arányi' caught his eye, 'an electric shock' went through him. Days later, Ruth received a letter from a Miss d'Arányi, whom she had never met. In an almost illegible giant looping hand, Jelly warned Ruth that Mr Mallory had flirted with her.

For Ruth to ask Jelly to tea shows that she (as Ruth's friend Hilda Haig-Brown told me in an interview in 2007) 'flowed against the stream'. Hilda is one of the Charterhouse families involved with Ruth's Montessori classes at The Holt. Along with everyone else I interviewed who knew Ruth, Hilda assured me that Ruth was not the compliant, conventional, soft focus woman that Adrian Harding's double portrait implies. The story of Ruth and Jelly's friendship that follows was, in Hilda's opinion, typical of Ruth.

It begins when Ruth receives Jelly's letter telling Ruth that her husband was not to be trusted. Ruth replies that she is sure George had not meant to flirt. He was simply enraptured by Miss d'Arányi wonderful playing. She assures Jelly that she trusts George 'as I would trust God', but even this unequivocal declaration is not enough for Ruth.

When the anti-Hun hysteria is at its height in the middle of the war and Jelly and her friends are being targeted, Ruth makes a point of having a regular and very public tea with Jelly in the Lyons' tea room near her Montessori training centre in London. Ruth deliberately chooses the window seat, to make sure she can be seen. She could have avoided Jelly for two reasons: as a threat to her marriage and as a threat to her patriotic reputation. She does not.

Back to December 1914, and Ruth is falling off the mountain, that ridge up to Snowdon in the hurricane snowstorm. She is so contrary, so determined to 'flow against the stream' that she deliberately refuses to follow George's instructions to dive off the ridge and is fully aware that she must accept the consequences.

But Ruth doesn't just accept consequences. Beridge (Berry) is born on 16 September 1917. Shortly afterwards, on 13 November, the man Jelly loved, Frederick Kelly, was killed in the war. Ruth invites Jelly to be Berry's godmother. By doing so she is inviting Jelly to be part of her family. Since Jelly will never marry, Berry becomes the daughter that she will never have.

There is more war to come following Beridge's christening. The end is captured in a momentous historical letter, which Ruth starts in wartime and finishes in peace: 'I don't think I can possibly write you an intelligent letter,' Ruth tells her husband trying anyway. 'I am too full of waiting emotion.'

The date at the top of the letter is 11 November 1918. George is finally back in France, having missed most of the war. First he was held back in terrible safety in the classroom. Then he was invalided home to have his ankle operated upon – an old climbing injury rather than a war injury. And finally instead of being posted back to France, he was sent around 'endless training camps' in the United Kingdom. (From his exhaustive research, Wade Davis suspects that friends in high places – perhaps Edward Marsh, Winston Churchill's private secretary – may have been protecting him. Marsh had edited George's published graduate thesis on James Boswell and had perhaps fallen in love with George.)

As she writes, Ruth is 'waiting and listening to hear the first thing that shall tell us the news of peace has come. We may hear any time now.' Frankly she is hoping for something dramatic, a band marching up over the hill banging drums, a blasting trumpet or two perhaps?

In France, George's commanding officer Major Gwilym Lloyd George, who is Prime Minister David Lloyd George's son, has been called to Versailles, where the negotiations are taking place. 'Lucky dog!' writes George. He is jealous of the men who can be witness to history. He is also envious of the men who have really embraced the most danger that the war could offer, those who have been mentioned in despatches, who have receive medals for valour and for reckless bravery. George tells his father that

> If I haven't escaped so many chances of death as plenty of others, still it is surprising to find myself a survivor, and it's not a lot I have always wanted … Anyway, it's good to be alive now.

In the Westbrook school room where Ruth is writing her letter, she listens as the grandfather clock ticks loudly towards 11.00 am. (Her father collects grandfather clocks and it appeals to him to have each one wound to go off at a slightly different time.) Blocking out the plucking tick, Ruth tries to organise her thoughts. She has just received a letter from George. 'The only possible jar to our happiness,' he tells her, 'will be my personal ambitions … You must be patient with me, my dearest one.'

How does Ruth hear this? Her 'personal ambition' was for George to be spared. One of the techniques Ruth has used to manage her anxiety was to picture the worst. What if George were killed? To brace herself she has visualised that terrible alternative reality in vivid detail. In that reality she turns the handle of the front door of The Holt and walks in alone. 'Think what this would have been if you had been killed,' she tells George to bring him to reason: 'Think what this would have been … if I had been going … to live there alone with only the children.' But in warning her of his personal ambitions, George is confessing that for him, survival is not enough. If he is to be alive at the end of the war: 'I should have liked to return home, if not a hero, at least a man of arms more tried than I have been.'

As Ruth listens to the clock ticking towards 11.00 am in the Westbrook school room in 1918, she can remember their first letters as an engaged couple. Back then before the war in 1914 George, was watching a cricket match at Charterhouse and she was suffering that fishy holiday in Ireland. Back then George's brother-in-law Ralph Brooke's team won and Ralph was the winning captain. 'Wouldn't you like me to be a hero like that?' George asked Ruth. From his most recent letters, that it is not only Ruth's desire for him to be 'a hero' that counts. George wrote not to Ruth but to Mary Ann,

> I was wishing the other day that I could know the individual minimum, as I call it to myself, for everyone – the least a man would be content to leave behind as his share of life accomplished wouldn't one know something if one could know that?

What will George 'leave behind'? On the cusp of Armistice, even before George is demobbed, Ruth realises that her experience of vicarious danger is not over. Perhaps it has only just begun. Ruth has yet to experience being George's wife without the threat that she may become a widow; that his children may be made fatherless by that random bullet, that artillery shell or that deadly gas. 'But darling,' she tells him, 'after this war I don't think I shall want you to do anything very dangerous for a long time, certainly not unless you take me with you ...'

If George is going to be in danger again, Ruth wants to be in danger with him. The not-knowing of vicarious danger is worse than being in danger herself. The war has convinced her of that. George agrees. The vicarious danger that he experienced when she was giving birth, or on the arête, was much worse than the quasi-adventure of fighting a war. Ruth declares that she will choose to join him if he chooses danger, but will she? Ruth is torn:

> It seems a pity to live and not experience all as much as possible, without stopping ordinary life which I believe to be the biggest experience of all ...

> I should love the expeditions with a spice of danger in them specially if I had no babies. I shouldn't be much use now for very strenuous expeditions. If I hadn't got babies or a husband I think I could be quite brave.

Ruth has told him 'if only I were a man & could be there with you. You would like me to be with you and have the experience you are having wouldn't you?'

But she doesn't want to be a man all the time, she wants to be a wife, a mother: the mother of his children. At the moment she is writing the letter, the church bells of St Peter and St Paul begin to ring out. The war is officially over. Ruth can hardly believe it. There are no trumpets. There is no band marching over the hill. She is still sitting at her desk in the schoolroom when she sets her pen back on the paper to finish her letter to George: 'It is over dear, the bells have begun.' Ruth does not have personal ambitions that involve danger for her or George, but it is her, rather than George, who will come closest to dying next.

When George receives the telegram that Ruth is dangerously ill, he is still in France waiting to be demobbed. Ruth is supposed to be safe at home, but the world has tilted and their positions are reversed. In reading the telegram, George recalls that abysmal sense of danger and vertigo; a sensation he is immune from even on the most precipitous rock face.

Ruth must have caught a form of Spanish flu after the packed Armistice church service in St Peter and St Paul that she rushed down to straight after finishing that letter. Or perhaps she caught it from the flag waving crowds on the streets of Godalming afterwards. George thinks she might die. The disease is taking the young and strong. Autopsies reveal lungs drenched in fluid. A report in the *Surrey Advertiser* of 26 October 1918, under the heading 'A WIDESPREAD EPIDEMIC' reports schools closed, medical staff stretched to the limit and suggests the use of face masks and rigorous handwashing techniques to prevent the 'wildfire' spread of the disease.

When Ruth finally emerges from the sickroom she has no sense of how long she has been ill. She was unconscious for most of it. When she is finally allowed to wield a pen, she tells George that it was 'a lucky let off I think'. She refuses to give into anxiety. Sickness, she concludes, is just 'a waste of time and money'. The doctor later informs her, on 19 November 1918, that she was 'the best pneumonia patient he has had'. George, by now used to Ruth's determined stoicism, is not convinced that she is beyond danger. He is still worried: 'I am sorry you have been distressed and made unhappy by my being ill,' Ruth tells him on 26 November 1918, '… [but] it might easily have been worse …'

Is that what she thought as the rope brought her up short on the ridge on Bwlch Glas in 1914? At least it did not break like Edward Whymper's rope on the Matterhorn: 'it might easily have been worse …'

# Chapter Ten

# Survivors' Meet

Two group photographs, Pen-y-Pass Party,
Geoffrey Winthrop Young,
Easter 1919,
Pen-y-Pass Scrapbook,
Alpine Club Archives,
(Please see plate section for reference.)

In the first photograph, on which this chapter is based, Ruth is about to be put through the toughest climb of her life. It is Easter 1919 at Pen-y-Pass – the survivors' climbing meet. Twenty-three of their Pen-y-Pass climbing friends are dead, eleven are maimed, yet George has survived intact. Those few survivors gather with their wives outside the Pen-y-Pass Hotel as shafts of sunshine sweep over them and on down Llanberis Pass.

Ruth, thin and pale but clad in her tweed climbing togs, stands on the road outside the hotel. She is squinting into the sun at the photographer. She wears her hair in a practical low pony tail at the nape of her neck. The wind blows wisps of hair out behind her. Most of the photograph is taken up with a large open top car with spoked wheels. It is the blue second-hand American Studebaker-Flanders that George has just bought to drive Geoffrey, now an amputee with one leg, to the beginning of the day's climb. Geoffrey is determined that his injury will not hold him back. He has fashioned a special climbing foot to screw to the bottom of his false leg. This will be a hill start in every sense. Geoffrey's caption to the photograph reads:

> To carry GWY [Geoffrey] (now wed to Eleanor Slingsby) nearer to Lliwedd, Mallory (now wed to Ruth Turner) drove his blue car to Llydau, backing into the lake to turn.

Geoffrey's new wife Eleanor, 'Len', comes from a climbing family. She first met Geoffrey when she was 6 and has been coming to Pen-y-Pass to climb since she was a child. Normally, Len would be right there, pushing the car with Ruth. Instead, newly pregnant, Len sits primly in the seat behind her now one-legged husband. Ruth is smiling but behind her amusement she senses danger. There is danger in George's post-war ambitions to become 'more tried', to take his place amongst the ghosts, the missing men at Pen-y-Pass. On 20 October 1918, Ruth tried to reassure him that

> whether you [came] back as a war veteran, or whether you [had] only been out six months. You have done all you could do, and I am so glad that you should be left to live and work for the sake of the world ... I am also very very glad that your nerves have not been ruined by shell shock ...

The group preparing to push the Studebaker outside the Pen-y-Pass Hotel, try to focus not on their dead comrades, but on the future. There is only one word on everyone's lips: 'Everest'.

Many of those present are members of the Alpine Club. Together with Pen-y-Pass climber and president of the club Captain Percy Farrar, they have just attended a meeting at the Royal Geographic Society headquarters on Kensington Gore on 10 March 1918. 'Now the poles have been reached,' said Major John Noel at that meeting, 'it is generally felt that the next and equally important task is the exploration and mapping of Mount Everest.' But was it important or was it, as George described it to his sister: 'a merely fantastical performance'?

George was at Winchester College a few years below explorer Apsley Cherry-Garrard who had narrowly survived Captain Robert Falcon Scott's 'fantastical performance' at the South Pole before the First World War. With the wisdom of post-war hindsight, Scott's 'performance' now seemed curiously naïve. But it seems that having lost the race for the North Pole to the Americans in 1909, and the South Pole to the Norwegians in 1912, Francis Younghusband and others at the RGS are keen to focus on a British success at the 'Third Pole'.

Ruth agrees with George's views on the British attitude to expansionism or, as he calls it, the 'Grab-Policy which has prevailed in the past'. He is preparing to chair a debate at Charterhouse where he has returned to his role as a schoolmaster: 'This House Deplores the Extension of Our Colonial Responsibilities'. George associates expansionism with the misuse of power. It is precisely this 'greed' that the newly formed League of Nations is desperately trying to check. The League's peace keeping role is essential as the victors of the First World War try to claim the territory they 'won' at the expense of the overall good. But Everest may be part of that retro-politics, the grab policy of Empire colonialism. George and Ruth are focused in the opposite direction. They want to promote nation-blindness, internationalism and cosmopolitanism.

In a second photograph from the same climbing meet, Ruth stands in a group lined up outside the porch of the Pen-y-Pass Hotel. To her left is the

Irish climber and sailor Conor O Brien. This is the man with whom George has sailed, climbed and circumnavigated a room using picture rails alone. O Brien is a Home Ruler at a time when the Irish Question is becoming a pressing political issue. George suspects that he is running guns. O Brien is prepared to run the risk for a cause in which he passionately believes.

If Ruth glances left, she can see George sitting two beyond O Brien as they pose for this photograph. Although Ruth has made it clear that she would like a reprieve from anxiety, George is considering visiting Ireland himself. This is the big picture, but looking deeper into the Brownie black and white image of the group outside Pen-y-Pass, there are different shades of danger, different threats to Ruth.

Third in from the right, sitting on the ground just in front of George, is a man in a jelly bag hat. His name is Ferdy Speyer. Ferdy's wife, at the time this picture is taken, is Stella Speyer but her maiden name is Cobden-Sanderson. Decades into the future, Stella's letter will be found in the breast pocket of George's jacket. For the moment, all Ruth knows about Ferdy is his connection to Captain Scott.

Before the First World War, banker Sir Edgar Speyer who came from a prominent German Jewish banking family, was on the Privy Council. He was also the treasurer and major donor for Captain Scott's *Terra Nova* expedition (1910–1913) and therefore the father of that epic 'noble failure'. After the declaration of war, Speyer was accused of spying for Germany and hounded out of the country by the anti-Hun hysterics. How will the expedition to the 'Third Pole' be funded without him?

Ferdy Speyer, Sir Edgar's nephew, may believe that the British public are fickle, but Ferdy is fickle too. He has just fallen in love with his sister-in-law Dorothea (Dricks) Cobden-Sanderson. In the near future, Ferdy and Dorothea will divorce their respective spouses and marry each other. Stella Speyer will revert to her maiden name, Cobden-Sanderson.

For Ruth, the hidden dangers of the future are obscured for the moment by George's plans for the day's climb. He wants to invent a new traverse on the East Buttress of Y Lliwedd from the Bowling Green to the East Gully. 'This climb,' said Harold Porter, who wrote it up later in the November 1926 issue of the *Alpine Journal* was 'peculiarly typical of Mallory ...'

Ruth was already pushed beyond her limit in Snowdonia back in December 1914 with George and David. Now in Easter 1919, she finds herself back with the same climbing partners on a harder route. Ruth may have been 'the best pneumonia patient' just five months earlier, but now George expects her to keep up with him pioneering the Girdle Traverse. She has now been climbing for four years and he wants her name to be linked to a new route.

The first pitch of the new Traverse climb is, according to Harold Porter 'of unique character ... exceptionally severe'. In the *Alpine Journal*, issue 38, under the title 'Garter Traverse – Lliwedd', George describes it as 'sensational'. It is worth imagining Ruth completing this move.

> It is necessary to grasp a small square bracket on the wall with both hands and make a clear swing. Once he [no mention of 'she'] has arrived and recovered his dignity the climber finds a convenient leaf for his left hand, which renders his situation unexpectedly comfortable; and by turning his body until he can use this with his right hand, he finds himself ready to start along the traverse.

Later, Ruth's son-in-law David Robertson (Beridge's husband) learns that 'though tired by the climb [Ruth] responded to George's by no means unaffectionate prodding and finished like a veteran.' Was Ruth ever 'unexpectedly comfortable' on a rock face? Even in the act of falling off a rock face after being pushed? I try to imagine her grasping that small square bracket at the beginning of the Girdle Traverse, launching her whole body to swing from her hands to the next foot hold. She made that sensational, exceptionally severe move, not at ground level but on the near vertical surface hundreds of feet up.

In a two-page typed mini-biography *An Impression of Ruth Leigh-Mallory in the 1930s*, George's niece Barbara Newton Dunn describes Ruth as 'a strong person'. She writes it by way of explanation. Ruth was 'quiet and didn't push herself forward but she was by no means a nonentity'. To complete the square bracket swing George describes for the Garter Traverse, requires not just strength and technique but grit. Ruth had an inner strength that enabled her, somehow, to keep up with George's requirement not just for classic climbs with the 'spice of danger' but for new routes offering a hotter spice that was in his opinion: 'sensational'.

Chapter Eleven

# Bouldering and Bloomsbury

The 'Snuff Box' boulder,
Zennor, Cornwall, 1920

Virginia Woolf's diary entry,
30 March 1921

Letters from Lytton Strachey to Vanessa Stephen

Letters from George Mallory to Lytton Strachey,
June 1915,
Auctioned at Bonhams

The next piece of evidence is not a photograph but a granite boulder known as the 'Snuff Box'. The boulder, approximately 10 or 12-foot square, is in the garden of Eagles' Nest; a house set on a rocky outcrop just west of St Ives in North Cornwall. From the top of the boulder, there is a panoramic view west down to the Atlantic Ocean and east up to the moor where in summer there are patches of sulphur yellow gorse. George and Ruth's friends, Will Arnold-Forster and his wife Katherine Laird Cox, known to all as 'Ka', bought Eagles' Nest after the war. Until then, Will and his family friends the Stephens, knew it as their childhood summer holiday rental.

Virginia Stephen, now Virginia Woolf, described Eagles' Nest as a cross between castle and a boarding house. Just over the Eagles' Nest garden wall lived Arthur Westlake Andrews, the 'father' of Cornish sea cliff climbing. Andrews is the Geoffrey Winthrop Young of Cornwall. He founded the unofficial Cornish Climbing Club and produced the *Climbing Guide to Cornwall* with E.C. Pyatt in 1950. Will Arnold-Forster and the Stephen girls, used to climb the Snuff Box when they were children. Now in the early 1920s, their childhood games have become formalised and Virginia Woolf describes Cornwall's early 'bouldering scene' in her diary: 'Visited Arnold-Forster's at Eagle's [*sic*] Nest … Endless varieties of nice elderly men to be seen there, come for the climbing …'

Ruth knows that Leslie Stephen (Virginia Woolf and her sister Vanessa Bell's father) was a keen Alpinist. Will and the sisters spent their summer holidays with their nannies on the beach at St Ives while Leslie Stephen was away climbing in the Alps. Stephen is one of the only climbers to have attempted a theory about the 'permissible level of danger for quiet fathers of young families'. He compared it with hunting:

> Many more men are given to hunting than to climbing, and yet many more are killed on the Alps than in the hunting-field. But hunting is an amusement which reaches the greatest permissible standard of danger for quiet fathers of families. Therefore, by an easy syllogism, it follows that Alpine climbing is too dangerous for quiet fathers of families. It may not be more dangerous than steeple-chasing; but who would recommend a middle-aged gentleman, with a wife and children, to ride a steeple-chase?

If he was going to do anything dangerous, Ruth had asked him to 'take me with you', but George did not take Ruth to the Alps in summer 1919. Why? Earlier she told him that the only thing that would prevent her coming was a baby:

> I shall be thrilled when we go there together, but there is no telling when that will be, a baby may always get in the way for me. It will be worth it.

Ruth did not have her next child until August 1920 so although I do not know why she did not accompany George in 1919, I do know that she eschewed a mountaineering holiday the following summer of 1920 because she was in the last months of her third pregnancy. Perhaps Cornwall with its Snuff Box might have offered a more appealing alternative at this time?

When George took Ruth to stay with the Arnold-Forsters in the early 1920s, some enthusiasts were pioneering bouldering as a form of climbing in its own right. The traditionalists were hard to convince. Pen-y-Pass climber Oscar Eckenstein started informal bouldering competitions in 1902 in the Himalayas as a way of training local porters. At the time he and fellow Pen-y-Pass climber Aleister Crowley were planning to climb K2, the second highest mountain in the world, just 781 feet lower than Mount Everest. But on page 139 of *Mountain Craft*, Geoffrey could not bring himself to see bouldering as more than 'the pleasantest of off-day distractions'. Geoffrey regarded it as an exercise in problem solving. The real value of bouldering '... is only for the expert who has learned to treat every rock with the same respect, be it five feet or five hundred feet.'

As an experienced climber by the 1920s, Ruth can imagine that the Snuff Box boulder in the Eagles' Nest garden is not just 'five but five hundred feet' above the ground, as Geoffrey suggests. She can practice her balance climbing technique where the challenge, as essayed in *Mountain Craft*, is to climb an easy block without your hands, or balance up with such light fingerholds that a friend can pass their hand under yours.

The sea cliffs at the foot of the slope falling west from Eagles' Nest is the Atlantic Ocean, offer sensational climbing. This is what excites George. In their bachelor days he and Geoffrey used to swim naked in the sea and clamber, still naked straight up those cliffs. As Geoffrey claims, those cliffs have many devotees:

> their wave-polished and often undercut bases, their summits artificially sculptured and constantly strained and fractured afresh by the fall of the cliff below.

Although the crumbling sea cliffs may represent some of the most dangerous climbing, there are other local threats that are more insidious. Ruth knows that in 1905, Oscar Eckenstein's former climbing partner Crowley reached the highest altitude recorded at 25,000 feet, on Kanchenjunga in the Himalayas. Although Ruth has probably not met Crowley, she knows that he is no longer welcome at Pen-y-Pass. But in the early 1920s, by the time the Mallorys visit Eagles' Nest, his influence was beginning to be felt in Cornwall.

Cambridge educated Crowley disgraced himself with his mistreatment of his porters and fellow climbers on Kanchenjunga. Since then he has become a satanist and styled himself 'The Beast'. The Arnold-Forsters are determined not to let Crowley pollute their Cornish haven. However unpredictable the sea cliffs are for climbing, and however 'ghost proof' the four friends claim to be, they regard Crowley and his Cornish-based satanic acolytes as unpredictable and unwelcome. On the scale of danger with steeplechase and satanism – bouldering on the Snuff Box just '5 feet' from the ground might seem relatively safe to Ruth.

When it comes to bouldering, it is not the danger that draws George, but the problem solving. A century later, standing in the garden of Eagles' Nest watching my 20-year-old son climb the Snuff Box, I imagine the four of them, Ruth, George, Will and Ka standing together devising new routes. I can imagine George and Will circling the boulder, pointing at possible lines up with the stem of their pipes. Arthur Andrews might join them. Eventually, between them, they settle on six routes of varying levels of difficultly. Andrews will later use the Snuff Box as a set piece to test new recruits for his climbing club. Anyone who can climb the sixth, the hardest route on the west face, can probably manage the sea cliffs, where a fall would be much more serious than a tumble into the Arnold-Forsters' flower bed.

George might encourage Ruth, who he still regards as his 'pupil', to try the route he has devised up the west side of the boulder. It involves an overhang.

Ruth has small hands. She struggles to stretch her fingers to span the holes to play her father's silver flute, but perhaps by 1920 her fingers are stronger. Clare remembers her father, George, doing his climbing exercises every morning: naked. He performed pull-ups hanging by his finger tips from the door frame of his dressing room where she often slept at The Holt. (They all know that Oscar Eckenstein was a pull-up machine. He could do one-armed pull ups until you told him to stop.)

After climbing, both couples might swim naked in the sea. Is this the moment when Ruth confides in Ka that, after two daughters, George really wants a son? Ka, also newly pregnant, wants a son too. Ruth may be aware of the rumour that, as Rupert Brooke's girlfriend, Ka may have borne his child. Ruth knows that when Rupert was dying from an infected insect bite in Skyros in 1915, he wrote to Ka telling her she was the nearest he would have to a widow. Does Ka ask Ruth for advice on childbirth? Do they discuss the relative danger of delivering the first child by comparison with subsequent deliveries? At that moment early in 1920, neither woman realises that they are they both pregnant with boys: John Mallory and Mark Arnold-Forster. Through entangled futures, their sons are to become step-brothers.

Although they cannot see into that future, or any future, Will and Ka are part of the Bloomsbury set. They know more about George's 'past' than Ruth does. Ruth appreciates George's good looks, she loves to watch his athletic form in motion. On 25 November 1916, Ruth expressed her response to the male body to George:

> So far I have always loved men running best ... It is a glorious thing to see a strong young man run. I remember seeing you run once with great pleasure when I first knew you. I was playing Lacrosse at Shackleford and you ran past along the foot path with a glorious long swift springy run.

Ruth may suspect that both men and women are attracted to George. But she probably does not know, as Will and Ka do, that George once had a brief homosexual affair with Lytton Strachey's brother James when they were both students at Cambridge. Weeks before marrying Ruth, George assured Lytton that marriage would not change him: 'probably nobody is monogamous'. Perhaps George's comment to Lytton on monogamy was worded purely for Lytton's delectation. It is significant from Ruth's point of view that monogamy and sexuality were openly discussed amongst their Bloomsbury friends. Ruth refuses to recognise the stigma of illegitimacy and is committed to reversing prejudice.

Time spent in bohemian Bloomsbury company has an impact upon her. When describing Will, Ruth admits to George that she not only loves Will but she is 'in love' with him. In other letters, Ruth might tell George that she loves someone but not that she is 'in love' with them. Staying with the Arnold-Forsters at Eagles' Nest, George does not hear her declaration as a danger to their marriage or as a statement about her view of monogamy. But Ruth does not lie. Her statement reveals that her love for Will is, if not overtly physical, romantic rather than platonic.

Ruth does not emphasise Will's wholesome nature as she does with the nurturing Ka whom she describes as 'a richly ploughed field', but tells George that

I'm in love Will quite a lot, I was trying to think just how I love him. I think I love him very much as I love flowers and trees and streams and all beautiful places, he is like the spirit of them ... a delicately tuned spirit ...

The dangers in Cornwall are multilayered. From the Bloomsbury Group's attitude to love, to Crowley's satanism and George's enthusiasm for climbing crumbling sea cliffs. Ruth focuses on the Snuff Box boulder, her eyes the colour of the Atlantic Ocean that is just behind her.

Looking up at the boulder 100 years later, I can see where Ruth might have placed one toe of her rubber climbing shoes into the base of the over-hang. I imagine her hooking the tips of her fingers into the stone here, feeling the grainy texture of the greenish rock. From watching George, she knows that good climbers are good planners, economic with their moves, efficient with their energy. They do not scrabble for a foothold; they have 'quiet feet'. She must remember George's route up from this position.

Some people climb better with an audience. Does Ruth? The second she takes her other foot off she is going to have to hold her whole weight on her hands before reaching up to the next hold. The faster she can become vertical the faster she can reduce the strain on her fingers.

Under the boulder there is soft earth. In that earth Will nurtures his prized collection of alpine flowers brought back from trips abroad. (Will has sent children and their entire families home for accidentally crushing a flower.) Although Ruth will only be 5 feet off the ground rather than 500, the stakes are high. Her audience is comprised of three people whose opinion of her matters: men she is 'in love' with and Ka, a woman she admires perhaps above all others. As she grips the rock and pulls herself up, she tries not to lose all dignity, grace and good will by a tumble into the tulips.

Ruth is falling again off that ridge in Snowdonia in winter 1914. Perhaps George wants her to feel the 500 foot-fear; to make her perform at the top of her game. But Ruth's rare combination of wisdom and innocence has already seen to that. Ruth expresses it to George, on 26 June 1916: 'Life is not an easy flower garden existence ... But something far finer and more difficult and stern.'

\* \* \*

In December 1920, after John's birth and an autumn term, George finally makes his long planned visit to Dublin. It is at the end of what the Irish newspapers called 'a black year'. With Ruth's agreement, George takes the risk of visiting the epicentre of a civil war, in order to prove his usefulness to the League, more specifically, to Gilbert Murray who founded the League of Nations Union with H.G. Wells in 1918. George teaches Gilbert Murray's son Basil at Charterhouse. Basil has probably visited The Holt. (Most Charterhouse boys remembered Ruth's Bournville chocolate cake for the rest of their lives.)

George's visit to Dublin was probably made possible by his climbing contacts including Conor O Brien who was at Pen-y-Pass with George and Ruth in 1919. O Brien is a staunch Home Ruler. Murray is known for his controversial pro-Home Rule and anti-colonial views. Ruth, who has never been afraid of controversy where her convictions are concerned, has been reading up on Irish history. She is dismayed at the attitude of the English landlords to their Irish tenants. Ruth is a Home Ruler through and through.

Will Arnold-Forster knows Murray and has already worked with the League. Will does not have to prove his credentials to Murray. If Fletcher had released George from the classroom to that job at the Admiralty back in 1915, perhaps Ruth might not have to brace herself for a second stint as the wife of a man in a war zone.

When George returns from Ireland, Ruth learns how dangerous the visit really was. One night George was woken at 1.30 am with a torch in his face. The man had a loaded revolver in his other hand. He asked George if he was a Protestant. George told him that his father was a clergyman in the Church of England. Fortunately, it was the right answer.

How does Ruth feel when she hears this? George explains that it was not the revolver in his face that worried him most; it was something far worse. George saw the body of a child who had just been killed. He believed that the child had been shot by mistake by English troops. He thought he had become inured to death but the image of that juvenile corpse haunts him. What can they, the Mallorys, do to protect children from becoming the collateral damage of war?

Ruth is already aware of Eglantyne Jebb, not just because she is George's mother's second cousin. Eglantyne has recently founded the charity Save the Children with advice from John's godfather, Geoffrey Keynes. Ruth may have met Eglantyne. 'All wars whether just or unjust, disastrous or victorious', stated

Eglantyne, 'are waged against the child.' Ruth knows that Eglantyne has a reputation, in the family, for being curiously detached. It is the theoretical child rather than the actual child that interests her most. But although Eglantyne does not enjoy fraternising with children as Ruth does, she is bold, business like and very effective. The previous year in 1919, she'd been arrested for distributing leaflets in Trafalgar Square with pictures of emaciated children in rags. The leaflets were headed: 'Our blockade did this'.

In almost every exchange of letters during the war, the Mallorys discussed the morality of nations and what form the peace should take. In their opinion, the children of the enemy are innocents. Like the dead child in Dublin, they are the collateral of a dangerous situation created by adults. But the Treaty of Versailles requires the former enemy to pay reparations that will keep Germany in poverty. The Mallorys sense that a punitive peace could be dangerous; brutalising the former enemy into retaliation. Ruth has never hated 'the Hun'. If those children inherit the prejudices of their parents, there will never be peace between nations.

The evidence for this part of Ruth's biography comes from my interview in 2007 with Marianne Nevel (wife of Franz). Ruth first hears of Franz through fellow climber Mabel Barker, a Quaker humanist and educationalist. Mabel knows that Ruth runs a Montessori nursery and that she wants to put Maria Montessori's theory of internationalism into action. At some point, Ruth adds her name to a list of British hosts who offer to have the children of their former enemy to stay. In 1921, at the time that George is writing up his report after seeing the dead child in Dublin, a young Czech orphan Franz Knefel (later Nevel) receives an invitation at his orphanage, the Kinderheim, in Vienna.

As Marianne recalls, 9-year-old Franz is given a copy of a letter agreeing to release him to visit an English family. It is conditional upon him passing a medical. Franz has another letter from 'the lady in Godalming' agreeing to be responsible for his maintenance while he is in England. All he knows about the family is that they have three children: all younger than him. Franz begins practising his English and his smile. He is given a label to wear around his neck during the sea journey across the English Channel planned for summer 1921.

Franz is not, technically, an orphan, but he has been placed in an orphanage by his mother. It is not clear when he first became aware that he was illegitimate; the result of an extramarital affair between a married employer and his housekeeper. Ruth and George refused to accept the conventional attitude to illegitimate children of their time. They do not want children like Franz to be the victims of prejudice or war.

When Ruth is 'saved' by a rope that prevents her from falling down the slope in 1914, the danger she feels then, the fear for her safety, is over in a moment. For children like Franz – hungry, socially excluded and nationally shamed – danger is a constant state of being.

# Chapter Twelve

# Pinnacle Club

Ruth Mallory's application form for the Pinnacle Club,
7 March 1921,
Pinnacle Club Archives

Would Ruth have become a climber without George? He was happiest on a mountain, perhaps happier still on a mountain with her. But both before and after having children, in what Ruth referred to as 'ordinary life', she takes every opportunity to push her body. 'These warm days,' she says as Godalming pitched into the winter frosts one November during the war, 'make me feel gloriously full of life. I long to run and use my body. I am glad if I am late for a train and have to run for it.'

Ruth devises her own triathlons. 'I shall have to go out for a run,' she says at a time when to see a woman jogging down the street caused shoppers to jump into door-ways in alarm. Instead of giving the grocer's boy the basket to carry up the hill from Godalming, she did it herself because 'I'm sure I am stronger than they are.'

She re-digs the garden (out of Beagly, the gardener's sight); she drags the water bowser around (after her father declares that a woman can't do it) and she gets so hot proving him wrong that she has to plunge (naked) into the Wey. (Where were the shoppers by then, one wonders?) Ruth loves to dance. She puts the gramophone on the garden wall and teaches her Montessori pupils to perform the intricate patterns of English country dancing. The elegance and exercise required by rock climbing suits Ruth perfectly. But there *is* the danger. Was it 'ordinary' danger, or did Ruth try to make it so to justify it to herself?

In the mini biography of 'Aunt Ruth' by Barbara Newton Dunn, we learn that

Though seeming on the surface good-tempered and placid, she was intolerant and could even be scornful of what she considered to be 'silliness' – frivolity or affectation of any sort.

Ruth has no tolerance for silliness, most of all her own silliness. She does not let herself give up; she throws herself into every climb and chases herself up it. Ruth's 'intolerance' is a personality trait that means, by 1921, she will be invited to become a founder member of the first all-female rock climbing club in Britian, the Pinnacle Club. It seems that she was the tenth member of that still thriving club.

Ruth fills out the application form on 7 March 1921. The list of climbing routes on this form is extensive, from her strenuous mid-winter novitiate in 1914, to spring 1921. Four years of her climbing life are against a background of world war. Most of the climbs are done when George is home on leave. During this time she has been pregnant for twenty-seven months and breast feeding for eighteen. But Ruth has balanced the danger inherent in childbirth with the danger of war and somehow, the equation resolves in favour of embracing the danger inherent in climbing.

## The Holt – 1921

Ruth is sitting at a desk holding a pen with a sheet of paper before her. She has her back to the mantlepiece. The pose is languid, elegant, a Dutch interior transposed to Surrey. She rests her chin on the back of her left hand with the finger tips pointed towards her neck.

Over the title 'WOMEN'S ROCK CLIMBING CLUB', Ruth can see founder Martha Emily 'Pat' Kelly's hand-stamped capital letters: 'THE PINNACLE CLUB'. The stamp is slightly inclined at an angle like the rising ground up to a crag. The ink across the stamp is inconsistent and makes a lighter print at the end of the title. Ruth's form is numbered by hand in the top right corner as number '10'.

Date:                    7 March 1921
Name:                    Ruth Mallory
Address:                 The Holt,
                         Godalming

State whether the
application is for
Full or Associate
Membership:              Full

Particulars:- [*sic*]
(If possible, state when climbs were done.)
Tryfan                   Grooved arete
                         Milestone Buttress (leading)
                         South Buttress

|            |                                |
|------------|--------------------------------|
|            | Central                        |
|            | North                          |
|            | Craig y Isfa Great Gully       |
| Llewidd    | E Peak Rout [sic] II           |
|            | Roof Rout [sic]                |
|            | Garter Traverse (1st ascent)   |
|            | Parsons Nose                   |
|            | Clogwyn y Dilysgyl Gambit      |

continued:- [sic]

|             |                               |
|-------------|-------------------------------|
| Scawfell    | Steep Ghyll travers & Moss Ghyll |
| Pillar      | New West                      |
| Great Gable | The Needle                    |
|             | Arrowhead Arete               |
| Skye 3 days climbing ...  |                 |

The qualification for the Pinnacle Club is that she can lead; that she can go first. Ruth cannot only lead but has even put up a new route: a first ascent. Setting her pen on the paper Ruth writes: 'Skye 3 days climbing – Sgùrr nan Gillean, Bartair Tooth & other unremembered names including a first ascent.'

Ruth is motivated by physical challenge and by using her body, more than a summit or abstract heroics – 'unremembered names' – sums up her attitude well.

Like Ruth, Pat Kelly, the club's founder has only been climbing for seven years. She works with her husband, a clerk in an insurance firm in Manchester. They do not have children. Pat may have made a deliberate decision not to. Following the death of her mother, Pat spent her young adult life as a guardian of her younger siblings. Now, Pat choses to climb. As her husband later observed: 'she called [the Pinnacle Club] more than once, her child'.

After the devastating losses of the First World War, there were fewer men available to take women climbing. Pat founded the Pinnacle Club because she became tired of having to wait patiently for a man to become available. Once, in the Lake District, sick of waiting, she soloed Owen Glynne Jones's route up Scawfell Pinnacle from Deep Ghyll. After the initial shock, the men suggested that solo climbing might not be the only way of dispensing with the requirement for a man. With Geoffrey and Len Winthrop Young's encouragement, Pat wrote a letter to *The Manchester Guardian* proposing an all-female rock climbing club.

Ruth met Pat Kelly at Pen-y-Pass. Slight and smiley, Pat is according to Geoffrey 'an entirely generous person'. On a rock face she moves with a deftness and a lightness that is extraordinary. Ruth admires Pat's breed of feminism.

Pat simply wanted to 'stand on her own feet without in any sense wishing to compete with or outrival the male sex …'

Ruth wants her daughters to be able to stand on their own feet, regardless of the angle of the surface on which they stand. Instead of offering women a needle and thread to sew a different future, as her mother had with the Women's Guild of Arts, the Pinnacle Club offers them a rope and pitons.

It is important to briefly establish Ruth's stance on suffrage. She wasn't a suffragette, but she wanted to empower women to become economically independent of men; 'to earn their own living decently'. She also wanted them to be educated equally with men. She never addressed the issue head on in letters so we must deduce her opinion from glancing mentions in her letters to George.

Nine days after the Representation of the People Act 1918 was passed, Ruth told George that if she was voting 'I should vote coalition'. Ruth's aunt Theodora Powell established the Guildford branch of the National Union of Women's Suffrage Societies in 1909. Ruth, like her mother May, seems to have focused on empowerment through enabling women to achieve financial independence rather than on politics with a capital P. The Turners stance on feminism (as embroidered on the 1908 suffragist march banners by Ruth's aunt Christiana Jane Herringham née Powell) was 'Alliance not Defiance'.

In another anecdote, on 5 November 1918, Ruth admitted that she 'simply roared with laughter when [she] read the parliamentary discussion about whether women should sit in parliament or not'. A Mr Hobhouse 'asked what would happen if the Prime Minister were a woman and were in that state that every loving wife should be.' If a woman can climb and have babies, a woman could surely balance politics and family. 'Isn't it ridiculous and childish of people to talk like that …' concluded Ruth.

Ruth does not want women to be confined to a domestic sphere. She wants women to be equal to men, or she would not have kept up her membership of the Women's Guild of Arts, or joined the Pinnacle Club. The difference between those two feminist groups is that only the Pinnacle Club involves danger.

As a mother, Ruth is conflicted. Unlike Ruth, Len Winthrop Young, Geoffrey's wife, learned to climb with her father William Cecil Slingsby, the father of Norwegian mountaineering. Len and Geoffrey's first child, a son Jocelin, was just 1 and a ½ when Len agreed to become president of the Pinnacle Club in 1921. They all regret that Owen O'Malley ('something of a professional pessimist' in George's opinion) has banned his wife Mary Ann from climbing.

Ruth's inclination to embrace risk, what she calls her 'brave[ry]', is linked to her attitude to being a wife and mother. But on some level, she thrives on danger. Barbara Newton Dunn remembered that after playing Kick the Can (a form of 'tag' which Ruth called 'Lurky') one evening in Savernake Forest,

Ruth led the children back through the dark woods telling scary stories. 'Woe betide any faint heart who cringed at the sound of an owl or the breathing of an invisible cow behind a hedge,' wrote Barbara remembering years later. 'Don't be so perfectly ridiculous!' Ruth would say. 'It won't hurt you!'

When Ruth was pushed off that ledge in Wales, before she had children, did she enjoy the scare? Did she relish the sudden frisson of shock, of a near miss? For her, ordinary life does not mean 'a flower garden existence'. It is something far finer and more challenging. On a crag with the Pinnacle Club, Ruth can be scared but can also take charge, empower herself to face her fear. She can tell herself not to be so 'perfectly ridiculous' and extend her reach beyond her grasp. But she cannot in all honesty declare to her fellow climbers that: 'It won't hurt you!' The dangers in climbing are real.

# Part II

# Everest

## Snowdonia, Wales – September 2022

I arrive at the Pinnacle Club hut in Nant Gwynant, in failing light in September 2022. It has been raining hard 'biblical weather' even for Wales. The path leads over a stone bridge to the hut, The Emily Kelly Hut. As I stand on the bridge looking down, I see the stream in full spate. I am wondering what to expect from the 'Spartan Pinnacle Ladies' – I have heard that in wet weather, a stream bubbles up through the stone floor, sweeps across to a specially excavated channel by the wall and exists via the front door.

Teresa, a long-time member of the Pinnacle Club, opens the wooden door. Inside to my right there is a cosy woodburning stove flickering in a deep stone fireplace. To my left is a shiny modern kitchen. Around the walls are framed photographs of Pinnacle ladies hanging off overhangs, perched on precipices and generally defying gravity in unlikely and spectacular ways.

Teresa remembers meeting the original president, Len Winthrop Young. By that stage, Ruth's friend Len was a white-haired old lady with bad arthritis in both hips. On one occasion, navigating long corridors to deliver a climbing talk for the Pinnacle Club, she refused a wheelchair but agreed to be pushed on a tea trolley. Len was fun. She is known, in the climbing world for her spectacular guided traverse of the Hohstock in the Alps in 1931. She also ascended the Rimpfischhorn in the same year and, with a guide, made the first ascent of the southernmost peak of the Fusshörner. Even in her dotage, Teresa remembered that Len's bright eyes that lit up at the mention of climbing.

Formerly a school teacher, Teresa was involved in the kind of outdoor education that the Mallorys and Winthrop Youngs promoted. I tell her that I am learning to rock climb with my now teenage children. We have been indoor bouldering on coloured holds like liquorice allsorts across a wall with deep crash mats beneath. Vanessa, a friend, and I have recently been signed off to belay each other on a climbing wall, but I have yet to take those skills outside. It will take me years to get to the heady heights of expertise required of the Pinnacle Club, but Alex, the president, has kindly invited me to be a guest at this autumn meet where they are trialling new recruits.

As Teresa and I are talking, other ladies appear out of the night. They switch off their head torches and sling their wet rucksacks on the wooden floor. Many have left their cars far away by the road block caused by a recent landslide. They have walked down in the pitch dark. To start with, I dig for a towel and rush to the kettle to make tea, but then I realise that these ladies are completely unfazed by 'weather' and 'night'. Walking in the mountains in the dark by the light of a head torch is as familiar to them as a pavement under streetlights.

The experienced climbers begin carbo-loading before tomorrow's climb. They discuss where we could go that would be dryish. Big plates of rice and pasta begin steaming on the hut's stove, there is beer and wine. These women are not masochists, they find climbing restorative, an essential corrective to their busy working lives. In 2020 they tackled the classic British climbs. The president's favourite was the 468 foot multi-pitch climb up the Old Man of Hoy, an iconic stack which rises from the Atlantic Ocean, off Orkney.

After supper we sit around chatting and I ask them about Alison Hargreaves, hailed as one of the finest climbers in the world. Alison climbed with the members of the Pinnacle Club. She intrigues me. None of us who are mothers and climbers (imposter-climbers in my case) can let her go. She had a young family, yet she climbed. The difference perhaps was that climbing was her job. She was the family breadwinner. She died on K2 in the Himalaya on 13 August 1995 when her two children, Kate and Tom, were very young.

By chance, I met Alison's family when I came back from Ecuador in the mid-1990s. I was temping at BBC Books in London when they came in to discuss the book spin off for the programme: *One And Two Halves to K2*. I have a clear image of Kate and Tom, two little blonde people peering over my desk. We made paper clip chains while the 'adults' talked.

In 1993, Alison was the first person to climb the six north faces of the Alps by herself and in one season. While I was preparing for this visit to the Pinnacle Club hut, I read her account, *A Hard Day's Summer: Six Classic North Faces Solo*, published by Hodder & Stoughton in 1994. Alison's family, Jim and their two children pitched a tent at the campsite nearest each north face. Jim looked after the 2 and 4 year old when Alison left for 'work'. He found a kind of celebrity with admiring observations of this 'new modern man' alone with his children.' Alison set off for each climb, acknowledging wryly that looking after the children was often more exhausting than climbing. 'People have asked me if I think what I do is reckless,' she writes on page 39, 'I would hope not … as every good girl guide or boy scout knows, the trick is to be prepared …'

'I would often return from a long run or a climb,' continues Alison, and Kate would ask unconcernedly, 'Have you been up the mountains?', and when I said yes, 'Which one?' she'd ask and I'd point, even if she was none the wiser.' This puts me in mind of my husband telephoning from Heathrow Airport as he boarded the plane to Katmandu. Our 5-year-old asked him if he'd got to the top of Everest yet. Young children have no idea of the risk involved, even if they are camping right under the mountain.

As the conversation about motherhood and climbing lifts and falls around The Emily Kelly Hut, members chat amongst themselves. I am reminded of snatched phrases from different interviews recorded for the documentary film, *The Pinnacle Club: The First 100 Years*:

Mother didn't work, was always tied to the kitchen sink. That was not going to be the life for me.

I'm not interested in shopping or clothes or, you know, having a big posh house, I'm not interested in having kids, we discussed having children, … I don't want to give up this life, it's too good.

We'd put the babies on the ground, you know, on a blanket and then we'd go climbing. We were never any distance away. There was no danger of them being eaten by a sheep while we were doing a route or anything like that …

Before we turn in, I ask the Pinnacle Club members whether it is important to have a very highly developed sense of the consequences of an action if you are going to climb. There is a pause, and finally someone says, 'That and the ability not to think about the dangers'.

That night, I get into my husband's Everest sleeping bag on the slatted sleeping platform in the attic. My face is inches from a square window set into the deep stone wall. There is no light pollution here. Through the window I can see a dark sky scattered with brilliant stars. I am thinking about Ruth in the Pen-y-Gwryd Hotel on her first climbing trip to Wales in 1914. Ruth knew of K2, the mountain on which Alison's body still lies. She knew it as the mountain Pen-y-Pass climber Oscar Eckenstein had led the first attempt on in 1902. Ruth had been to Europe, she had an idea of the scale of European mountains. But in 1921, when Ruth was filling in her Pinnacle Club application form, she could barely imagine the scale of the Himalayas, the scaling up of the danger.

I try to sleep listening to the gentle rise and fall of breathing from the others around me. I look out of the tiny window. Before mobile phone satellites winked across the sky, George tried to close the gap between him and Ruth with letters.

My mind has cast loose in pre-sleep and I am thinking of things that are so big that they are unknowable, bigger than the Himalaya, bigger than the star studded universe, things like the future. George described marriage as a weaving loom, with brightly coloured threads shuttled between man and wife. I have always had the sense that time is like this. For me, it is not linear, except biologically, the obvious part, the bit we can see. For me, time is a mesh with a warp and weft, a matrix for brightly coloured threads thrown from past to future and back. I drift off trying to imagine what Ruth felt when George threw her that first shuttle with the thread: 'Everest'. What colour was it? What colour *is* it. What is the colour of danger?

# Chapter Thirteen

# 'Pye has got it all wrong'

Geoffrey Winthrop Young's scribble
in the margins of a copy of
*George Leigh Mallory: A Memoir* by David Pye,
Oxford University Press, Oxford, 1927,
Royal Geographical Society Archives, London

It is a boiling hot summer day in July 2023. I drive into Godalming past the Arts and Crafts low-gabled Prior's Field, where Ruth was a pupil, then past Charterhouse, where George was a schoolmaster. After forking right, I drive along Frith Hill contouring along the edge of the ridge. I park outside a sign which reads 'The Holt'. George could probably have made it from his bedroom to his classroom with a brisk five minute stroll.

The Holt is positioned on a steep slope so that I must walk down a series of steps from the road to get to the front door. This is the house that Thackeray Turner gave Ruth and George as a wedding present, along with her allowance of £750 a year. Laura, an environmental lawyer and mother of two young children, welcomes me in. We walk round into the back garden to stand in the shade of the covered terrace, the loggia. It is still just as Mary Ann described it on page 83 of her handwritten biography:

A big bricked loggia was thrown out beyond the drawing-room & continued in a broad low parapet wall overhanging the steep lower reaches of the garden, a perfect place to sit & swing the heels in discourse … and for those who objected to sitting on brick, an oaken seat of vast & dignified proportions waited in the formal garden above the lawn where two ornamental lily-ponds at once delighted the child & threatened the peace of the parent.

I walk down the loggia steps. This is where George's friend the improbably-named 'Sligger' Francis Fortescue Urquhart took the only double portrait of George and Ruth other than Adrian Harding's portrait in The Barn Studio. In Sligger's photograph Ruth is once again actually and metaphorically 'behind'

George. I walk back to the loggia and sit on the low brick wall (I don't object to sitting on brick). I sit precisely where Ruth sat. I can see that there is only just enough space between square wooden pillars for two people to sit together with their backs to the pillars, their knees angled in. On the day that the photograph was taken, it must have been cloudy but warm; no shadows to speak of but Ruth is wearing a long white 'Watteau' dress. (Ruth's 'Watteau' is actually her customary fashion-proof, home-made, round necked, loose fitting shift with a dark belt and a necklace.)

For me, this photograph is very important. Ruth is about to take a big risk. Before she does, I want to try to build up an image of the drawing room off this loggia, back in January 1921, more than a century ago. To start with, I need to re-examine her priorities.

Ruth made a point of staying abreast of developments in the news. During the First World War she read *The Nation* from cover to cover before forwarding it to George in France. One night she woke up with her head resting on the magazine. She had been reading Foreign Secretary Edward Grey's speech: 'I was a little disappointed that he was not more definite,' she tells George, on 16 October 1918, unsticking her cheek from its pages:

> I don't think he said anything that seemed new to me about the guarantees for peace that the League [of Nations] would have ... He evidently thought that the great hatred we all have for war now was the greatest guarantee. But although I agree, we still must have some force ready in case anyone breaks out again as the Germans have.

Sligger, the man holding the camera as Ruth and George sit on this loggia wall, was a Balliol College don. Ruth, described by Owen O'Malley as 'uneducated', has nailed one of the main problems with the League of Nations. Without a 'force ready' how could the League of Nations hope to enforce its decisions? From his study at Oxford, Sligger wrote pamphlets on 'Restorations of the Law of Nations' to the effect that nations should be bound by moral law as much as individual people. Even before Sligger's visit, Ruth felt instinctively that the peace process was not something to be delegated, it was each individual's overwhelming personal responsibility. For Ruth, peace was *the* priority.

This turning point in Ruth's life is passed to us as a scribble, a piece of marginalia in George's 'Life'. It is scribbled up the side of page 106, a page of printed text in George's biography. The scribble is in Geoffrey's handwriting: 'Pye has got it all wrong'. At the time, Geoffrey was disappointed that David had given him such as small role in George's 'Life'. Geoffrey had declined to write the memoir himself precisely because he was *too* involved, too essential to

George's story. By the time he was writing that frustrated margin note, it was 1927 and George was dead.

## The Holt – 25 January 1921

Geoffrey gets out of the taxi and, sweeping aside his circular cape, holds the metal handrail with his right hand, his crutches in his left. He can see his breath. The steps might be icy. It is more difficult to correct a slip with one leg. As George's climbing mentor, Geoffrey knows that, but for the missing left leg, it might be his name rather than George's on Captain Farrar's invitation to join the expedition to Everest.

Geoffrey reaches the bottom of the steps and knocks on the door of The Holt. He may have saved Ruth from a dangerous Alpine honeymoon, but what will she do with his next piece of advice? She is no longer a newlywed, a novice, she is an experienced climber and mother of three.

The door opens, Geoffrey catches a waft of beeswax furniture polish. As he gives Ruth his cape and cap, he may see the envelope on a chest in the hall. The address: 'Capt. P. Farrar, Alpine Club …' is in George's familiar angular hand. It is George's letter declining the invitation. Last night, Geoffrey telephoned asking himself to tea. He told George not to post that letter until he had seen them. He wants to see them both, to see George and Ruth together.

Geoffrey swings across the hall into the drawing room and moves over to the mantlepiece, where the fire is throwing out a good heat. Leaning his crutches against the wall, he manoeuvres around until he can lean his left arm on the mantlepiece. On his right are the west facing glass doors to the loggia, a place which he knows George loves. The orange sun is setting. The flames of the fire glow in the grate.

The tea tray is set; Ruth pours. She might be using one of the Wedgwood tea sets she has hand painted; perhaps one of the sets exhibited at The National Gallery. They may begin discussions by talking of Ruth's application to join the Pinnacle Club. But Ruth's Pinnacle Club invitation is not the reason for Geoffrey's visit.

Geoffrey adjusts his position at the fireplace, takes a breath and begins. Have they (George *and* Ruth) considered that Mount Everest is not so much retro-British-Empire posturing, as the key to its equal opposite? Not so much what George might call 'merely a fantastic performance' but a 'label'. Geoffrey suggests that it might not only be *a* label but *the* label that George requires to deliver on his – his and Ruth's – post-war ambitions for peace.

If their ambitions lie with founding a new school to raise 'cosmopolitan citizens' who are nation-blind, they will need leverage. They will need to inspire confidence in potential investors, teachers and pupils. If, on the other hand, they want a more direct access to the peace process, to securing George a position with the League of Nations Union or even the League of Nations itself, how much more likely with the cachet, the label of Everest?

He might mention Arctic explorer Fridtjof Nansen? George and Ruth know about Nansen. He was the first man to cross Greenland. He now represents Norway at the League of Nations. He and Eglantyne Jebb of the Save the Children, are working on a declaration of the rights of children. He might also mention T.E. Lawrence 'of Arabia'. Lawrence will be at the Cairo Conference as Winston Churchill's chosen assistant. These are both examples of men who have converted the 'label' of exploration – the Arctic Circle and the Middle East – into real international influence.

As Ruth sips tea, bitter tannin on her tongue, she may remember George's warning. His 'personal ambitions'. George wanted to coat-tail the prime minister's son to Versailles at the end of the First World War. He has walked through danger in Dublin in an effort to land a job offer from Gilbert Murray at the League of Nations Union. George wants to be in the room where it happens. Everest could put him in that room. That mountain could enable them, the Mallorys, to have a voice in the peace process. The peace.

After about fifteen minutes, Geoffrey stops talking. Outside, the sun has sunk beneath the horizon. Inside, embers glow. Geoffrey lights his pipe. He has climbed with both George and Ruth in Pen-y-Pass. They will read this gesture as it is intended. Geoffrey always lights a pipe before a difficult route. It allows one to look for handholds, ledges, wrinkles, and to calm the nerves. The atmosphere is tense. They are so near the war where it was Ruth's selfless duty to endorse George's decision to fight. Peace. Freedom. These are heroic words that cannot be domesticated. Where does the word 'family' fit amongst them?

There is the tinkle of a porcelain cup as it is set back in its saucer. The scent of Geoffrey's tobacco as it curls across the room. From the day nursery two floors above, faint voices can be heard. George looks towards Ruth. Those are the voices of their young children; their youngest John not yet walking.

George does not want to make the decision. He has batted the weaving shuttle across to Ruth. George waits. Geoffrey waits. Both are looking at Ruth.

\*   \*   \*

'What happened was,' Geoffrey scribbles up the margin of his copy of David Pye's biography of George, he 'left it to Ruth'. 'She was against it. He was going to refuse. I saw them both together ...' Here his pen comes off the page. Is he pausing to think of the consequences of his action? If George and Ruth had posted that letter, that refusal to Captain Farrar, George might still be alive.

But six years before, in the scene he is picturing in his mind as he writes that margin note, Geoffrey is pushing Ruth metaphorically rather than physically. He knows that she has already endured sixteen months on a ledge – sixteen months of precarious living in the presence of vicarious danger whilst George was away at war. But neither he nor George are taking the pressure off. Ostensibly, Ruth is the one with the power here; she is the one making the decision. But is she really?

The phrase 'left it to Ruth' is in quotation marks. All the people in this triangle: the husband, the mentor and the wife know that, as a 1920s wife, Ruth's is not a real choice. Leaving it to her is a courtesy; a chivalrous gesture typical of 'Sir Galahad', perhaps, but a formality. George does not step in. He does not break the silence. He is 'forcibly' pushing her.

A century later, I am standing in The Holt drawing room where a short man (Geoffrey was a head shorter than George) who has only his right leg to stand on might naturally stand. I survey the room. There is George brushing up his thick brown hair with his hands as he does when he is agitated. There is Geoffrey his pipe between his teeth, a curlicue of smoke rising. And there is Ruth.

Will she jump before George pushes her this time? What will she do?

On page 25 of Geoffrey's book *Mountain Craft*, he writes a paragraph subtitled 'Vertigo'. He describes the 'inclination, sometimes felt on the edges of sheer walls or cliffs, to "throw oneself over". We have all felt it.'

Is it a way of surrendering to the inevitable, or taking control of a situation to empower oneself? A decisive jump just to get it over with. To accept the consequences even though they will probably be fatal.

Twenty minutes is nearly up. Ruth, as Barbara Newton Dunn observed, was 'strangely silent'. She had no small talk. She did not chatter nervously into a silence. She let it stand. And so do I. When does she realise that her only choice is the manner in which she answers, not the answer itself. Perhaps her mind glances back to 8 August 1916 when she was cornered by an unpopular village lady, a Mrs Kendell, who asked her to come for tea, 'not a great joy,' observed Ruth to George wryly, 'but I could not possibly get out of it and so submitted gracefully & readily.'

I am standing here in the room where Ruth was pushed to the edge; not on a ridge in a snow storm with a wind of hurricane strength, but in air filled with the comforting scent of pipe smoke, over a china tea set, in a room furnished with affection; a place where she was so safe it was dangerous.

Six years later, Geoffrey set his pen back on the page to continue his correction of David Pye's biography: 'and in 20 minutes talk, Ruth saw what I meant; how much the label of Everest would mean to his career, and educational plans' and then? She dived over the edge 'gracefully and readily'.

'She told him to go.'

'I am just fixed for Everest,' George wrote to Geoffrey on 10 February 1921.

> ... I expect I shall have no cause to regret your persuasion ... at present I am highly elated at the prospect and so is Ruth: thank you for that.

# Chapter Fourteen

# The Right Kind of Wife

George Mallory's Medical Report,
Mount Everest Committee, 18 March 1921,
Royal Geographical Society Archives, London

On the left of the headed paper on the document on my desk at the Pepys Library in Cambridge, a diagonal line reads 'Telephone Paddington 5042' and the address on the opposite side: '75 Harley Street, W1'. It is dated 'March 18th 1921 and headed 'Report [three letters illegible] Mallory'. The illegible handwriting is that of one of the two doctors selected to put both George and his fellow climbing partner George Finch, though the prerequisite expedition medical. But before the medical, the Mount Everest Committee conduct discreet unofficial background checks to make sure that Mallory and Finch are the right kind of men to represent the British Empire on this iconic expedition. One of the unofficial qualifications is their family. Who are the women 'behind Everest'? Can they be trusted to toe the line?

The MEC is a combination of Alpine Club and Royal Geographical Society members. The AC provide the climbers, while the RGS supply the surveyors, the geographers. The AC wants to make sure that their men are properly equipped and matched in expertise on the rope, but they are poor cousins to the wealthy nerve centre of the British Empire: the RGS. For the secretary of the MEC, Arthur Robert Hinks (an RGS man with a bulldog jaw, a bulldog manner and no climbing experience) it is simply about putting a British 'gentleman' on the top of that mountain.

As a confirmed bachelor, Hinks regards one wife (or widow) as much the same as another. Hinks predecessor, Sir John Scott Keltie was secretary at the time of Captain Scott's tragic expedition to the South Pole before the First World War. Hinks picks up negotiations from where Scott Keltie left off. As far as he is concerned, the beginning of the Third Pole expedition dovetails with the end of the South Pole expedition.

Arthur Hinks is in regular contact with Kathleen Scott, the widow of Captain Scott. Kathleen is the role model for any future explorer's wife. Hinks is also in touch with Emily Shackleton the wife of Scott's arch Antarctic rival, the explorer Sir Ernest Shackleton. Ruth will know both Kathleen and Emily in due course; the first as Geoffrey's sister-in-law and the second as a fellow leader in Robert Baden-Powell's Girl Guide movement. But for now, in 1921, she only knows *of* them.

Ruth knows that Kathleen Scott actively encouraged her husband to go to the South Pole and never regretted his death, his 'sacrifice'. Following that heroic tragedy, Kathleen became Lady Scott. She was considered to be the right kind of wife and offered honorary fellowship of the RGS at a time when female members, 'Fellows', were a rarity. If the MEC investigate what kind of wife Mrs Mallory might prove, Geoffrey, an advisor to the MEC, could vouch for Ruth. He knows that Ruth not only supports George's application, but that, like Kathleen Scott, Ruth is the one who 'told him to go'.

Any further background checks will confirm Geoffrey's description of Ruth as an independent woman and a member of the Women's Guild of Arts, but not a suffragette and certainly not a militant brick-hurling 'bounder'. Hinks may wonder whether George is the right kind husband. Is he the self-funded gentleman explorer-type of which the RGS approve? Are any of Farrar's 'confounded climbers' gentlemen?

When Captain Scott's frozen corpse was discovered in a tent just 11 miles from a depot in the Antarctic, a message was found at the back of his diary. The message titled 'Message to the Public' was published in the newspaper in 1913. The most effective line was Scott's last, a pencil scrawl: 'For God's sake look after our people'. The outpouring of public sympathy amounted to £75,000 (equivalent to £7.9 million in 2024). It is the public who 'looked after' the South Pole widows.

Hinks does not want the MEC to be responsible for dependents of the 'Third Pole' any more than the RGS wanted to be responsible for those of the South Pole. Ruth, it is established, as the granddaughter of the wealthy philanthropist Thomas Wilde Powell and can 'look after' herself. She will not become a drain on RGS funds, she is not associated with any scandals and she has 'told him to go'. Ruth ticks all the boxes. The final official test is George's medical.

## London – 17 March 1920

George stands naked against the wall in the doctor's surgery at 75 Harley Street. Dr Anderson and Dr Larkin are about to put him through his paces. He has a berth on *Sardinia* leaving on 8 April 1920 for India. When he reaches that country he will trek overland to Tibet. For some unknown reason, the MEC has elected to leave the deciding medical until the last minute, just three weeks before departure.

Teeth?
'Four missing. Two stumps.'
Previous illness?
'Rheumatism.'
Urine?
'No sugar.'
Height?
'... five foot eleven inches.'
A scale and with adjustable weights along a cantilevered arm.
'159 pounds.'
A tape measure around the chest.
Exhale.
'Thirty five inches.'
And inhale.
'Thirty seven.'
An inflatable rubber sleeve wrapped around the lower section of the right arm.
'A pulse of 68 and a blood pressure of 115.'
Nutrition is good. Skin healthy.

George is told to get dressed. The report will be sent on directly to the secretary of the MEC, 'A. Hinks Esq.' When George leaves the room the doctors both agree: 'This man is in every respect fit.'

Shortly after George shuts the door of the MEC approved doctors' practice behind him, his fellow climber, George Finch walks in. Captain Farrar has emphasised to Hinks that:

If for any reason either of the men, Finch or Mallory, were to fall out, I know nobody who would be capable enough to take their place.

As a climber herself, Ruth knows that the two Georges are vital to each other's safety. There are so few climbers left after the war that Finch is the only one left who can match her husband. She knows that George Finch is an Australian graduate with a chemistry degree from the University of Geneva. Finch has more Alpine experience than Ruth's husband and an MBE awarded for replacing the fuses on over 60,000 bombs during the war.

Finch approaches the problem of scaling Everest as a scientist. He believes it may be necessary to use supplementary oxygen at the highest altitudes but he knows that there are those in the MEC who regard the use of artificial aids like supplementary oxygen as ungentlemanly cheating.

After his medical, Finch walks out of Harley Street and straight to the Strand Palace Hotel, Piccadilly where he enters a pre-booked room. He takes his clothes off for the second time that day. 'The witness' sees Finch entering the hotel and sees the five prostitutes. But is 'the witness' the only eyewitness to Finch's complicated love life?

Finch's first wife is not dead, as he has told president of the Alpine Club, Captain Farrar, but they are getting divorced. 'Their' son, Peter, is not biologically his, as he also told Farrar, but the result of her affair with another man. (Finch has beaten that other man to a pulp.) Finch suspects that words like 'divorce' and 'illegitimacy' may sit awkwardly with the traditionalists and he does not want to jeopardise his chances of Everest. Having staged the divorce-requisite 'adultery' in the Strand Palace Hotel, Finch gets dressed and goes home. It has been quite a day.

* * *

While Finch is 'staging' his affair, Ruth is buying George's expedition clothing in Godalming High Street. She has knitted his socks, mittens and long johns, but she is improvising. The local expert on cold weather gear is her late headmistress's husband Leonard Huxley who edited Captain Scott's diaries for publication in 1913. George has handed in his notice to Charterhouse. Without his salary, Ruth will have to be careful with her father's £750 allowance, but Everest equipment is very expensive and the MEC is being stingy with money.

On the second page of a two-page letter written to Hinks on 27 March 1920, George tries to ask for cash. It is ungentlemanly to be direct. Instead, he informs Hinks that he 'is a married man and can't go in bald headed'. George hides behind a metaphor, he does not mention his children Clare, Beridge and John. The word 'married' is probably enough to make bachelor Hinks wince. After his initial elation, George soon has moments of 'complete pessimism' as to their 'chances of getting up or getting back with toes on our feet …' Captain Farrar tries to appeal to Hinks's polar experience:

> the risks of this expedition are at least as great as those of a Polar expedition … The [Mount Everest Committee] will be open to criticism if they tried to economise on equipment for men making the final push.

But Hinks does not react to Farrar or to George's description of himself as 'a married man'. It is not Hinks's concern if George has chosen to get spliced. Instead, he pointedly asks George whether he expects the MEC to fund his passage to India.

Peter Gillman (co-author with his wife Leni of *The Wildest Dream: George Mallory – The Biography of an Everest Hero*) told me that Ruth's family money enabled George to go to Everest. The Gillmans' fantastic narrative only hints at the fact that when George left teaching, Thackeray Turner's suspicions about him marrying 'a girl with her own income' were reignited. George must have been aware of the problem when he told former pupil Robert Graves that Ruth was 'bravely content to be comparatively poor for a time, but I must make some money one of these days.'

On 20 March 1920, when Ruth is sewing on name tapes at The Holt, the results of the MEC medical reports come in. George has passed, but Finch has failed. Geoffrey Winthrop Young and Captain Farrar are apoplectic. As experienced climbers and members of the Alpine Club, they held out for expert climbers as a non-negotiable condition of advising the MEC. Without a man like Finch, even a non-climber like Hinks must understand that the risks are significantly higher. Without Finch, George is in danger. George Mallory could and should resign.

(Does no one consider that the alternative would be to recruit a female climber to make up the team? A member of the Ladies' Alpine Club? Or even a member of the emerging Pinnacle Club? Ruth is not a 'bank holiday' climber. Even the first few climbs on her Pinnacle Club application form are evidence of that. If the sleeve used to measure blood pressure in Harley Street was applied to the arm of Arthur Hinks as George floated the name 'Christiana Ruth Leigh-Mallory' past him as a possible candidate, it might be Hinks rather than Finch who failed that medical.)

When Ruth hears that Finch has been rejected at the last minute, and that the circumstances seem suspicious her first instinct might be to confront Hinks, to demand the truth. But George is a 'peasant slave' where headmaster Hinks is concerned: 'And how different [I am] from you, dear Ruth, who would so readily give him one of your direct hits, no matter who he might be!'

Ruth does not give Hinks one of her 'direct hits'. George does not resign. They are climbers. George acquires some copies of Younghusband's photographs of Everest that were taken from a distance. He and Ruth study the mountain. Even in grainy black and white, 'the photos all show comparatively easy angles on the north side.' George concludes that it would not be so much a question of 'technical skill' as of endurance.

Ruth has told David Pye that she has 'never seen a mountain without wanting to be at the top of it', but she is not at the mercy of that desire. George has seen the summit of Everest. Even in black and white, and in two dimensions – it is enough to induce the first rise in temperature; the first symptoms of summit fever. Ruth is pushed to the edge. Should she agree that George should accept the higher risk of climbing with a less experienced second?

Geoffrey has observed that George has a habit of leading those with less climbing experience into danger. With days left until his ship sails for India, George voices his concern to Hinks: 'we ought to have another man who should be chosen not so much for his expert skill but simply for his power of endurance.' Fortunately Guy Bullock, George's old Winchester College friend who has some climbing experience is available. Bullock is an excellent long-distance runner.

# Chapter Fifteen

# Jealousy and 'Dangerous' Love

Letters from George Mallory to Ruth Mallory,
1921,
Magdelene College Archives,
Cambridge University, Cambridge

Letters from Ruth Mallory to George Mallory,
1914–1918,
Magdelene College Archives,
Cambridge University, Cambridge

Letter from David Pye to George Mallory,
17 July 1921,
Magdelene College Archives,
Cambridge University, Cambridge

The next time we hear from Ruth, via George, she is jealous. As George sails out to India on the *Sardinia*, he finds a sheltered position on the upper deck and settles to write Ruth a letter. He explains that she has no need to be jealous of the women passengers for not even 'the circumstances of the voyage will greatly interest me in anyone else.' Ruth was never jealous before, what has changed?

During the war, the Mallorys tried to continue their physical relationship through letters. Back then George visualised kissing Ruth. She replied saying she could feel his embraces, physically:

Dearest, it feels very nice to be kissed even at the awful distance you are from me, but the best of all is that you should want to kiss me so much. It takes a big lot of the sting of being apart away … because we both want to be together & both know we do and both trust the other entirely.

But now she is jealous. Does she no longer trust him entirely? What does jealousy mean to Ruth? During the First World War, she assured George that 'Now surely we neither of us feel [jealous] in the least.' Two years later and she is not so sure.

Perhaps Ruth has heard rumours of 'the fishing fleet', the single women encouraged to sail out to the colonies to marry colonial bachelors; lest they marry 'native'. With a month on board in which to cast their siren nets at her handsome husband, Ruth feels uneasy. George's name has begun appearing in the newspapers. The Everest explorers are already celebrities. George is entering a glamorous world and he is leaving Ruth and his young family behind.

During the war, Ruth and George wrote daily letters. The army postal service between Britain and France was efficient and ensured that she could send food, clothing, books and packets of vegetable seeds for George to do a little light midnight gardening at his post. But now with letters taking weeks to arrive, it is difficult for their pen and ink conversation to achieve the same flow.

The Everest expedition will have to carry everything they need. The long supply caravan of mules, yaks, men and wagons must march overland from northern India through Sikkim and the planes of Tibet to the base of Everest. George's letters to Ruth must be carried first by runner, then yak, train and finally mail boat from India through the Suez Canal to the Mediterranean and by train and ferry to England. The last town before Everest, Kampa Dzong has a telegram office. The expedition has an exclusive sponsorship deal with *The Times*. Ruth subscribes to the newspaper. Its disinterested despatches will provide the most up to date news of the expedition and by implication, her husband.

George has asked Ruth to write regularly. He also welcomes letters from his family and friends. A letter from David Pye to George is a rare domestic vignette gleaned from 17 July 1921. For me, it scans like a card game with three players. George is on Everest whilst David and Ruth are at The Holt. Ruth's card hand (where the cards are her letters) is the only one with 'danger' in it or at least the word 'dangerous'. When Ruth uses the word, it is not to do with George's vulnerability either to the fishing fleet or the mountain, it is to do with the danger of being in love with the wrong person.

Shortly before this scene begins, Ruth has read in *The Times* expedition despatches that one of the climbers in George's team has died 'of a heart attack'. They haven't even reached the mountain. Dr Alexander Kellas, who was eighteen years older than George, was the only one with high altitude Himalayan experience. To Ruth, reading the newspaper despatch in Godalming, the risk to her husband seems to be increasing.

## Godalming – 17 July 1921

It is 1.00 pm precisely as Ruth welcomes David Pye into The Holt. He can hear a young child's muffled sobbing in the background. It is a hot summer's day and yet the rich aroma of roast beef drifts into the hall. Within a few paces he enters the dark William Morris wallpapered dining room. Blinking behind his round spectacles as his eyes adjust, David tries to adapt from the bachelor world of Trinity College Cambridge, to a crowd of females. Three adults, two young girls and an infant boy emerging feet first from under a dining room table. Ruth begins the introductions: George's sister, Avie Longridge; Violet Meakin, the nanny; Clare, his goddaughter; Beridge and baby John.

Ruth begins to carve the joint of beef. David realises that she is managing without a cook to save money. He has never seen a lady cook or carve, but he is used to Ruth's revolutionary ways. It would never be allowed in Cambridge, or at least, Ruth would be ostracised from polite society if it were discovered that she was her own 'cook and bottle washer'. There is no denying that the smell of a good roast is mouth-watering, even in mid-summer. David realises that Ruth is rolling out the red carpet for him; it is, almost, as if by feeding up David in Godalming, she can send nourishment to George on Everest.

As David takes his place at George's table, he knows that, on Everest, George has a confession. He confides only to David that he is consumed with guilt for having abandoned Kellas to the back of the caravan of supplies in the long trek to Base Camp. Kellas died alone. Where was the team work, where the spirit of climbing camaraderie? George is appalled: 'can you think of anything less like a climbing party?' he asks David rhetorically. Perhaps Ruth will conclude her husband has still not learned to put 'personal relations before mountains'. David promises not to tell Ruth: 'of course I shall be very careful not to spoil her peace of mind by speaking of your difficulties …'

Looking at David from the opposite end of the dining table, Ruth sees a neat bespectacled bachelor with a trouser brace that needs mending. She does not tell David that George has told her of David's passion for Jelly d'Arányi. David had taken Jelly to dinner without her customary chaperone. Although it was a bachelor error, David now wondered whether he should propose. Ruth observes that 'in the best sense [Jelly] flirts a lot … but then I wonder if she is in love with him.' She will try to talk to Jelly but she is extremely 'shy about discussing love affairs.' On 26 November 1918, Ruth explains 'I should feel very afraid of advising anyone to try at all to fall in love with Jelly because I think it rather dangerous.'

As Ruth passes around her Yorkshire puddings, David pronounces them 'a star turn'. Ruth knows that 'star' status is one of the reasons that David put forward against proposing. His reluctance stems from a concern that Jelly would not be like an average wife. On 12 November 1918, David states:

if one made up one's mind to ask her to marry one … it would mean arranging one's life accordingly – I mean that she has her art & her own success to make & nothing must stand in the way of that – She's is not a person who could – or ought to – fit herself to a way of life as most women do …

David wonders whether he should take the easier path, and submit himself to academic bachelorhood, at least until a girl who can 'fit herself to' one's way of life 'as most women do' chanced along.

From the other end of the table, David gives no hint of his secret dilemma and Ruth assumes that David is here to send George a report on the children. 'What I couldn't get over all lunch time was the growth of Berry,' he will later write to George, 'not so much in size … but as a person … I do think she has an unusually expressive face & her hands too are always part of what she is thinking.'

Blonde and extremely talkative, Clare has what Ruth calls 'some difficulties of character'. She cannot sit or be silent for more than a few frustrated seconds but she is fiercely clever. 'Clare had been a little tearful about something just before lunch,' the source of the sound of weeping on David's arrival, 'but cheered up all right about half way through'.

And John – the longed for son with what his father proudly described as 'fighting fists'? David tells George that

John was amazing in his masculinity! … & flattered me with an unwavering attention all the afternoon – probably I was one of the first men he had seen since you left & he may not have distinguished between us.

But John has just had to be fished out of one of the two ornamental lily ponds in the formal garden by his britches. Avie feels, along with Mary Ann, that Ruth is 'too casual about potential risks', those ponds are dangerous. Ruth does not want to remove all hazards, she wants her children to learn to manage them. She has placed a short wooden ladder against the house for Clare to strengthen her climbing arms by monkeying up the wrong side. She has put two planks along on bricks in the garden for Beridge to balance along. But the ponds threaten the peace of visiting parents most. From Everest, George will later write a letter to Clare and Beridge reminding them: 'don't drown John'.

After lunch Vi takes the children into the garden. Ruth, Avie and David sit in the loggia fanning themselves. The day has become even hotter. Ruth reads George's letters slowly with a low voice that David describes as musical. Avie has spread the expedition map published in *The Times* on the single-legged table. She draws a fingertip across the page tracing the route that her brother describes in his letter. While Ruth is reading about frostbite and frozen billy cans, it gets hotter and hotter until suddenly, there is a crack of thunder above the house followed by 'a terrific down pour with rain drops the size of marbles'.

> Ruth stood up with her back against one of the pillars on the house side of the loggia and pointed out how the garden and everything in it seemed suddenly to have come alive – for as one looked down the slope every leaf was dancing up & down …

After his afternoon at The Holt, David, a bachelor, is even less inclined to think of proposing marriage to Jelly. Life with three young children looks exhausting. He must have asked Ruth how she is managing to balance managing the household with managing to control her anxiety. He informs George that 'during the day Ruth doesn't give herself time to think too much …'

David knows that she is too busy to think, but what about at night? David does not like to ask a lady what she thinks about after lights out, so he has to speculate. On Tuesday, 19 July 1921, he writes to George, 'I hope at night she is tired enough to make her sleep soundly'.

But there are more than three people in this card game. Avie has seen over David's shoulder, she knows which cards he is going to play. Suspecting that David might serve up roast lunch at The Holt for her brother's delectation, she wants George to know the truth. Whatever David might tell him, Ruth's cheer conceals just how 'strung up and anxious' she is about George's safety.

On page 413 of *Into the Silence: The Great War, Mallory and the Conquest of Everest*, Wade Davis describes Ruth as 'gravely ill' when George was away on Everest in 1921. I know, from our discussions, that Wade took no license with that seminal book, but the only reference I can find is a letter from George to Ruth which mentions that she had been suffering with boils. These are painful infected lumps under the skin, often a stress-related illness. At this time, seven years before Alexander Fleming discovered penicillin on a petri dish of staphylococcus bacteria, infections were indeed 'grave'. (When my husband was away on Everest, our 4-year-old required intravenous antibiotics. That same son, now in his twenties, has the Alexander Fleming blue plaque on St Mary's Hospital, London as his screen 'saver'.) But David doesn't mention that Ruth was gravely ill in July 1921. Perhaps she became ill after his visit? Now, in July 1921 as David drives away from The Holt and back through the summer thunderstorm to Cambridge, he concludes, 'I think Ruth really is as happy & brave as she could be in the circumstances'.

At the conclusion of the card game, Ruth has managed to conceal just how 'strung up and anxious' she is for George's safety. She has also sidestepped discussing 'love affairs' with David. David has not revealed George's guilt at marching ahead and abandoning Kellas to die alone. And George? After receiving David's vignette, George realises that Ruth must be exhausted and begins to think about how he can give her the holiday 'she so richly deserves'. He wants to bring her nearer, to close the distance between them. During the war on 16 July 1916, Ruth wrote: 'I want more and more some day to see where you are now, it would make it more real & vivid to me. I wonder if I ever shall. I was by you last night in imagination as you sat in the map room at a night watch. I wonder if you were there.' Is she thinking of him now? Is she imagining herself beside him here on a mountain she has never seen? Looking up at the sky on 6 July 1921, five years after Ruth was 'by [him] last night', George signs off with the St Augustin 'star' quote transporting himself momentarily from the Himilaya to the loggia in Godalming where he imagines Ruth 'doing this and that':

There'll be something to be told even if we don't climb Everest, as I hardly think we shall … Goodnight and great love to you. We see the same stars.

## Chapter Sixteen

# The Heroics of Ordinary Life

Frantisek Binowetz Knefel, Nationality
and Naturalisation Certificate AZ4400,
issued 15 June 1934,
The National Archives, Kew

Ruth Mallory's letters to Arthur Hinks,
of the Mount Everest Committee, 1921,
Royal Geographical Society Archives, London

George Mallory's letters to Geoffrey Winthrop Young,
Royal Geographical Society Archives, London

### Godalming – late summer 1921

Ruth, Clare and Beridge turn to face the train as it steams into Godalming
Station on a windy autumn day. The brakes hiss and steam curls under the station
canopy as a boy steps down from the train. He has a paper label around his neck.

| | |
|---|---|
| Name: | 'Franz Knefel' |
| Date of Birth: | '31st March 1911' |
| Host: | 'Mrs Leigh-Mallory' |
| Destination: | 'The Holt, Frith Road, Godalming, Surrey.' |

Franz is olive-skinned and dark-haired with kind eyes behind his small round
spectacles. He has a lovely smile. Clare, Beridge and John have been told that
they must give the new boy a big welcome. Ruth and George have noticed that
Clare is at her best with older children. Having a boy who is four and a half
years older than her seems ideal. Clare tells Franz that she is learning German.
Beridge is silent, but Clare explains to him that Beridge is also learning German.
At just over 1 year old, John is in a push chair. He can't talk in either English or
German yet but he can show Franz how to climb into the garden pond. Clare
quickly concludes that she will probably marry Franz. Her mother sees hunger
behind the sharp cheek bones, the toothy grin.

As Eglantyne Jebb of Save the Children says 'Every generation of children offers mankind the possibility of rebuilding his ruin of a world'. Children can lose the dangerous prejudices of their parents. If every British mother took in a Franz, old grudges could be erased. Back in January, Geoffrey described Everest as 'a label' but for Ruth Franz's label is a real label. It may only be a piece of paper with a domestic address but it represents the potential for children to realise what the League of Nations is struggling to achieve.

Although the United States had not joined the League of Nations, Margaret Wilson, President Woodrow Wilson's daughter, was in discussions with Maria Montessori to extend the system to the Haus der Kinder in the very city Franz had come from, Vienna. Franz becomes an important member of Ruth's Montessori 'staff', and classes gain popularity. As Hilda Haig-Brown remembers it, Jebb's message about rebuilding the world, became Ruth's central theme.

\* \* \*

I never asked Franz's widow, Marianne, whether that paper label around Franz's neck still exists. But the document lived in her memory and the scene is taken from our conversations about Franz's arrival at The Holt while George was away on Everest on his first expedition. It shows that Ruth was not just waiting while George was away on Everest, she was busy transforming lives.

However, the obsession amongst Everest historians is the gap. The silence from Ruth during the Everest years. Where are her letters? Only one survives. And yet there are letters that are written by Ruth. They are in the Royal Geographical Society Archives because they are addressed to the MEC secretary, Arthur Hinks. The letters that form the basis of this chapter are from Ruth during 1921. For me they are evidence of Ruth's dangerous trust. In late September 1921, when the leaves of the beech tree outside the drawing room window at The Holt are turning gold, she sits at her desk, takes out her black fountain pen and leaning her chin on the back of her left hand writes:

Dear Mr Hinks,

I think the only thing I can do it to send you the typed coppies [sic] of my husband's letters that I have had made to pass round to some of his friends. Yesterday I received three letters from him which will be of chief interest to your committee.

... I am also enclosing some earlier letters. If you look through them you will be able to pick out better than I can what your committee would like to hear.

Yours sincerely,

Ruth Mallory

The minute her undated letter arrives at the RGS offices on Kensington Gore, Hinks takes out his ink stamp and bangs it onto the top left corner: 'N.GEOG. SOC 26 Sep[tember] 1921'.

Two days later and Ruth is desperately trying to remember exactly what was in George's letters to her. Were there any lèse-majesté, that Hinks could interpret as treason, or even a breach of contract? Perhaps she has been too honest and trusting. Should she have sent them whole or edited out the bits that George probably did not want Hinks to see?

'You will remember won't you,' she writes to Hinks in a panic,

> that the letters are mearly [*sic*] personal ones sent to me and if I should have coppied [*sic*] out anything that could be considered indiscreet I hope you will leave it out. You see I have sent them quite without my husband's leave …

Ruth has just remembered that there are parts of George letters where he has used Ruth as a confessional, one such ('a horrible confession') is that he and Guy Bullock (George Finch's replacement) fell out suspecting each other of eating more than their fair share of food.

But when Hinks receives Ruth's panicked addendum, he tries to allay her fears with compliments. He does not want Ruth to vet George's letters – knowledge is power. He notes that Ruth has sent him 'a tracing of the map that I have made'. When Hinks first sees Ruth's map, he is angry that George has wasted his time and states: 'In the absence of a map, I spent laborious days trying to recognise bits of detail to fit photographs together.' Hinks knows that Mrs Mallory is an artist and the map is good, but he is aghast at her audacity. That a woman should presume to send a map drawn on the kitchen table at Godalming to *the* map room of the world. It is almost inconceivable. 'Thank you for the tracing which tells me quite a lot more than I knew before,' he replies tactically, instead of highlighting her temerity, 'You need not be anxious about your extracts from your husband's letters. I have no intention of publishing them as they stand …'

On 30 September 1921, instead of warning George that his letters to Ruth are effectively public, he informs George that 'Mrs Mallory has very kindly let us see extracts from some of your letters to her, which have given us details that we did not get in your Chief's letters or telegrams …' (The implication is clear. Hinks is not happy that Mrs Mallory has more information on the Mount Everest Committee-organised expedition than he does.) But to ensure Ruth's continued co-operation, Hinks suggests that she might like to come up to London to see the expedition photographs that George has sent back so far.

Ruth is proving more co-operative than her husband. Hinks wants George to know that he and Ruth now have an understanding '... and I hope that she is coming up in a few days' time to see the photographs which make a beautiful show.' She does, and they do. In a letter Hinks stamped 8 October 1921, Ruth writes that

> I immensely enjoyed seeing the photographs on Friday and hearing you [*sic*] ideas about what they have actually been doing. Thank you very much for the trouble you took in showing me everything.

In the same letter, Ruth tells Hinks that George is planning to sail home on the *Malwa* leaving Bombay (today's Mumbai) on 29 October 1921.

George is not the only person using his wife as a bucket into which to pour his unsayable self. Bullock confides in his wife, Laura, just as George does in Ruth. Laura will later claim that her husband

> considered Mallory ready to take unwarranted risks with still untrained porters in traversing dangerous ice. At least on one occasion, he refused to take his rope of porters over the route proposed by Mallory. Mallory was not pleased. He did not support a critical difference of opinion readily.

But she will only make this statement after her husband's death in 1956. Ignorant of this opinion, Ruth assures herself that Guy Bullock (whom George calls 'my stable companion') is a stabilising influence. Guy can check George's tendency to take 'unwarranted risks'. George has told her that he wishes it was Ruth rather than Bullock in the sleeping bag next door. He dreams her into being until it is almost as if she is physically there, beside him, roped to him.

Increasingly George feels torn. He uses the language of romance for both his flesh and blood wife and his snowy mistress. 'I can't tell you how [Everest] possesses me ...' he tells Ruth. He describes the North Col, the saddle en route to the summit, as 'the Col of our desires'. George is joking, but he is also deadly serious. He is becoming dangerously infatuated with the mountain, but he can still feel 'the pull the other way'.

It is as if George is on that ridge on Snowdon now. He is roped in the middle with Ruth on one end and Everest on the other. How can Ruth's 'pull the other way' match the pull from Everest? By 9 September 1921, when they are about to make a push for the North Col with plans to camp there and go on to the summit, George is so conflicted that he begs Geoffrey for advice:

at what point am I going to stop? It is going to be a fearfully difficult decision and there's an incalculable element about other men's physical condition ... I almost hope I shall be the first to give out!

George has assured Ruth many times that he will know when to stop, that he recognises that it would be 'bad heroics to take wrong risks'. But what are 'bad heroics' exactly? What are 'wrong risks'? After the war he told her that 'I should have liked to return home, if not a hero, at least a man of arms more tried than I have been.' Without Ruth's perspective, Everest is becoming less a label than a second chance.

George chooses Geoffrey as his confessor rather than Ruth, editing what she hears. Ruth was aware of necessary censoring of news during the war: 'Tell me if you can,' she asked George back then, 'how much danger you are in.' Now on Everest he is self-censoring, 'making light the dangers' as Ruth observed that his hero Edward Whymper did even in the lead up to a tragedy.

Ruth is in Godalming. She is not in a position to catch him on a rope if he falls but ignorance of the danger that he is in at any time, is the greatest source of her anxiety. As she explained to him during the war, 'I don't think it makes me less frightened, when you hardly tell me anything about [the danger you are in].' The difference between being in a war zone and being on Everest, is psychological. George wants to be the first to give out to become physically unable to continue climbing. He wants the choice to be made for him. Only then will he be able to deliver on his promise to Ruth to avoid 'bad heroics' and 'wrong risks'. Only then will he feel able to stop.

# Chapter Seventeen

# Luxury and British Empire Politics

Arthur Hinks's sealed letter to George Mallory,
carried by Ruth, November 1921,
Magdelene College Archives,
Cambridge University, Cambridge

The next time we meet Ruth is on the train to Marseille. George contemplated a reunion in the Alps 'but I feel so sure you wouldn't come,' he tells Ruth, 'on grounds of expense that I make no suggestions'. Naturally thrifty, Ruth must now be particularly frugal with only her allowance to live on. Since George's ship back from India is docking in Marseille, she has suggested a walking holiday in Provence rather than an expensive climbing holiday in Switzerland. Ruth has packed her rucksack for walking, but it is not as straightforward as a visit to Pen-y-Pass.

Before they stride off into the sunset (and in spite of what George knows about the state of their finances) George feels that Ruth deserves a little amusement. He wants to splash out on a night or two in splendour at the Prince of Wales's favourite, the Hôtel Louvre et Paix in Marseille. Ruth, delighted at the prospect, does some research. The façade is all baroque marble opulence with sculpted female caryatid pillars holding up the building. Maps show that it is on La Canebière; an historic high street in the old quarter. The name Canebière stems from the French word for hemp. Canebière was the centre of the rope-making business; the business on which the life of a climber literally hangs.

Ruth has read George's letter outlining their final attempt on Everest; the gale-force winds that nearly swept them off the North Col. Ruth knows what it is like to stand on a snow ridge in a screaming gale. How long could they have survived that? Others in the team, including Canadian expert climber Charles Wheeler, concluded categorically that 'no man could have existed'. But George was not so sure. He could breathe, just. He could stand, in a manner of speaking. He could probably have crawled and continued ascending.

But in the end, George cheated his mistress and now, at a lower altitude, the pull the other way has become strong. By 1 September 1921, he wanted to see the children, 'dear souls', far more than Ruth might think. He does not ask that the nurseries are moved yet further away from his study. Instead he writes 'I don't think I knew before how much they are a part of life ... What can I bring them home from the East?' But he doesn't want to see any of the children, just yet. Or at least not as much as he aches, physically, to see her.

Sitting in the train trundling south through war torn France bound for Marseille, Ruth is longing to see George. He has told her to meet him in the vast lobby of Hôtel Louvre et Paix at 9.00 am. He will be at the front desk at 9.00 am and then, lest her train is delayed, he will return to the hotel desk every two hours to see whether she has arrived. Ruth has a sealed letter from Hinks in her rucksack, which he asked her to deliver. She has no idea what is in it. She does not suspect that as she is travelling south, Hinks is writing to the Mount Everest Committee: 'I regret more than ever the death of Kellas, who would have shown Mallory in two days how far he was negligible as a mountaineer.'

As for the walking holiday Ruth has mentioned in passing to Hinks, he now notifies the MEC

[it was Mallory's] intention is to dally in [France] instead of coming straight home helpful as usual. I am writing to try and get him to get that idea out of his mind. His ideas of responsibility want a little stirring up and strengthening.

On 20 November 1921, in the privacy and intimacy of their luxurious suite at the Hôtel Louvre et Paix, George tears open the envelope from Hinks. He finds a summons. Hinks's politeness is deadly. When George has quite finished amusing himself with his wife in Marseille, he might remember his responsibilities to the late Dr Kellas and the rest of the expedition. George is expected to file his expedition report immediately. There will also be a short interview (interrogation). Hinks would like to corroborate the facts already reported by those of the expedition who have remembered their manners. Ruth has been used. But she is not the only one. They are all pawns in a dangerous game of British Empire strategy.

Although none of the players in this story know it, in exchange for access to Everest, the British government in India have promised the Dalai Lama weapons. Everest is effectively a Trojan horse. The British have promised to arm the Tibetans to protect their own borders from the Russians and the Chinese, thereby protecting the northern borders of British India. But Tibet is split between the traditionalists in the monasteries (who want the British out) and the Dalai Lama (who sees them as necessary allies).

Charles Bell, the man who negotiated for George's expedition to be able to have access across Tibet, is a friend of the Dalai Lama's. Bell has received death threats from the monasteries. The situation is unstable, close to civil war. Frederick Bailey, one of the men who invaded Tibet with Francis Younghusband back in 1904, will be taking over from Charles Bell. He is making secret plans to stage 'a very British coup' within Tibet.

Bailey may not recognise that his efforts are in opposition to that of the Mallorys. He may however be aware that they are in direct opposition to one of the Mallorys' closest friends, Will Arnold-Forster. The Union of Democratic Control was formed by Will and his friends when they realised that the last war (the First World War) resulted from largely secret international understandings. There is no democratic overview of the secret strategy being rolled into Tibet under cover of access to Everest.

## Marseille to Godalming – November 1921

The Mallorys jump off the northbound train at Avignon for a foreshortened holiday, bridging Ruth's disappointment with a quick dash to Le Pont d'Avignon. Returning to the station, Ruth tells herself that although their walking trip may have been cut rather short, they are at least travelling together. Instead of writing to each other, they can talk. Ruth can read what George is writing because she is sitting close, within touching distance. 'What I want,' scribbles George with his black fountain pen, 'is to see is the faces I know, and my own sweet home … an English river, cattle grazing in western meadows.'

Signing off on family letters, George finishes a letter to his sister that he started on 10 November 1921, 'I wouldn't go again [to Everest] next year, as the saying is, for all the gold in Arabia.'

But as George begins opening new letters delivered by the Poste Restante from the Mount Everest Committee between Lyon and Paris, his tone changes. Hinks may or may not have mentioned to Ruth that the MEC plan to ask George to join a second expedition to leave the following year. 'I've said,' George tells his sister Avie, 'it's no use going out [to Everest] except early in the spring, to climb before the monsoon.'

Standing together with Ruth at the bow of the ferry to Dover, George explains:

[The Mount Everest Committee] can't possibly organise another show so soon, particularly as I've also said that it's barely worth while trying again, and anyway not without eight first rate climbers. They can't get eight, certainly not soon, perhaps not even the year after next.

Back at The Holt, after a brief reunion with his children, George is nervous that he may have burned his bridges with the MEC. Has he underestimated

Younghusband's messianic drive to put a man on that mountain? The MEC is recruiting climbers at a rate George never thought possible: 'I don't know precisely what I said in my haste from Marseilles,' he writes to Hinks 'but please don't tell the committee if the question arises that I don't intend to go unless they do as I wish. That's not my thought ...' George takes the train to London.

\*    \*    \*

Ruth has already been pushed to the edge and jumped. Back in January 1921 she 'told him to go'. Does George push Ruth to endorse his next expedition or has Hinks already pushed her as part of his photograph exhibition charm offensive in George's absence? Arthur Hinks is a dangerously manipulative Machiavellian. Hinks and Ruth both know that George is disappointed that the end of the 1921 expedition was so 'tame'. Has Hinks told Ruth to be grateful, for George's sake that the expedition is being reframed as 'successful reconnaissance' rather than as a 'failure' to reach the summit? How much does Hinks know of George's need to prove himself?

Hinks believes that George's sense of responsibility needs stirring up and that a man's first responsibility is to his country, to a 'national show' like the Everest expedition, not to his family. When Ruth agrees that George should return to 'finish the job', she agrees out of our hearing.

# Chapter Eighteen

# Priorities and Prejudice

Kate Nicholson's conversations with Marianne Nevel, 2007

Jan Levi,
*And Nobody Woke up Dead:*
*The Life and Times of Mabel Barker –*
*Climber & Educational Pioneer,*
The Ernest Press, UK, 2006

Ruth introduces George to Franz Knefel for the first time on George's return to The Holt in November 1921. Franz is 10 and George is 35. For Franz, hero worship is instant and enduring. From George's perspective, he finds a 10-year-old boy willing to believe that his theory of the ideal 'cosmopolitan citizen' is a realisable goal. Together the man and the boy try to imagine a future in which they would not be British or Czech, but nation-blind citizens of the world.

Some of their conversations are more prosaic. Franz never had enough to eat at the orphanage. He was often in trouble for leading his fellow orphans in raids on the kitchens. George and Guy Bullock had fallen out over the issue of food on Everest. George knows that hungry feeling too. Franz imagines a world in which it rains sweets. George tells him that he often takes a linen bag of sugar climbing though sometimes it spills, raining all over his rucksack. Perhaps that sugar is raining through Franz's dreams. Both Franz and George both know that although Ruth is careful about money, her favourite treat is melted chocolate spooned straight into her mouth from the pan.

Franz and George manage snatched conversations, but they are mostly conducted on the move. George barely has time to sit down and light his pipe. His MEC contract requires him to give thirty-three Everest lectures in three months while preparing for the next expedition. Ruth swings into action. The Holt becomes a maelstrom. There are various widths of hemp, manila and cotton climbing ropes knotted to the bannisters. Chairs are strewn with Everest clothing. Ruth and Vi take the Montessori pupils into the garden to climb the wrong side of Clare's ladder and balance along Beridge's raised planks where they can be out of the way. But back inside, more climbing equipment is delivered every day as sponsors realise the that being associated with the expedition, is good advertising. Ruth, battles through the boxes piling up in the dining room to conjure roast joints of beef amongst canvas tents and climbing boots.

To have any hope of keeping control, Ruth, Clare and Franz march down Frith Hill to Godalming to buy more nametapes. Clare is buying wool. She is learning to knit socks. She tells Franz that they must make sure that her daddy comes back 'with the toes on his feet'. Even with her modest Montessori nursery income to supplement her allowance from her father, Ruth runs out of money. She has a meeting with her bank manager, a Mr Raxworthy, about taking out an overdraft. For the first time in her life she is in debt.

*   *   *

On the way from The Holt to Gammons, the drapers on the High Street, Ruth, Clare and Franz walk over the bridge that crosses the River Wey. On their left, they pass Godalming's *Titanic* memorial, the Phillips Memorial Cloister on the Lammas Meadow. The memorial was designed in 1914 by Thackeray Turner and Gertrude Jekyll. It commemorates John 'Jack' George Phillips, son of the owners of Gammons and the local hero.

Jack was one of the Marconi radio operators on *Titanic*'s maiden voyage. He and his fellow operator Harold Bride stayed at their posts to transmit the distress signal but only Bride survived. Whilst Jack is memorialised, Harold Bride slipped into obscurity. The paternalistic Birkenhead drill: the order to save 'women and children first'? It purported to protect women but did it actually disempower them? In later life Franz will wonder whether historical obscurity is the inevitable price for survival.

Ruth and the two children open the door of the Godalming branch of Gammons drapers, activating a small bell. Inside, the shop is lined with shallow wooden drawers filled with ironed cotton shirts and school ties. It smells of starched linen. This is the place where the Charterhouse pupils buy their uniform. But today, they are here for silk shirts. George has told Franz that a silk shirt, or even two, will be the warmest thing he can take to Everest.

George Finch has reapplied for the 1922 expedition and been accepted. He had proved the 1921 medical a fraud with an impressive mountaineering season in the Alps. Now it seems that the MEC are willing to overlook illegitimacy, divorce and 'cheating' with supplementary oxygen, if it means getting a British Empire man on the top of that mountain. George told Franz that Finch was thinking of taking a quilted jacket stuffed with down feathers. He has never seen one, never tried one but it might catch on.

Although George could be fearless on a rock face, Ruth knows that he can be reduced to a stammering heap when confronted with an audience. On page 42 of her hand written biography, Mary Ann describes George:

> his hands round his knees unclasped now & then to throw back his hair stammering a little with his eagerness & impatience & the difficulty of getting out what he had to say, but getting it out all the same ...

Now the Mallory income will derive from a percentage of Everest lecture ticket sales. With thirty-three lectures to give, Ruth calls in Mary Ann whose maiden speech to the Ladies' Alpine Club was 'mentioned in despatches'. Ruth knows that Mary Ann is desperately unhappy in her marriage and that Owen is publicly unfaithful. Coaching George in public speaking at The Holt gives Mary Ann a reason to be out of her house. Ruth adds Mary Ann's children, Jane and Patrick O'Malley, to her Montessori class. As Mary Ann describes it on page 86, Ruth had been raised to offer

> almost medieval traditions of hospitality & welcomed everyone [George] brought from the smallest boy to the most learned don with the same simple direct cordiality.

In just over a year's time, George will invite George Finch and his family including his illegitimate son Peter, to experience Ruth's legendary hospitality for a weekend. But for now, on 2 March 1922, Ruth is on the Liverpool dockside watching George's receding figure on the deck of the *Caledonia*. Part of her would like to go too. Ruth is determined to content herself with 'ordinary life', but she is not ordinary.

Watching George's ship as tugs pull it out of the harbour, Ruth recognises that she has been pushed to accept a protracted postponement of her adventures. In a letter written during the First World War, Ruth dreamt a stream of travelling consciousness. Scribbling an ink route down the page, she visited continents and castles:

> I do want to see some of the far away wonderful places of the world. I would rather go somewhere into Asia than into Africa because the civilization is old in Asia & that would make the people and things so far more interesting. I don't want to go till we are too old. I think perhaps we ought to wait till we have as many children as we want in case it is dangerous. Then we will go away for six months and see wonderful places. I suppose you will want to mingle climbing with it. I don't mind that at all so long as it's not too dangerous.

Ruth longs to see beyond Europe, to see the world. She wants to find the sweet point between having young children and being too old to stand really adventurous travelling. She is wary of danger, mentioning it twice in one paragraph. Instead, as George leaves for another expedition to Asia, she tries to refocus. She looks away from 'dangerous' and 'too dangerous'-climbing trips, channelling her urge for adventure on the 'biggest experience' she can wring from 'ordinary life'. When she gets home she will at least climb trees.

'I love to see you climb the trees', she tells George as she swings from bare branches beside the Wey with Franz and the children. 'I tried the difficult tree with my shoes off but I did not succeed. I think it is just possible I might in rubber shoes. I tore the gathers out of my dress swinging down.' She does not tell the children to take care (Mr Cockerall does 'and I think he has made both his [children] rather silly and nervous') but in the past she has told George that 'I do hope you don't find that you are getting careless yet, please don't. I don't think you will be only constant care always gets so boring.'

Franz becomes a decent tree climber. Ruth knows that although she is trying to solve world peace one child at a time, if Franz's mother asks for him to return to Vienna, she will have to relinquish him. His mother is his legal guardian but Franz 'dislikes' her. She makes him spend every Sunday praying for forgiveness on his knees in church. The Children's After Care Committee secretary, Mrs Levin who acts as a go between the British hosts and the Kinderheim, asks that Franz's mother has 'regular news' of Franz. 'I am continually having complaints made to me, so I do hope you will see that a postcard is sent regularly.' Franz does not want to send postcards. He knows that he will have to go back to the orphanage in Vienna shortly. Ruth prepares the ground by asking her climbing friend Mabel Barker to 'order' Franz from the Kinderheim on her next summer holiday school trip to the 'Camp Schleifstein', near Mayrhofen.

Franz is not an orphan, but he will return to an orphanage. Peter Finch is not an orphan, but George Finch, though not his biological father, is bringing him up. Shortly after George leaves again for Everest, Mary Ann finds herself pregnant. Owen declares, with characteristic malice, that the baby cannot be his. Even if Mary Ann's child is not Owen's, it will grow up an O'Malley – anything else would publicise the suspicion that Owen is a cuckold. He may not be, and he will not be, that. (In a future none of them can imagine, Peter Finch becomes a famous actor and Franz runs a successful furniture business. Grania O'Malley, who follows her siblings Jane and Patrick, changes her name to Kate to be more in line with theirs.)

Ruth, as usual, sympathises with the women and does not subscribe to the conventional view of them as blameworthy but as victims. '... in many ways you can point to definite right and wrongs ...' she told George back on 22 July

1916 'although some points are still controversial. Such as having babies without being legally married ...' At the time, Ruth had taken to visiting 'three poor unfortunates ... who were not married' at the maternity hospital on her way back from wrapping bandages at the depot.

Why is it always 'fallen women', but never 'fallen men' however far they fall? The default understanding of a fallen woman, was (and is) that for a woman, it is a moral fall, but a fallen man is a man who has fallen in battle, or fallen on a mountain. The understanding in Ruth's time for almost everyone except for Ruth herself, was that a fallen woman had jumped willingly, not that she'd been pushed.

# Chapter Nineteen

# Death on the Mountain

Letters between George Mallory, Ruth Mallory and David Pye
are supplemented by an account of
Martha Emily 'Pat' Kelly's accident and information in
*Presumptuous Pinnacle Ladies:*
*A Selection from the Early Journals of*
*Britain's First Rock Climbing Club*
Millrace, UK, 2009

'Dearest love,' George writes from the *Caledonia,*

is it a very bad gap now that I'm gone? I hardly like to ask for fear of suggesting loneliness to you, but with the children you'll know how to put that away. I hate the fact of your not being with me and even more the thought of my not being with you as though I had been cruel to you; and I don't want ever to hurt you the least little bit.

Ruth is not hurt but she is jealous of the ladies on board. They have leisure time to talk without having to balance the demands of the Mount Everest Committee with the responsibilities of a young family. George tries to allay her fears:

If you were to see the women folk on board, dear, even the faintest glimmering of jealous feeling would be laid to rest – I haven't even spoken to one yet.

To salve his conscious, George writes from the *Caledonia* in March 1922 and asks David to take Ruth to the Easter meet at Pen-y-Pass. He tells Ruth that he wants her to go so 'you won't be dull without me ... Be gay as you can.'

He has also sent a Tibetan fox skin in the post: 'She'll probably say she can't wear it,' George says to Ruth's sister Marby on 1 July 1922. But it has not arrived by early April as Ruth shoulders her rucksack, puts on her dark cloche hat and three-quarter length mackintosh and walks down the hill to Godalming train station.

Ruth's letter detailing her climbing trip no longer exists, but George's reaction to it does. Lining up the Easter meets at Pen-y-Pass, it seems that Ruth and David may have crossed over with Ruth's friend, the Pinnacle Club founder Pat and her husband Harry Kelly.

## Snowdonia, Wales – Easter, early April 1922

It is early April in Wales and, after a day in the hills, Ruth and David are lined up in two rows opposite each other in the Pen-y-Pass Hotel lobby. They are about to start dancing the English country dance, Roger de Coverley. The hotel owner, Mrs Reade, lowers the needle on the gramophone and the music begins. The couples link elbows and turn each other, they move in a pre-arranged pattern weaving in and out in figures of eight. Much as Ruth sees the advantages of the Pinnacle Club, it is a relief to get out of her female household and into mixed adult company at Pen-y-Pass. Dorothea Pilley claims that the club gave 'us a better chance of climbing independently of men' but as much as Ruth values independence, with George away, she and David climb and dance. They dance at the foot of a crag to warm up, at the top of a climb just to celebrate and in the evenings they dance just for fun.

Ruth is grateful that George has arranged this break for her

it made me extra thankful as well as joyfully glad, which I always am, that I had married you because you don't let me sit down & comfortably deteriorate.

At least that was how she felt back in 1918, but with George away, she is torn. Unlike dancing, climbing comes with 'the spice of danger'. With George on Everest, she does not want their children to have to worry about her safety. She remembers her anxiety when she realised that her mother May, whom she adored, was in danger with pneumonia. 'I know how horribly frightened you can be when you are a child, especially if you love your mother very, very much,' she confides to George.

Nobody must ever talk about climbing accidents or dangers when the children are there and they mustn't see photographs of narrow edges or steep precipices below and people walking along them.

But although she does not want their children to have to fear for her safety, she relishes the physical challenge of climbing and the time spent in the glorious Welsh mountains.

The music is still going, the dancers clap and peel off, skipping down the outside of their respective lines where they meet and form an arch with their

Ruth as a baby, c.1892, The Cameron Studio. (*Courtesy of John Mallory*)

Ruth as a teenager, c.1907. (*Courtesy of John Mallory*)

Ruth's mother, Arts and Crafts embroiderer and founder of the Women's Guild of Arts, c.1855–1907. (*Courtesy of Frank Arnott*)

Ruth's father, Hugh Thackeray Turner, Arts and Crafts architect and secretary of Society for the Protection of Ancient Buildings, c.1853–1957. (*Courtesy of Frank Nevel's album – Marianne Nevel*)

Ruth pushing the car outside Pen-y-Pass, Easter 1919. George driving, Geoffrey Winthrop Young is a passenger with Len Winthrop Young sitting behind him. This is the first photograph referred to in Chapter Ten. (*Courtesy Alpine Club*)

Ruth and George at Pen-y-Pass, 1919. *Back row:* (*left to right*) Marby Turner, Kitty O Brien, Ruth Mallory, Raymond Bicknell, Conor O Brien, Harold Porter, Geoffrey Winthrop Young and Elliot Rathbone; *middle row:* Len Winthrop Young (wearing headscarf is sat in front of Ruth); far right is George (with a pipe) and third from right is Ferdy Speyer (sitting down). This is the second photograph referenced in Chapter Ten. (*Courtesy of Alpine Club*)

Easter meet at Pen-y-Pass, 1922. *Front row*: Mabel Capper, H.V.R. (full name unknown), Ursula Nettleship, Nancy Blixam, Len Winthrop Young, Gillian Elliot, Ruth Mallory, Rupert Thompson (John's godfather). *Back row*: sixth from left Conor O Brien, nineth David Pye and twelfth Harold Porter. (*Courtesy Alpine Club*)

Page for 1925 from Geoffrey Winthrop Young (GWY)'s Pen-y-Pass album including a picture of Mary Ann and Ruth (*bottom left*) and the Pinnacle Club (*middle right*). Using GWY's descriptions: (left to right top) Popham & Son, Maxwell & Son E.A. Gill & the Maxwells; the Mid. Ass. M. tramp up the track; Climbers Club – go daily past the door! (*Left to right middle*): Dr Adrian, Mrs Adrian, Claude; MOM [Mary Ann] Dyne, the Adrians, Tony, Norah Topham; The Amph. Butt. Pinn. AND Claude Elliot; Pinnacle Club start out. (*Left to right bottom*): Denis Pilkington, Brown, Budenturz; M. O'Malley [Mary Ann]; Ruth Mallory; Norah Lawrence, Hester Adrian, Tony Popham; Mrs Adrian, M. O'Malley; Tryfan Summit [with Adam and Eve summit stones visible] Norah, G.W.Y.; Cwm Tryfan: (in baking sunshine) Norah Lawrence. (*Courtesy Alpine Club*)

Everest Base Camp, 1924. Plate from *The Epic of Mount Everest* by Francis Younghusband, Edward Arnold & Co., London, 1926. Ruth did not 'see' the mountain in colour as we can through modern photography and film. She knew it through George's descriptions, John Noel's silent black and white film and photographic reproductions like this one. (*Courtesy of Edward Arnold & Co.*)

Everest expedition members having crossed a ford, 1922. (*Left to right*) Howard Somervell, Arthur Wakefield and George Mallory. (*Courtesy of John Mallory*)

(*Left to right*) Sandy Irvine and George Mallory. Ruth wrote to thank Arthur Hinks at the Royal Geographical Society for sending her this photograph; taken by Noel Odell, 7 June 1924. 'Dear Mr Hinks', wrote Ruth, 'I want to thank you and the Everest Committee for so very kindly sending me the last photograph ever taken of George.' Letter stamped on receipt at RGS with 4 August 1924. (*Courtesy of John Mallory*)

George and Ruth in loggia at The Holt, 1915. This is the photograph referred to in Chapter Thirteen. (*Reproduced by kind permission of the Master and Fellows of Balliol College, Oxford University. Francis Fortescue Urquhart Album 7, FFU07-30k*)

Portrait of Ruth, *c.*1916. (*Public domain*)

Portrait of George, *c.*1923. 'George Leigh-Mallory 1923, Underwood & Underwood photographers New York, Emery Walker ph sc.' Ruth sent this to the RGS on their request for a portrait to hand out to the press in July 1924. Frontispiece of David Pye's biography of George Mallory, 1927. Following the request for a portrait of George for 'the Society' Ruth wrote to Hinks: 'I am sending you [a portrait photograph] taken in New York when George was there. Its [*sic*] good but I don't know that it is better than any other. I have no portrate [*sic*]. PS. It's the only copy of this photograph I have so I shall want it back.', 7 April 1926. (*Courtesy John Mallory*)

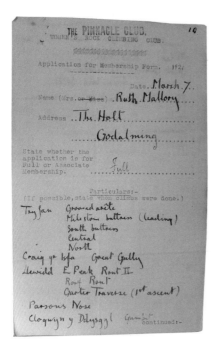

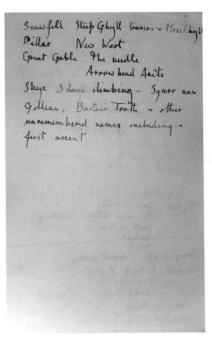

First page of Ruth's application form for membership to the Pinnacle Club. (*Courtesy of Pinnacle Club*)

Second page of Ruth's application form for membership to the Pinnacle Club. (*Courtesy of Pinnacle Club*)

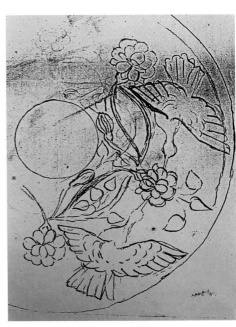

The catalogue cover for the Arts and Crafts exhibition in 1916 at the Royal Academy at Burlington House, London where Ruth exhibited her hand painted bowl. (*Private collection*)

Ruth's sketch – design with birds. 'This is very rough and bad,' Ruth told George, 'and as the circle is flat instead of sticking up as the bowl does the birds come too big & then don't fill the space. Still, this will give you some idea …' Ruth to George, 21 August 1916. (*Courtesy of John Mallory*)

Great Gable war memorial dedication service, 8 June 1924. Ruth is far right in profile. (Press photograph). (*Public domain*)

A picnic, *c.*1935. (*Left to right*) Ruth, Marby, Beridge, Clare and John, and unknown (perhaps Violet Meakin). (*Courtesy of John Mallory*)

Ruth with Marby's dog *c.* mid-1930s. (*Courtesy of Frank Nevel's album – Marianne Nevel*)

Ruth sitting on a wall at Westbrook, *c.*1938. (*Courtesy of John Mallory*)

Will & Ka (Cox) Arnold-Forster in Eagles' Nest garden, *c.*1918. (*Public domain*)

(*Left to right*) Marby and Ruth at Westbrook. (*Courtesy of Frank Nevel's album – Marianne Nevel*)

Author's middle son (6 foot 4 inches) on 'Snuff Box' boulder with corner of Eagles' Nest in the background. (*Author's image*)

raised arms. The floor boards creek and the needle skips. They must be lighter on their feet. Pat Kelly does not seems as fit as usual. Later she admits to feeling below par. Climbing is about balance. Her days off work are precious but, it would not be sensible to climb. She agrees that she will be the guinea pig for a young man who wants her to trial a new configuration of climbing nails hammered into the sole of her boot.

In the morning, the meet splits into three parties according to ability. Pat's husband, Harry, is leading the group climbing the Wrinkled Slabs on the west face of Tryfan. The others will climb the buttresses and the least experienced will practice balance climbing on Tryfan Bach, Little Tryfan. Pat confirms that she is not going to climb, but she will watch. She sets off to walk to her vantage point in a grassy gully, while the climbers start their ascent.

It is nearly the end of the climbing day when there is a shout. Someone has fallen. Harry and others rush toward the fallen figure to find Pat. She is lying awkwardly at the bottom of the gully. She is not moving. The canvas stretcher they always bring is rolled out. They slide poles into long pockets down the side and lift Pat on carefully. The walk in was steep. They will need to tie Pat down lest she slides off as they run her down the mountain. One of her boots is missing. Another party has split off and run to get the car ready at the road running through the Ogwen Valley. They must drive Pat with all haste to the hospital in Llandudno.

*    *    *

Was Ruth there? If she was there, Ruth would have helped. During the First World War, Ruth learned first aid, she even trained other people. Whenever any of her friends needed her, wherever they were, Ruth went, immediately and without question, just to be there.

Pat recovers consciousness at the hospital. The next day she rallies and is able to answer questions. Pat tells whoever is there at her bedside, possibly Ruth, that she rested her hand on a rock to steady herself when it gave way. She was pitched a few feet before she rolled down the gully over grass and stones. Those with her ask what happened to her boot. It seemed extraordinary that a fully laced-up boot could have come off. But instead of continuing to recover, on Tuesday, Pat begins to deteriorate, experiencing facial paralysis before slipping into unconsciousness. Pat Kelly dies on Wednesday, 26 April 1922 with Harry at her bedside.

I have never seen Ruth mentioned, specifically, in connection with Pat's death, but Pat was a friend and Ruth wanted to support her club. If it was possible for an experienced climber to die like an amateur, a 'bank holiday corpse', Ruth cannot rule out the possibility that George, also an expert climber, could die in a similar fall. The death of an experienced climber while not climbing is the 'random bullet' but outside a war zone. Nothing is safe. While Ruth is back at The Holt with the children processing all this, George is still on Everest and he is about to receive the letter describing their time at Pen-y-Pass.

### Tatsang – 17 April 1922

It is only six months since George was here on this blasted plateau believing that he wouldn't see it again 'for all the gold in Arabia'. He has no gold. As his father-in-law has made clear, the G. Mallory Esq. family coffers are emptier rather than fuller. George is struggling to embrace the adventure. He would much prefer to be at Pen-y-Pass with Ruth at that moment. 'I function in a sort of undertone,' he explains to her. 'Life seems more of an endurance and a waiting than an active doing of things that seem worthwhile.'

When George receives his letters from Ruth describing the Easter meet at Pen-y-Pass, there is no mention of Pat Kelly's death. George tells David that

> evidently [Ruth] enjoyed herself immensely and I'm very glad she was able to do so much climbing. It is delightful to hear about it all, though I am almost painfully reminded that there are pleasures in the high endeavour of mountaineering – this sentiment comes naturally on the eve of another attempt on Everest.

George finds it exhilarating to hear from David of the elegance and grace with which his wife climbed in Snowdonia. He thinks of the other climbing couples, Geoffrey and Len, and Harry and Pat. In the same way that those couples dance together on a rock face, Ruth is essential to him. She is his wife and his muse. On 12 May 1922, George writes to his wife:

> the spur to do my best is you & you again – in moments of depression or lack of confidence or overwhelming fatigue I want more than anything to prove worthy of you.

### Godalming – April 1922

Ruth receives a letter from Blanche 'Gabriel' Eden-Smith, Pat's friend and recording secretary of the Pinnacle Club. The letter, to all club members, urges Ruth to ensure that the club must be kept going. It was the biggest interest in [Pat's] life & it would be just a waste of all that work, enthusiasm & pluck of hers for us to let it go down now.

From George's letters, it seems that Ruth never told him about Pat's death while he was away in 1922, in the same way that she never told him when she was 'gravely ill' in 1921. Later, some members of the Pinnacle Club find Pat's boot lodged in a rock on the gully. They realise that the new nail configuration in the sole may have been the cause of her death. They do not want to upset the young man who persuaded Pat to try it out. They bury the boot. They agree never to mention it until everyone who might be upset by the discovery, has passed on.

## Everest – May 1922

George holds the 'Mount Everest Expedition headed letter paper down on the mess table with his left hand against the incessant wind and writes: 'May 28 1922, My dear Clare & Beridge, Thank you very much for all your nice letters.' Ruth has been asking him for parenting advice and he is trying to engage. 'Clare', he tells Ruth, has 'little troubles of competition with other children, [she should] think of herself full of love & delight'. And the others, often suffering from childhood illnesses, should focus on an 'image of themselves with boundless energy & large appetites'. The advice gives a rare insight into his attitude to parenting. It betrays, perhaps, how theoretical it is.

The letter blows into a stream. He chases it and he fishes it out. As he waits for it to dry, he might think of the other children, the Sherpa 'coolies'. Though, like the colonials George refers to all porters as 'coolies', George regards them 'like children where mountain dangers are concerned … and they do so much for us'.

The Sherpas are his allies, but George has developed what he calls, a 'Finch complex'. Finch's daily sport is the humiliation of the coolies. He complains that they smell but so do they all. None of them have washed for weeks, least of all, Finch.

George knows that Finch would be the best climbing partner to keep him safe but Finch's treatment of the coolies has made him a much less attractive prospect. Instead of insulting or ridiculing the porters, George memorises their names, asks them about their villages and their families. Some of them, George learns, are fathers like him. They are here not interested in heroics or glory; they are embracing risk by necessity as a way of earning a living wage.

George confides to Ruth that he would still prefer to climb Everest without breathing supplementary oxygen. As Finch leaves with his oxygen cylinders on his back for an attempt on the summit, George writes a separate letter to Ruth, desperately trying to check his competitive instinct.

> I shan't feel in the least jealous of any success they [Finch's climbing party] may have. The whole venture of getting up with [supplementary] oxygen is so different from ours that the two hardly enter into competition.

But whilst separating oxygen, from oxygen-less worked in theory, when Finch walked into camp with a new height record of 27,235 feet, the reality was hard to swallow. George knows that he has told Ruth that he shouldn't feel 'the least jealous'. He shouldn't. But without Ruth there on the rope to reinforce what he knows he ought to feel, George can't help himself.

# Chapter Twenty

# Collateral Damage and Hope

*The Times*,
4 July 1922

George Mallory's letters to Ruth Mallory
Magdelene College Archives,
Cambridge University, Cambridge

Ruth Mallory's letters to Arthur Hinks
of the Mount Everest Committee,
Royal Geographical Society Archives, London

Mabel Barker's report
in her biography
of summer camp 1922

On 4 July 1922, two months after Pat's tragic death, Ruth is flat out with 'ordinary life' at The Holt when the newspaper boy delivers the daily copy of *The Times*. She does not need to turn to the despatches from Everest. The newspaper's main headline reads: 'Avalanche' and 'Seven Dead'.

For a heart-stopping moment, Ruth must have wondered whether George had been killed, but under the headline 'Seven Dead', Ruth quickly realises that all seven casualties are Sherpas. Her immediate thought, in the past, has been 'for those left behind'. Who are the survivors? Who witnessed the tragedy? Who are the families about to learn of their bereavement?

So far the letters Ruth has received from George have been full of criticism for Finch's callous treatment of the Sherpas, and George's determination to be more responsible. In a letter that has yet to reach her, he writes:

> There is no obligation I have so much wanted to honour as that of taking care of these men … now through my fault seven of them have been killed.

Weeks later, George's explanation finally arrives at The Holt confirming that he conducted the kind of avalanche tests that he would have done in the Alps.

'The three of us [European climbers] were deceived,' George told Ruth, 'there wasn't an inkling of danger among us.'

Hinks is in his office at the RGS in London when he opens a letter from Ruth with George's account enclosed: 'I think,' Ruth states in her covering letter,

> George's feeling that the accident was his fault is the result of the shock … He appears to have taken the greatest care all through and to have been at the time of the avalanche quite unconscious of danger.

Is 'unconscious' a good word for Ruth to use in connection with the word 'danger'? Perhaps better than George's word 'inkling'? A few days earlier, Hinks confirmed to Ruth that he was irritated that some of the other climbers left Everest 'without doing anything geographical' rushing home with unnecessary haste. He did not tell her that when those climbers eventually arrived at his office to deliver their reports, they told him that her husband's 'judgement in purely Alpine matters was bad'. If George is 'quite unconscious of the danger', as Ruth suggests, if George really has 'no inkling of danger' as he writes in the letter Ruth encloses to Hinks, perhaps he is even worse at assessing risk than Hinks suspects?

Without knowing of his peer report, George confirms to Hinks the names of the dead men – Thankay, Sangay, Temba, Lhakpa, Pasang Namgyn, Norbu and Pema. He wants their service and their sacrifice to be officially acknowledged. Two of the men, like him, were fathers. The Mount Everest Committee decide that the families of the Sherpas will be offered compensation as if their men were soldiers killed in battle. But in the official account of the expedition, George must understand that there will be no specific mention of the dead Sherpas.

During the First World War, George told Ruth that he felt as if it would be selfish to keep safe for her sake. One of the other European climbers expressed a similar sentiment immediately after the avalanche when he said

> I would gladly at that moment have been lying there in the snow, if only to give those fine chaps the feeling that we had shared their loss, as we had indeed shared the risk.

The incident seems to add to George's malingering post-war sense of survivor's guilt – he wants to hide. 'I shan't feel much like showing my face' in public, he says.

Ruth knows that George wanted to be 'more tried' during the First World War and after it return home a 'hero'. Four years later, he feels as if he is returning from Everest with blood on his hands. George is in the middle of a nightmare from which he cannot wake, it is a nightmare in which seven men tumble over the edge of a cliff in an avalanche. George did not push them, but he feels so responsible that he might as well have done.

Pat Kelly died at Tryfan. Ruth has not. Seven Sherpas died on Everest. George has not. How much is skill and how much is in the roll of the dice? Francis Younghusband advises George that he speaks from experience – it was bad luck: 'for I have done precisely the same thing myself in the Himalaya, and only the purest luck can have saved me and my party from disaster.' But 'purest luck' is no good to Ruth. She needs to believe that George's expertise can reduce the risks on Everest. Pat's death makes that belief hard to sustain.

In an ugly twist, Lieutenant Colonel Edward Lisle Strutt suggests that after a heavy snowfall 'seventeen persons on the North Col was fifteen too many'. In the circumstances,

> the British Public, the middle classes, shop-keepers, gillies, etc., who alone show a real interest in the expedition, these rather welcome the accident (dead bodies always appeal to them) and think us real 'eroes in consequence …

Ruth's reaction to Strutt's racist and elitist British Empire babble is not recorded, but from England, she seems to have refocused on collateral damage that she can have an impact on. Mabel Barker writes from Camp Schleifstein, near Mayrhofen in the Alps, where she has arrived with thirty people – adults and children – for a school camping trip. On Ruth's recommendation, she has invited Franz Knefel from the Kinderheim in Vienna to be a companion for her younger brother Patrick and to teach him some German.

'Franz is a very delightful child', writes Mabel in a letter quoted on page 108 of Jan Levi's biography of Mabel *And Nobody Woke up Dead*, published by The Ernest Press in 2006.

> Most helpful around camp and rather worried by Pat's untidiness in the tent, I gather! They hoisted a flag in camp yesterday. I was told that it was of combined British and Austrian colours, but as it was made of paper it had already dissolved into a rag by the time I saw it!

The two boys became totally absorbed in an Austro-English climbing club of which they were the committee members.

A joint flag, a couple of nation-blind children, these are the proto-cosmopolitan citizens of the future. This for Ruth, is progress. The Austro-English club is proof, if Ruth needed it, that the child can lose the prejudices of their parents. That the peace depends upon it. The dissolved rag, is a flag worthy of a summit.

But for all her joy, it is quickly obvious to Mabel that Ruth is right. There is very little future for Franz at the Kinderheim and 'no chance of a happy homelife'. They must contrive a way of bringing him safely back to Britain. The paperwork takes time.

\* \* \*

## Queen's Hall, London

Although George does not feel like showing his face in public, the Mount Everest Committee contract obliges him to deliver post-expedition lectures. The auditorium of the Queen's Hall smells of cigarette smoke and perfume. There is a rustling as those who have bought tickets for the event, settle to listen to George relate the story of his nightmare. The lights go down and George is alone on stage in a spotlight.

Just as the two parties move off, George tells the audience that he heard a noise that sounded like the report of a gun.

> I had never before been near an avalanche of snow, but I knew the meaning of that noise as though I were accustomed to hear[ing] it every day ... And then I was moving downward.

Ruth does not need to hear more, but George has captured his audience in a way that he never did with the previous expedition. She knows that the public thrill to a tragedy. The deaths emphasise the danger, but the risk will never directly affect them. It is not their husband or the father of their children who died leaving Sherpa widows, and fatherless children. It is not their husband, the father of their children, who nearly died. It is danger so safely packaged as to be almost fictional; like reading a tragic novel. It takes her back to George's first engagement present to her: Edward Whymper's *Scrambles Amongst the Alps*. Is the story better because four men died falling to their deaths from the Matterhorn? Is George's story better because seven Sherpas fell to their deaths on Everest?

Ruth is being pushed to accept the validity of using tragedy, real tragedy, for entertainment. Worse than this she is obliged to accept that the tragedy is now hardwired into their income since George is being paid a percentage of lecture ticket sales. Without the 'spice of danger', George has told her, climbing would 'lose its allure'. But what about the people left behind – the Matterhorn families, the Sherpa families and Harry Kelly? Ruth is expected to listen to her husband's lecture without identifying with those families and without allowing herself to think that their fate might become hers.

Chapter Twenty-One

# Ruth, Kathleen, Pat and Stella

The letter that does not exist is
Ruth Mallory's letter to George Mallory,
which we only hear in his reply

The letter that has yet to be written is
a letter from Stella Cobden-Sanderson
to George Mallory,
which was only found in 1999,
perfectly preserved in the pocket of
George's tweed jacket
Magdelene College Archives,
Cambridge University, Cambridge

This chapter is based on letter that no longer exists and another that does but, at this stage in the early spring 1923, has yet to be written. It starts with Ruth back on the Liverpool dock waving at the figure of her husband, but this is the first farewell with no obvious risk attached. George is off to the United States. This time Hinks has made sure that George is travelling in 'style' on *Olympic*. Ruth has convinced George that this is a vote of confidence from the experts; a clear declaration that the Mount Everest Committee do not believe the avalanche disaster was his fault. But the MEC do not seem to have offered to pay for Ruth to accompany him. When *Olympic* docks in New York, on 17 January 1923, George writes to Ruth:

It is much more difficult to go without you in this country than ever it was in India … I don't know why, but I don't feel I can really be happy at all without you.

He is nervous. He needs her. He is booked to speak at the Broadhurst Theatre in New York, which has 1,100 seats to fill. There is a risk that George may be empty seated. Since their income relies on ticket sales, George warns Ruth that 'Everything depends on this'.

Ruth has tried to fit her housekeeping expenditure around George's uncertain income. She knows that George doesn't want her to be consumed by housewifery. Ruth's father has not offered her an increased allowance or lent her one of the many Westbrook maids, but he has acquired an expensive Marconi radio set. Perhaps he's bought it in order to listen to Richard Hughes, a Charterhouse master like George, who had been commissioned to write the first ever 'listening play' to be broadcast on the BBC. Scheduled for 15 January 1924 it will be called *A Comedy of Danger*.

The day before George's ill-attended and, therefore, ill-paid lecture in Detroit on the US-Canadian border on 16 February 1923, Ruth joins her father at Westbrook for what will become compulsory attendance of the radio 'performance' in the drawing room. The programme is Act 4, Scene 3 of *Julius Caesar*:

CASSIUS
You love me not.
BRUTUS
I do not like your faults.
CASSIUS
A friendly eye could never see such faults.
BRUTUS
A flatterer's would not ...

George has always been able to rely on Ruth's unflagging reassurance to give him the confidence to take to the stage for lectures. Now as he realises the lecture programme is not going to pay, he admits to Ruth that they would be 'poorer than I'd hoped'.

From The Holt, where Ruth is trying to economise, she reads that George is being introduced to the 'swellest of New York clubs' and forbidden prohibition wine cellars, where he drinks gin into the early hours. He has just met Stella Cobden-Sanderson, the 'poor deserted little wife of' Ferdy Speyer. Stella is not 'poor' her divorce settlement from the wealthy Speyer, means she is financially independent, though she chooses to become a buyer for Peter Jones. She is petite, fashionable, gossipy, intimate and bright. After one lecture George tells Ruth that they 'go for ices'. When George's lectures are not as successful at filling theatres as he hoped, he is determined not to be despondent. Stella has been deserted and yet is not despondent about it. She is, George tells Ruth '... very nice'.

Ruth knows the Cobden-Sandersons. Until Stella's father, Thomas, sabotaged the Arts and Crafts Doves Press by throwing the metal type over Hammersmith Bridge, they had been close family friends. In earlier, happier times, Thomas

Cobden-Sanderson even coined the term 'Arts and Crafts' when he exhibited with Thackeray Turner and his future wife, May Powell, at the New Gallery, Regent's Street in 1888. When May died in 1907, Cobden-Sanderson came down to Westbrook to comfort his widowed friend. Cobden-Sanderson had loved May Turner. She was restful, unlike his fiery militant suffragette wife, Annie. He told Ruth's father that he could feel the spirit of May moving in that garden. Thackeray Turner later created a rose garden as a memorial to May with a gap in the wall so that passers-by could appreciate the blooms.

But in New York in 1923, George tries to be as upbeat as the newly divorced and disgraced, Stella Cobden-Sanderson. Stella's divorce is controversial, her ex-husband is divorcing her to marry her ex-sister-in-law. Although Stella comes from a family that courts scandal, she is keen to be out of the way of the wedding. The United States suits her. This is the country where her parents were welcomed as celebrities. She does not relish the idea of returning to London – too many awkward memories.

Back in England, Ruth receives George's letter about meeting Stella and his admission that they 'would be poorer than I hoped'. Ruth is already struggling. She is overdrawn at the bank. Her father considers debt of any kind to be immoral. Ruth is out driving their latest car 'the Albert' that George bought before he left, when it breaks down. Repairs will be expensive. They have still not finished building it an even more expensive garage. Ruth has a weary trudge home with tired fractious children. She is trying to keep the 'big nature' Geoffrey praised her for, but she is worn out. She cannot keep deferring to the Everest label for peace. For the first time, Ruth tells George exactly how hard she is finding it to cope.

Perhaps the final straw is George's answer to a reporter in New York on 18 March 1923. When asked 'Why climb Everest?' he replied, 'Because it's there'. Ruth reads the phrase requoted in the British newspapers. 'Because it's there' will become George's catchphrase and then his epitaph. It will be adopted as a universal advertising strapline for self-justification. George's climber son-in-law Glenn Millikan will later observe that 'Some adepts quote it as they quote bits from difficult poems, with knowing half-smiles, as if to say, "You and I can grasp the sense without asking more".' Mary Ann, like most of George and Ruth's climbing friends, wants to dissociate George's name from it completely. Mary Ann will tell George's future biographers to 'slap it down'.

But in 1923, when George receives Ruth's letter telling him how hard she is finding keeping their ship afloat, he is 'greatly distressed'. He does not like her 'despondent tone … My dear I am sorry but it's a day's work with the car I suppose.' He would take a burst magneto over empty theatre humiliation any day. George cuts short his lecture programme. Having delivered his last talk on 23 March 1923, he returns to New York where Stella is waiting.

* * *

When the Treaty of Lausanne is signed on 24 July 1923, it is heralded as the formal end of protracted post-First World War peace negotiations. Geoffrey and his brother Hilton Young are there in Switzerland to witness the moment. Hilton has brought his new wife, once Kathleen Scott, now Kathleen Young. She is just pregnant with their first child.

Kathleen chose her first husband, Antarctic explorer Captain Scott, for his genes. He was, in her opinion, a 'lion' and, therefore, suitable as the 'father for my son'. She believes that a son, a 'man child', delivers the father's immortality. Now in 1923, Kathleen is in her mid-forties and recognises that at her age, pregnancy might be dangerous. (She writes a letter to be delivered to her first son, Peter Scott 'in the event of my death' in childbirth.) But she believes the risk of this second pregnancy is worth it if it means delivering her second husband, Hilton's genetic immortality. In this respect, Kathleen and Ruth hold similar views. During the war, when Ruth did not know whether George would be killed, she told him, on 2 November 1916, 'I want children. If I did not admire you I would not want them so much but I want to make you go on for ever [sic] as much as I can.'

Unlike Ruth, Kathleen prioritises accompanying her husbands over being with her children. Back in 1910, Kathleen left baby Peter in England to accompany Captain Scott to New Zealand, the last port before Antarctica. Although Kathleen was a committee member of the Women's National Anti-Suffrage League (of which Lord Curzon was president) she expects her husbands to consult her on their decisions. (Captain Scott acknowledged that many women were 'the power behind the throne'.) In 1923, Ruth stayed behind while George toured America. Kathleen decides that rather than staying behind while Hilton goes to Lausanne, she will accompany him. (She has the added incentive of seeing her friend the Arctic explorer and League of Nations representative for Norway, Fridtjof Nansen.)

In many ways, Ruth is more adventurous than Kathleen. Kathleen has no desire to become a climber, but she is not Ruth's only role model. Before 1912, Robert Falcon Scott and Ernest Shackleton were in direct competition for the South Pole. Emily Shackleton offers an alternative to Kathleen's interpretation of the role of an ideal explorer's wife.

When Emily Shackleton accompanied her husband on his post-expedition lecture tour to the United States and Canada in 1909, the newspapers suggested that she must have heard rumours of 'the kisses with which the American women are so free'. Ruth was jealous of the 'fishing fleet' aboard George's boats to India in 1921 and 1922, but by 1923 it appears that she trusts George with the free-kissing American ladies.

The Mallorys are already acquainted with Emily Shackleton through Ruth's mother's second cousin, Robert Baden-Powell, who founded the Scout movement. Now in 1923, in her mid-fifties Emily Shackleton is an established leader of the Girl Guides founded by Robert's sister Agnes and now run by his wife, Olave Baden-Powell. By the mid-1920s, Robert begins to turn his attention to mountaineering. He enlists Geoffrey Winthrop Young to provide information on 'climbing as an educative activity for the Scouts'. Ruth could have delivered the equivalent 'educative activity' for the Guides but the Baden-Powells believe that it is her status as an explorer's wife, rather than a climber in her own right, that makes her the ideal Girl Guide role model.

The Baden-Powells describe their movement as the Junior League of Nations. As the most prominent explorer's wife of the moment, Ruth is tempted by their invitation to join up. As with Montessori, the Scouts' philosophy could be applied in every country. (Since does not require an expensive outlay, to Ruth's mind, it has a greater chance of success than George's proposal for opening an international school.) But whilst Ruth prioritises any organisation that supports the League, she is effectively single parenting a young family. When Clare, Beridge and John are at school, Ruth assures the Baden-Powells that she will follow Emily Shackleton's lead, perhaps in the newly formed Ranger Guides.

Alongside 'peace' news from Lausanne, Ruth reads reviews of the late Sir Ernest Shackleton's biography in *The Times*. Most of the biography's reviewers focus on the answer Shackleton gave his wife Emily back in 1909 when she asked him why he had turned back within 100 miles of the then unconquered South Pole. His answer? 'Because I thought you would rather a Live Donkey to a Dead Lion.' For the first time, the question is laid out in black and white. Geoffrey, Kathleen's new brother-in-law, can assure Ruth that Kathleen defends Captain Scott, her 'Dead Lion' as the more heroic alternative. But Ruth knows that Shackleton did not have to sacrifice his life to his goal to receive his knighthood. The British public have never considered Shackleton to be a 'Live Donkey'.

Ruth subscribes to *The Times* to keep abreast of developments in Switzerland, but she cannot know that on 24 July 1923, the day that the Treaty of Lausanne is signed, the India Office in London, receive a telegram titled 'Secret Mount Everest'. In the telegram, the now retired British diplomat Charles Bell reveals that there is 'something behind' Everest. He is not talking about Ruth.

Regarding the expeditions to Mount Everest via Tibet in 1921 and 1922
… The Tibetans do not believe that explorations are carried out only in
the interests of geographical knowledge and science. They will suspect that
there is something behind what we tell them … Until the Tibetan question
is settled with China, these expeditions to Everest should not be allowed.

\* \* \*

George finally interviews for a salaried job lecturing for the Board of Extra-
Mural Studies, part of the Cambridge University extension programme. The
programme is in line with League of Nations ambitions to educate those working
men and women unable to attend university. Remembering his impromptu visit
to The Holt, back in January 1921, Geoffrey writes to George on 18 May 1923:

I said to Ruth, 'What George wants is a label, and this [Everest] will give it.'
And t' other day, when G.M.T. [George Macaulay Trevelyan] was talking
of your chances [of being offered the Board of Extra-Mutal Studies job]
he used the very phrase: 'You see, he's known about now – he's ticketed!'
And I chuckled!

Geoffrey is congratulating himself on having persuaded Ruth to agree to George's
expeditions. Although the lecturing job may not be the glamorous League role
George had hoped for, Geoffrey argues that educating working men and women
is essential, a work of 'national importance'. Geoffrey believes that George's job
opportunities have broadened, that Everest has already delivered the 'label', the
'ticket', even if it has meant some belt tightening for the Mallorys. He has no
idea of the extent of that tightening. The Mallorys are now seriously in debt.
When George is offered the job, Ruth is relieved and hopes that the role will
satisfy his personal ambitions. But on 10 April 1923 when the MEC ask George
to supply a list of possible climbers for the next expedition to Everest planned
for 1924, he writes – 'Self?'

# Part III

# 1924

## Pinnacle Club: Then and Now

Ruth did not have the dangers fact-flashing before her eyes. Now there is an area called 'the death zone'. The term refers to altitudes above 26,240 feet, where the pressure of oxygen is insufficient to sustain human life.

A brief internet search for 'list of deaths on Everest' brings up a chart with nine vertical columns: name, date, expedition, nationality, cause of death, location and remains status. The first on the horizontal column is Dr Alexander Kellas, 5 June 1921, and the seven Sherpas from 1922 are there too. Scrolling down the 'cause of death' column, I see: avalanche, falling into a crevasse, crushed by serac, high-altitude cerebral edema, exhaustion, frostbite, exposure and several described as 'disappearance – likely accidental death during climb'.

Today the dangers are infantried and searchable. Dead climbers are preserved cryogenically in the cold, like butterflies pinned to a board. There are over 300 butterflies on that board. Each one in their bright neon climbing suits with their bright plastic boots. High altitude climbing is known to be dangerous. To embrace that danger is a choice, a deliberate choice.

But it is on a scale of choice that we all make every day; it is just at the extreme end of that scale. In 2022, my children are grown up and I am invited to Snowdonia for a day's climbing with the Pinnacle Club. I am going to walk the unlikely tightrope that Ruth walked, the tightrope that the Pinnacle Club members articulated to me in the Emily Kelly Hut. I must be aware of the dangers whilst trying 'not to think about [them]'.

## Llanberis, Snowdonia – September 2022

After more heavy rain, the climb the Pinnacle Club have decided upon is on fast drying south facing slate. The Sidings is high up the side of a quarry in an area called 'Australia'. There is a ledge the width of a wide pavement at the bottom of an almost sheer face, with sheer drops below. We have divided into pairs with one climbing and one belaying from the bottom. The dark grey slate face above looks smooth to me. My partner assures me there are ripples and that the quartz lines have more friction than the slate. Rubber soled climbing shoes are less likely to slip on the quartz.

As the climbers are getting ready, I make a couple of notes:

Taste – chocolate eclairs and fear dry mouth.
Sight – wet slate with sun on it acts like a mirror, it looks like ice.
Sound – sound of rooks circling and clinking metal climbing gear.
Touch – smooth and warm.
Smell – petrichor.

'Your turn now.'

I think I was trying to be invisible, the person behind the notepad. But I am being asked to climb a 6a bolted route called 'Goose Creature'. I have a quick glance at the guidebook, its pages lifting in the light breeze:

A great route with a hard rock over. Climb up to a small ledge then foot traverse, then break until you can climb up past a bolt to a second break. Mantel this and clip a bolt on the right. Traverse left to another bolt and make a hard move past this.

I approach the rock face and reach up to the 'holds' my partner Emily has just used. They are difficult to see with the naked eye. Should I be climbing with spectacles? Somehow I use my fingertips and find myself 'foot traversing' along the small wrinkle of a ledge. I break right. I am now at full stretch, with my knee on my raised elbow, my body flat against the rock face. Somehow I must transfer my weight onto my highest foot. I have to do this without being able to counter weight by leaning forwards because the rock is in the way.

I think of George 'flowing up' a rock face. I think of Ruth, 'a natural'. What is the opposite of that? I come back down and approach the route with the other leg highest. Is that better? From the bottom my partner instructs me to 'reach left, a bit further, can you feel it now?' I can feel that the slate is slightly off vertical. Is that a hold? How the hell do they do this? It's at moments like this that climbers can get those 'sewing machine legs'. My legs seem to be all right but I can feel adrenaline. 'I've got you,' says Emily. 'If you want to come down and rest, I've got you …' Emily is kindness personified, but how can I come down a 'Goose Creature' without first getting to the top? Ruth wouldn't.

After I get to top, the sheer relief of having managed is amazing. I stop for a sandwich. Along the face, Teresa is complaining about slate. She doesn't like slate. She says it is like trying to cling to a mirror. She wants to get back to grit.

She'll take the gritstone over slate any day of the week. She finds the smooth surface unnerving: 'I'll relive the slips in the night.'

Clouds are scudding across a blue sky. When they obscure the sun, we put on a layer. When they pass, we take the layer off. Climbing is tiring, it makes you hot but belaying another climber is chilly. I am climbing with what I have come to think of as Ruth's Pinnacle Club. Suddenly, I am euphoric. The whole climbing thing is an art, I can see that. It is creative and like all creative things it is a confidence trick. Some of us need confidence more than strength. We climb all day, all along the Sidings until, at last, I finish with an easy climb up the slab and corner on the right hand side of the face.

This last climb is all joy. The knots are starting to become automatic, the boots are tight but I notice that the others tread the heels down when they are belaying to release the pressure on their toes. The helmet is becoming more familiar, the chin strap less noticeable as I crane my head back to look up for the next hold. My adrenaline is under control.

Most importantly, climbing like this feels elemental. It is like a natural puzzle, a game almost between me and the rock. When I reach the top of one route, I look west and there is Alex, the president of the Pinnacle Club. At that moment, the sun comes out from behind a cloud and glances off the slate face between us so that it shines like ice. And I find myself thinking of Ruth climbing here in Snowdonia at the same time that George was climbing Everest 100 years ago. Was there a moment when they were both ascending simultaneously on opposite sides of the world? Did they ever stop to think of the relative danger of their respective positions? Did they ever refuse an adventure because it was too dangerous? 'To refuse an adventure,' George Mallory once said, 'is to dry up like a pea in its shell.' But where to draw the line?

Jim Ballard, Alison Hargreaves's husband claimed that

> I've always thought there's quite a definite line between good adventure and danger. And the trick is to make sure you've always got your feet on the line.

Driving home, I realise that climbing is at once supremely selfish and also completely selfless – partnering another person means holding their life in your hands. It is way of achieving an almost sublime level of self-forgetfulness, a kind of moving meditation. That evening Alex sends me a photograph she took of me at the top of a route with four words: 'I wonder, I wonder'.

# Chapter Twenty-Two

# 'Self?'

Peter Gillman (interviewer)
Clare Millikan (née Mallory) (interviewee)
Script kindly lent to the author

George Mallory's letters to Ruth Mallory
and Reverend Herbert Leigh-Mallory,
Magdelene College Archives,
Cambridge University, Cambridge

Kate Nicholson and Audrey Salkeld,
Conversation, 2006

Until George leaves for Everest the following year, Ruth is as Robert MacFarlane describes her, 'inaudible'. The next time her name appears it will be as a signature on the lease to what will be their next home, Herschel House, Cambridge. George's name is not on that lease. The conversations ('girl-with-her-own-income' arguments) between Ruth and her father behind this situation are lost to us, but it is obvious that Ruth is caught between the two men in her life. Her only 'audible' comment is to agree to put her name only on that lease.

As Ruth is preparing to sign the lease in Godalming, in London Hinks opens George's reply to his request for a list of climbers and reads 'Self' at the bottom. Before we look at Ruth's reaction, what is George's 'Self'? Is it the selfless self-sacrificing 'patriotic duty' self as understood by the soldiers who served in the First World War, or is it (as Robert MacFarlane puts it in *Mountains of the Mind*), his 'selfish'-self? Is it just a question of context? At the Mallorys end of the twentieth century, the default understanding was that returning to Everest a third time would be an act of extreme selflessness, of putting duty to country before self-interest.

George was an agnostic, but he was the son of seven generations of clergy. His mind was set to think along lines of Christian self-sacrifice. His time in the army had honed his sense of the duty to his country. His upbringing and education had emphasised the responsibility that came with the privilege of his class. These are all values Ruth recognised. Clare (Mallory) Millikan would later insist, in an interview with Peter Gillman, that her mother understood her father's decision to put himself forward as a candidate for the third expedition as a moral imperative: 'go out there and save lives and finish the job.'

Who am I to question Clare? I, we, do not have to find some purchase on that refracting mirrored surface. I, we, do not have to believe an 'a posteriori'-justification to have any hope of living with the consequences. But since Clare, Beridge and John are no longer alive and vulnerable, I suggest that George writing 'Self' on that list was, and still is, more complicated than the self-justifying motivation of selfless-duty.

George does not tell Ruth that he has asked to be included on the expedition by writing 'Self'. Instead he gives her the impression that the invitation has come unexpectedly, almost against his will. He tells her that she needn't worry because the Reverend Cranage, his new employer at the Board of Extra-Mural Studies, will probably not release him. Ruth is packing up the house in Godalming preparing to move to Cambridge. George has already started the job and is living in temporary lodgings when he writes to tell her, 'Cranage has not turned it down definitely. But I don't think they will hear of my going.' It would be 'a big sacrifice either way'.

> It is wretched not being able to talk to you about this, darling. You must tell me if you can't bear the idea of my going again and that will settle it anyway.

The words are loaded with effort. A burden, the bearing of an idea that is as George recognises almost unbearable. Unlike the previous times he has pressed her, pushed her to the edge for an answer, this time he implies that she would be justified in saying that she could not bear it. Even worse, if she could not bear it, he would be released from the burden himself.

Ruth is back in the same position that she had been when Geoffrey first dangled the 'label' of Everest in The Holt drawing room in January 1921. She is being asked to make the decision. Is she any more empowered now than she was then? Perhaps she is. Back in the drawing room of The Holt, it had been two against one. Geoffrey and George on one side, her on the other. This time, Geoffrey advises George that he should *not* go. Even Mary, George's sister, has declared that they (she seems to be speaking for the whole Mallory family) emphatically do *not* think he should go. Ruth has support, but her answer is still the deciding vote.

In a letter George has yet to write, he will look back on this torturous time as one of the most 'difficult times' of their marriage. There may be other reasons, perhaps reasons that Ruth can only sense. Something has changed. To balance his new job and expedition negotiations, George is often in London. Stella Cobden-Sanderson, who had relished the chance to be in New York whilst her ex-husband married her ex-sister-in-law, is now back in London herself. From the address on her letterhead, it seems that she is frequenting the Forum Club, just along Hyde Park from the RGS offices on Kensington Gore. By March the following year, Stella will be living at 23 Hertford Street in London W1.

The first we hear of Ruth 'directly' is George quoting her to his father Herbert Leigh-Mallory on 25 October 1924 'instead of settling down to make a new life here [in Cambridge] with Ruth,' George tells his father that he has decided to return to Everest. Why?

> We have both thought that it would look rather grim to see others, without me, engaged in conquering the summit; and now that the prospect revives, I want to have a part in the finish ... Ruth comes in, of course. She has written that she is willing I should go ...

Is this George the 'Self?' of selfless duty or the competitive self who confesses that it 'would look rather grim' to see others conquer that summit without him? The rhetoric is one of conquest. Whoever conquers Everest will be a hero. George admits that he wants to have a part of that. He never uses the word 'want' in reference to Ruth. What does she want?

Ruth is in Godalming with the redoubtable Vi and the children waiting for the furniture removals. Was 'willing' her actual word or George's interpretation? It is not a word that carries a sense of 'elation'. It is not the kind of word she used when describing her attempts to make the best of being cornered. There is no 'grace' or 'joy' in 'willing'-ness. It seems more like weary, even painful, resignation. George's choice of words, or Ruth's word (we will never know whether 'willing' was a direct quote) acknowledges that he was pushing Ruth to the edge of what she could bear. And yet he did it.

George's father replies on 12 November 1924: 'Ruth, too, is very good to give you up again ...' Even Hinks is moved to comment on Ruth's predicament: 'I would like ... to thank Mrs Mallory for her consent to spare you once more for the work of the expedition.' All of them, George, his father and his erstwhile boss recognise that Everest has been, and will now continue to be, an endurance test for Ruth.

There are others who have their own version of Ruth's reaction. They are valuable 'live links'. Hilda Haig-Brown told me that Ruth believed that she could not live with herself if she held George back. That is all she said. But it is subtly different to Clare's point about safety and finishing the job.

If Ruth held George back and someone else had reached the summit without him, it would have cast a permanent shadow over the future of their married life. It is as if she could not live with herself if she prevented George from going, even if he died as a result. As if the choice was their relationship or his life. For me, it seems as if Ruth, at this point, is choosing between life and death, but I am aware that I have the curse of hindsight. Even without that curse, there is reason to suggest that Ruth sensed this choice. In later life, Clare remembered that before her father left, her mother had terrible premonitions. Clare was not specific. Perhaps Ruth was not specific when she told her about them. In her interview with Peter and Leni Gillman, Clare was clear that her mother had the strong feeling that some disaster was about to happen.

Despite her premonitions, Ruth hoped that George would return home safely. 'Hope can't be untruthful can it?' she asked him once. Evidence from the First World War and the previous two expeditions validated that hope. At times, Ruth must have wondered whether it was possible that George could climb Everest, like Sisyphus (Greek mythology), again and again and again. But when George told her after the war that he wished he'd been 'more tried', what did that mean in the context of Everest? Was his limit the summit of that mountain or his own death? Ruth cannot for a second entertain the possibility, surely, that they could be one and the same? The expression 'between a rock and a hard place' seems at once a perfect metaphor and a trite over-used phrase. Ruth found herself in an extraordinary predicament, on the edge of the worst precipice, on the brink of the deepest abyss.

* * *

The next piece in the puzzle is going to require a brief sidestep into non-climbing autobiography because the next piece of the puzzle is missing. I made this point to Everest historian Audrey Salkeld in 2007 as we were watching a video of John Noel's Everest film on the television at her home, Grumply Nook.

Audrey has authored and co-authored more books on Everest history than any other single author. She died last year at the age of 87. An obituary in *The Guardian* suggested that she was 'an unrivalled source of information, often opening new perspectives and contesting received truths'. Along with her extraordinarily generosity in giving time to researchers like me, that description fits my memory of her perfectly.

Audrey met many of the 1924 Everest team who climbed with George. Although she never knew Ruth personally, she knew people who did, amongst them Len Winthrop Young and Noel Odell.

I have trawled Kathleen Scott's diary in Cambridge University Library archives for any mention of George's visit to her (made just before George left for Everest in 1924) and I can't find it. I have seen it mentioned in other Mallory biographies, but I need the primary source to corroborate. Where, I ask Audrey, is the evidence? Audrey sets down her cup of tea. Where, she asks me, is the evidence that we are having this cup of tea? I know that George visited Kathleen Scott, or by then Kathleen Young,' Audrey tells me firmly,

> because Len [Winthrop Young] was there in the taxi afterwards as they all drove back to Euston to catch the train back to Cambridge. And she told me. I remember. She told me about it when we were on top of a bus in London.

Like the pivot stone on which Ruth swung herself across to begin the Garter Traverse in Snowdonia, this visit by George to Kathleen is for me an essential turning point in Ruth's story. At the time of the visit Kathleen had just given birth to her second son, Wayland. She had also endorsed an heroic equivalence between Agamemnon (Greek mythology) and her first husband, Captain Scott in the draft of a biography by Stephen Gwynn. Agamemnon was a classical figure who would rather die than (in literal translation) 'return with his task unaccomplished'.

Audrey and I talk about Kathleen's peer group. Her close friend, the Norwegian Arctic explorer Fridtjof Nansen, maintained that the only way to succeed in exploration was to burn the bridges behind you; to leave no means of retreat. Only total commitment, he told Kathleen, led to success. Kathleen agreed. To her mind, Scott had been a success. He may not have won the race for the South Pole, the Norwegian Roald Amundsen won that, but he had 'not turned back with his task unaccomplished'.

It is impossible to know exactly what was said between Kathleen and George in her home at Buckingham Palace Road, but whatever it was had a profound effect upon his attitude to his next expedition. He had returned twice from Everest alive but without the summit. In the taxi, George confided to the Winthrop Youngs that this third attempt would be 'more like war than adventure and that he did not expect to return alive.'

## Cambridgeshire – February 1924

It is 3.00 pm on 14 February 1924. Ruth is driving George to his Board of Extra-Mural Studies tutorial class in Raunds, Northamptonshire, a journey of over 30 miles. Ruth knows that Ka always drives Will to his League of Nations meetings because she thinks he will be too distracted to remember to turn the wheel. For Ruth, time in the car is precious time with George before he leaves for Everest. The car, the now mended 'Albert', is high sided and buffeted by cold easterly winds that rake the Cambridgeshire flat lands.

George's lectures start after the working day. They often return to Herschel House after midnight. He is juggling his work commitments with preparations for Everest. In the car beside Ruth, George can use the time to prepare his lectures. He will not tell her about his meeting with Kathleen Scott in London but seems unsettled by it. Ruth will not tell him about her premonitions. There is an uneasy silence, stiff with unsaid words.

'My impression of his state of mind,' said David who was worried about his friend,

> is that he would have been profoundly relieved if the whole expedition had been called off; but that in any other event he felt it as inevitable, and indeed he wished, to be there. He did not really want to go.

As Ruth drives through the silence, she might sense that she is as near falling as she was when George pushed her off that ridge. Can she step back from the edge? Should she tell him that, after some consideration, she can't bear it? That she is not willing? That he must not go? At this stage there is a chance that George could return alive, an adventure-sated paterfamilias. When something is too painful to think about, Ruth can use her wartime technique of not thinking about it – 'it may be cowardly but there are limits'. She has learned to distract herself by remembering happier times, summer and sunshine and holidays.

## Skye – August 1918

Ruth is surrounded by clouds of midges. The Cullins of Skye are spectacular, but the 'national bird' is a pest. The weather has been hot. The air smells of peat and vegetation, the rushing stream from the Fairy Pools is the only sound. Walking beside the river from the pools to the sea, Ruth gets nearer to the bay at Glen Brittle. The river becomes deeper with eddies in which Ruth can strip off and bathe. The mosquitoes are so bad that she tries to stay under water to evade them, but it is a technique, as David has wryly observed, which has 'limited usefulness'.

As Ruth rounds the corner to the sea, she sees green islands flung out across a shimmering Atlantic Ocean. The view is spectacular but will be even better from where George is on Sron na Ciche. If she looks up to her left, she might see the small figure of her husband moving crab like over high gabbro granite slabs.

Yesterday evening George set his heart on finding a way up Sron na Ciche, a 'precipice', rising to 1,000 feet that looks over the glen. This time, for the first time, Ruth has refused to accompany him. (It is the only recorded time that Ruth ever said 'no' to climbing with George.) The days preceding this have been long and unremitting. George has other experienced climbers who can climb with him. He does not need Ruth even though he might want her.

Later, she will find that George has made a first ascent. It will be called Mallory's Slab and Groove. It will be graded 'severe'. She will learn that George led out 70 feet without a belay and out of sight of his partner. If she had been there, would he have at least used a rope? How essential is she to his safety?

# Chapter Twenty-Three

# The Last Goodbye

Ruth Mallory's letter to George Mallory,
3–4 March 1924,
Magdelene College Archives,
Cambridge University, Cambridge

## Birkenhead – 29 February 1924

Ruth follows George up the gangplank onto the deck of the latest Anchor Line boat, the *California*. Although the air is freezing, George is in his white linen tropical suit. By now he is familiar with the pre-expedition publicity and the requirement to pose as the linen-suited gentleman explorer. George is the celebrity of the moment. He has a fan club, many of them young girls. To Ruth it must seem that these are people with no skin in the game. These are people who can incite a remote figure, a Mr Leigh-Mallory, to acts of classical heroism. They have nothing to lose. Ruth, his wife and the mother of his children, just wants him back.

Ruth tries to comfort herself in the knowledge that George has not forgotten his young family. A few weeks ago, he stayed with her youngest sister Mildred Morgan in Taunton before giving an Everest lecture. A man in the audience had exclaimed that Mr Mallory must be thrilled to be returning to Everest. Instead of agreeing, Mildred told Ruth that George replied almost reproachfully: 'You know, I am leaving my wife and young children behind me.'

Now on the deck of the *California*, the ship's boilers are being fired up. The press photographers are gathered between the after mast and the aft funnel. After the official team shot, one photographer wants a picture of just the 'Two Birkenhead Men in the Party', George and fellow teammate Andrew Comyn 'Sandy' Irvine, are both local lads. At 38, George is over a decade older than Irvine who was too young to fight in the war. Irvine's lack of war-weariness is refreshing, but he has hardly any climbing experience. He has been chosen for his youth, strength and his exceptional engineering genius.

Irvine interests Ruth. He is a typical Nietzschean 'superman' recommended by another Everest team member, Noel Odell. Odell (as distinct from the expedition's film maker John Noel) is a geologist and climber who had led the 1923 Merton College Oxford Arctic expedition to Spitsbergen. Irvine impressed him and he recommended him to the MEC.

Ruth has far more climbing experience than Irvine, but still, in 1924, the idea of taking a woman on the expedition is never considered. Ruth remembers Captain Farrar's warning in 1921 that George and Finch were essentially matched in skill and experience to ensure each other's safety. She knows of Geoffrey Winthrop Young's warning that George tended to lead the less experienced climbers beyond their ability. But there is a third conundrum. When Geoffrey first advised George not to take his novice wife to the Alps on honeymoon, the argument centred around the enervating effect of sex. The 21-year-old Irvine is notoriously promiscuous.

Irvine has been conducting a torrid affair with Marjorie Summers, ex-chorus girl and the step-mother of a fellow Oxford student who had booked a cabin in the expedition boat to Spitsbergen. (The husband, the student's father, is suing for divorce and proceedings 'Summers v Summers' will be published in *The Times*.) But for the Mount Everest Committee, it seems that Irvine's sexual activity is taken as encouraging proof of his virility, of stamina not unlike Guy Bullock's long-distance running. George seems to believe that with his experience and Irvine's potency, they will make an invincible partnership and 'stamp to the top' of that 'infernal mountain'. The photographers leave, shaking hands with the four explorers. It is time for Ruth to disembark. At some undocumented point, George and Ruth say goodbye.

The ropes tying the *California* are released from the stanchions and drop with a splash into the sea water where they are reeled in. The ship's horn sounds. The dockside is alive with handkerchiefs, tears, lifted children. How is Ruth at this stage in the story? During the First World War, Ruth told George that war toughened the fibres, that their repeated farewells meant she was learning to part with him 'in true British fashion', but those farewells had been simpler, easier to rationalise. War was duty. What was Everest? However Ruth appears to those on the dock, I am not convinced by Ruth's 'tough fibres'. Once she admitted that she felt as if her heart was trying to jump out of her body – to jump the gap between them.

An hour later, George's ship has still not left the harbour. There is a strong westerly blowing smuts from the central funnel across the dock. The *California*'s tall hull is acting like a sail and tugs cannot pull it against the wind. Ruth waves. Turns. Walks down the dock in the direction of the train station. She leaves before the ship is out of sight. Perhaps she has a train to catch. Or perhaps Ruth decides to play an active role. Perhaps she was trying to 'jump' to be proactive – to do the leaving rather than the being left. Ruth can walk away but she cannot walk away from her premonitions.

*    *    *

Ruth becomes at once elusive and extremely clear at this time. Herschel House in Cambridge has been pulled down. Although I cannot walk around the rooms, I can try to reconstruct it from snatches of letter conversations. It seems to have been cold, cavernous and expensive to heat. Ruth planned to go and stay with her sisters as soon as the children finished school for the Easter holiday. There is no trace of George's extensive library with the zigzag pattern curtains. There is no evidence for the porch where Clare 'belayed' Beridge up on a skipping rope. Looking over a fence, I see what must have been the Herschel House garden. Ruth hurt her back 'the fifth lumbar' digging the heavy clay soil in that garden. But although Herschel House is gone, less than half a mile away is the fullest documentation of Ruth's life in the Everest years. Amongst the boxes and boxes of Ruth's letters housed at Magdalene College Archives, Cambridge University, there is 800 words of pure 'Ruth'. It is the only one of Ruth's letters to George from this time that survives. (I have included the unedited letter in the Appendices.)

The undated letter starts on Tuesday, 3 March 1924 and finishes, probably, on Thursday, 5 March 1924. It is written between four and six days after she waived George off from Liverpool docks on the *California* when her head and heart are still full. There is no ghost of premonition stalking her careful script. Ruth starts with a lingering guilt for having left before the ship was out of the harbour.

The letter is soothing. It meanders into the Cambridge theatre to watch the Greek play. (Ruth could not read or speak Greek.) It continues through domestic detail, the servants, Clare's temper tantrum, Ruth getting her period (as usual she is extraordinarily frank about her body), but there are two points that give an insight into her state of mind.

In the letter, Ruth tells George that she fell off a ladder while trying to store their climbing things in the attic. 'Luckily I didn't hurt myself ...' Why were the climbing things still out? Perhaps George had been selecting pieces to take with him up to the minute before departure. Perhaps they had not had time to put them away after returning from a final snatched holiday 'walking' in the Peak District over the New Year.

They'd stayed at Castleton in Derbyshire, where George's family used to holiday when he was a child. George assured his sister Mary on 2 January 1924, that they had visited the 'great things' of their youth and in spite of the 'murky, murky weather' had fitted in 'quite a little climbing'. Perhaps they had ventured to the gritstone edges and limestone crags of the White Peak. (The most famous of the gritstone edges is Stanage which now has over 400 routes of all grades and is thronged with climbers of all abilities most weekends.)

George told his sister that he'd taken Ruth up Mam Tor, a 1,696 foot hill called 'mother hill'. The hill is so called because frequent landslips on its eastern face have resulted in many 'child tors' beneath. On their return to Herschel House for another maelstrom of packing, it seems they'd been so busy George had left the climbing gear for Ruth to put away. Ruth is fit and strong with excellent balance but Herschel House was known for its high ceilings. How high was that attic? How far did she fall?

In addition to her fall from the attic ladder, Ruth is shivering cold. Herschel House is perishing. The only solution is to use a few of the smaller rooms and to build up their fires. But on 14 February 1924 George admitted to Geoffrey that 'we [will] be poor at present after the move'. George suggested various solutions to Ruth. She could take in lodgers, she could sell her painted china but above all she must be frugal with the heating fuel. Returning from seeing George off on the *California*, Ruth entered a house that was colder than a morgue and something snapped: 'I am afraid I am going to do the one thing you told me not to,' she informed George, 'and use a ton of coke straight away.' Now, warmed by the fire of disobedience, Ruth reaches the end of her first letter to George since their parting. The vague, soft focus Ruth of Adrian Harding's picture, resolves into a clear portrait of a woman of business like precision:

I have heard from Mr Raxworthy. My bank balance is overdrawn £823 and yours £112 that is £935 in all. He suggests we sell of our £5000 Vickers 4% which would bring in £400 and £400 National War Bond for £420. If we get £2500 for The Holt we need only sell the Vicars [*sic*]. I think so I will tell him only to do that for the present.

Ruth's final paragraph changes character from the clinical, disinterested business woman. These are words loaded with heart felt regret:

Dearest one I do hope ... you are happy and having a good voyage. I am keeping quite cheerful & happy but I do miss you a lot. I think I want your companionship even more than I used to. I know I have rather often been cross and not nice & I am very sorry but the bottom reason has nearly always been because I was unhappy at getting so little of you. I know its [*sic*] pretty stupid to spoil the times I do have you for those when I don't.
    Very very much love to you my dear one,
    Your loving
    Ruth

The extent of their debt outlined in Ruth's penultimate paragraph is, in Thackeray Turner's opinion, an actual moral sin. None of Thomas Powell's descendants knew debt before Mr Mallory came along. The Holt was a generous wedding present. Thackeray Turner does not help Ruth out of debt even though he realises that selling The Holt, will be a wrench for both her head and heart. Ruth's husband must learn to accept his family responsibilities.

Ruth is realistic enough to understand that she has no option and lists the drastic cuts and sales they are going to have to make to become solvent. She does so without blame or emotion. She is going to have to sell off her assets – her insurance against George's non-return. Although the letter may seem innocuous, trivial at times, it is deceptive. It is a form of 'jumping' before she is pushed. More than that, this time Ruth is jumping without a safety rope.

Back on 13 February 1924, George signed a contract with the Mount Everest Committee, which is an important document in Ruth's biography. The most important clause as far as she is concerned, is this one:

I agree that I shall join the Expedition at my own risk as to the consequences and the Committee shall not be responsible for any damage, personal or otherwise, which I, or any dependents, may suffer during the continuance of the Expedition or on my journey to, or back from Darjeeling.

George is a risk taker where his own life is concerned. But it is not just his own life. There is no escaping the implications of George's decision to sign that contract, to sign away any responsibility for 'risk as to the consequences'.

# Chapter Twenty-Four

# '… you poor left behind one'

George Mallory to Ruth Mallory.
Magdelene College Archives,
Cambridge University, Cambridge

George Mallory to Marjorie Holmes,
Bonhams auction, London, 2015

### Cambridge – late March 1924

At Herschel House a parcel is delivered. It is addressed to: 'Miss Clare Mallory, Miss Beridge Mallory and Master John Mallory'. The postmark and the stamps on the parcel are from Port Said, an exotic whisper of Egypt – inside is a box of coloured jellies, Turkish delight. It is the most lovely Turkish delight with nuts slightly flavouring it.

George has also enclosed some Port Said stamps for Ruth to send on to King's Langley Priory, a Rudolf Steiner school in Hertfordshire 50 miles away, where Franz is boarding. When the school term finishes, Ruth will take all of them, her three biological children and Franz, to stay with her younger sister Mildred and her two children in Taunton, Somerset.

\* \* \*

'How are you feeling you poor left-behind one …' George asks in his first letter. In some respects, George is the 'left-behind one' this time, since she'd left the Liverpool dock before he did. Ruth still has an image of the last time she saw him standing on the deck. He'd changed out of his white tropical suit into clothes more appropriate to the season. He had just purchased a new book, André Maurois's *Ariel: The Life of Shelley*.

> I have finished reading Maurois' [*sic*] *Ariel* … an interesting story because, in so far as Shelley's relations with [his wife] Mary were impaired, it was simply by the friction of everyday life.

George informs her that 'He [Shelley] was the most unselfish of men but the glamour of Mary wore off a bit when he saw her as a housewife'. Was it that Shelley loved his mistress more than his wife, or just the fact that he did not associate his mistress with 'everyday life'? It was difficult to say. When Ruth reads this, does she see it as an oblique explanation for George's distance from her in those final weeks?

> [Shelley's wife] certainly had little enough of his society when he was making poems, but I'm inclined to think that she had Shelley all the time …

Despite his mistress, George seems to be telling Ruth, that Shelley's wife 'had' her husband all the time. He is distinguishing between having in the physical sense and having the sense of having inside one's head. If Shelley's wife had her husband all the time, Ruth could have George 'all the time' too, even when he was away 'making poems'. But why is George comparing the wife and the mistress and the parts of Shelley that each 'had'. Why is he telling Ruth about women whose relationship has never been tested by the 'friction of everyday life?' How much does Ruth know?

Ruth may have known that George asked some women correspondents to write 'Personal' on the envelope of their letters to him, to distinguish them from the normal mail. One of them, Miss Marjorie Holmes, a passionate fan of George's had forgotten. We only know that she forgot to write 'Personal' on her letter to George because in his reply (which will only be found years hence in Marjorie's effects) George chides her, telling her that she is 'naughty' for forgetting. She must remember to write 'Personal'. It is important. Why? Who had seen the letter? Was it Ruth?

The ten letters that George wrote to Marjorie Holmes were sold as Lot 114 by the Holmes family through Bonhams auctioneer in London on 11 November 2015. Marjorie, a teacher at Bentham Primary School in the Yorkshire Dales, first wrote to George after seeing him lecture, presumably somewhere local to her on his post-1922 Everest expedition lecture tour. At the time, she was in her late teens. On 4 October 1923, at the beginning of their correspondence, George asked her: 'Why should a letter from you have a strange effect on me? – Strange effect? Well, only this, that after reading it I wanted to kiss you …'

Although Ruth does not know it, Marjorie's latest letter from George is on an Anchor Line paper with the red embossed anchor upside down on a flag in the top left corner. It is from the *California*. Is Marjorie in his mind when George writes to Ruth of Shelley's mistress? Is she just one of many?

'Can you love a shadow', George asks Marjorie whom he has never actually met.

a mere hand that spins lame halting words and belongs in some way to a mere name in the newspapers? But words are thoughts, and thoughts are men and women. Can thoughts love each other? Clearly they must.

In one of the letters found amongst the ten, he is in a pub in Cambridge imagining her in the opposite chair:

> Guess what might happen if another spark glowed there in the chair opposite. Would two sparks make a fire? Suppose the other spark were you Marjorie? What is it all about this fire always wanting to blaze up? Shall we see it blaze or shall we hold the snuffer on it?

Now in March 1924, George signs off his latest letter to Marjorie telling her that he is going to go ashore at Port Said and will buy a box of Turkish delight to send home – 'the most lovely T.D. with nuts slightly flavouring it.'

> Now farewell dear Marjorie
> And believe me always
> Your affectionate
> George Mallory

Although those are the very Turkish delights that Ruth later received, we can know for certain that Ruth does not read this letter because George's letters to Marjorie were found by her relatives in a box after her death. Marjorie probably never forgot to put 'Personal' on her letters again. But if Ruth was the person who opened the one she forgot to mark, one was probably enough.

This is a different species of falling. How 'Bloomsbury' is Ruth, how invested is she in monogamy? From her letters, I would suggest that she has a traditional Church of England view of marriage vows, her children certainly thought so. If Ruth opened the letter which Marjorie forgot to mark 'Personal', she would be pushed to the edge. What could arrest her fall? In a few weeks' time, George will select a cotton rope with a red tracer thread to take to the highest slopes of Everest. The tracer thread has a lower stretch capacity than the rope itself. If the tracer at the centre of the rope is broken, the rope has been over stretched and lacks integrity.

This is the first time that George does not refer to Ruth's jealousy, in his initial letter after sailing away. Why? When George flirted with Jelly at the Charterhouse concert in 1915, Ruth dismissed it. She trusted him. Can she trust him still? After a decade of marriage, is there an unrecorded discussion between them on the propriety of George's writing to other women flirtatiously? Does

Ruth ever ask him not to? Perhaps. Ruth knows that George always uses the time on board to catch up on correspondence with their friends and family. So why on 7 April 1924, does George tell Ruth: 'I've written to no one but you this time ...'

*　*　*

As George marches north towards Everest, he has been waiting for Ruth's letters to catch up with him. The first one finally arrives. It is headed paper, with 'Herschel House' in royal blue copper plate at the top of a page that Ruth has folded in quarters. Opening it, George scans the text. He cannot bear that Ruth should feel she has to apologise for being 'cross and not nice': 'Dearest one,' he replies,

> you needn't worry that you haven't been an angel every day of your life. We went through a difficult time together ... but, though we were both conscious that we saw too little of one another last term, it seemed to me we were very happy and I often thought how cheerful and pleasant you were when life was not being very agreeable.

Even before he receives Ruth's delayed first letter, the distance, and reading Maurois's *Ariel: The Life of Shelley* 'has made me think about you very particularly.' The mistress versus wife debate has given him some perspective and with it, remorse. On 8 March 1924, George writes:

> I fear I don't make you very happy. Life has too often been a burden to you lately and it is horrid when we don't get more time and talk together ... Somehow or another we must contrive to manage differently; to have some first charge upon available time for our life together.
>
> What with a car & a stove and our new house altogether we seem to have got terribly stuck with material considerations & how often we talk of nothing but what has to be done to keep the ball rolling as though it [marriage] were so much business to be transacted ...

As he is writing, it seems George realises that someone must transact the business and that someone is Ruth. He assures her that he admires her housewifely skills. Whilst Mary Ann's servants are always handing in their notice, Vi, their nanny, is loyal and loves Ruth. Since George is never there, without Vi, where would they be? He regrets his criticism of Ruth's housekeeping. On 2 April 1924

George writes, 'I will try not to be concerned so much simply with efficiency, which is useful but not a god.'

From her letter, Ruth is obviously determined not to be despondent. George tries to make up for his distance over the last weeks in England by recovering some of the romance of their past relationship. He confides that he

> could almost whisper in your ears; and even now dear I do feel near you, though my state is loggish [*sic*], & I come very near to kissing you.

Why is he putting them both through this again? 'Dear Girl,' he tells Ruth and in telling her, tells himself, 'we give up & miss a terrible lot trying to do what is right; but we must see we don't miss too much.'

When Ruth receives his letter, she must realise that he can see through her bravery. She is trying to settle down in Cambridge but it is difficult to integrate into the exclusive and excluding clique of academic hierarchy. During the war on 4 July 1916, Ruth noted that:

> I think a good many of your friends ... label one ... rather. I mean they think you are funny or uneducated or clever or something and always answer or laugh at the same things ...

Clare remembered her mother returning from a dinner party in Cambridge shortly after her father had left for Everest, very cross and upset. Ruth told Clare that the hostess had deliberately changed the conversation about the Renaissance when Ruth tried to engage. Ruth may not have had a classical education but, before marriage, she had visited many of the most significant Renaissance churches in Italy with her uncle Hawes, keeper of The National Gallery, as her guide.

Even before Ruth's Cambridge humiliation, she told George that she wanted their 'daughters to be educated as well as their sons'. Sometime after the dinner party in spring 1924, Arthur Benson, George's waspish old Cambridge tutor pronounces that George's wife may be beautiful but she is 'a thin and truculent performer'. He concludes 'I really rather hate Mrs Mallory'.

# Chapter Twenty-Five

# The Last Post and Everest

Letters from George Mallory
to Ruth Mallory and David Pye,
May 1924,
Magdelene College Archives
Cambridge University, Cambridge

A photograph of the service of dedication
for the First World War memorial
on top of Great Gable,
8 June 1924

A walk, in Ruth's footsteps,
to a Remembrance Day Service
on Great Gable,
November 2022

George writes a note to Ruth from Everest. They will begin the first phase of the climb on 3 May 1924. He plans to get to the summit of Everest on 17 May. That, he reports to Ruth, is his goal, but by 11 May, they are forced to retire to Base Camp.

The second phase of the campaign opens on 17 May 1924. This time, George advises Ruth that they will summit on Ascension Day, 29 May. He has mixed feelings about Irvine. On 24 April 1924, George notes that he is

wonderfully hard working and skilful about the oxygen [apparatus]… but his lack of mountaineering experience will be a handicap. I hope the ground will be sufficiently easy.

George is not practical but Irvine is. He is also a gifted engineer. As a school boy he solved the problem of firing bullets through the propeller of an aircraft. On Everest, the oxygen cylinders are heavy but Irvine has reduced the weight of the back frame and made several improvements. Anyone who wants to try to make the summit using supplementary oxygen would do well to take Irvine along. But the second phase of the expedition is soon over. Although they reach the North Col cutting steps, George admits they had 'a very bad business on the descent'. His judgement is deteriorating – he'd walked into 'an obvious crevasse'.

They decide on a third attempt, a seven-day dash. Instead of writing to Ruth, on 26 May 1924 George writes part of the official expedition despatch: 'The issue will shortly be decided. The third time we walk up East Rongbuk Glacier will be the last, for better or worse.'

Next he writes not to Ruth but to David Pye. 'We are on the point of moving up again, and the adventure appears more desperate than ever ... All sound plans are now abandoned ...' The dangerous monsoon weather is almost upon them, 'it will almost certainly catch us on one of the three days from [Camp IV].'

Sound plans abandoned. A monsoon that will almost certainly catch them. These are 'bad risks'. George knows that the situation has become more dangerous but this is his third year on the mountain, his third expedition, his third attempt.

On 27 May 1924, George is at Camp I when he finally takes out his pencil to write to Ruth.

The physique of the whole party has gone down sadly. The only chance now is to get fit and go for a simpler, quicker plan. Norton [the climbing expedition leader Colonel 'Teddy' Norton] has made me responsible for choosing the parties of attack, himself first choosing me into the first party if I like. But I'm quite doubtful if I shall be fit enough ... The candle is burning out, and I must stop.

Darling, I wish you the best I can – that your anxiety will be at an end before you get this, with the best news ...

\* \* \*

## Great Gable and Everest

It is 8 June 1924, Ruth is scrambling up from Seatoller Farmhouse to the summit of Great Gable in the British Lake District. She is aiming for the summit, for the dedication ceremony of war memorial plaque that has been placed there. She is placing each foot with care. It is good to feel rock beneath her fingertips. She is finding her rhythm and breathing hard. On her right, there is the sound of crashing water. On the left, Herdwick sheep balance on the close cropped slope. When the path veers right, the air is rushing cool above the falls. Where it zags left, there is the warm dense smell of sheep droppings and new bracken. The scrambling is good. The automatic upward movement releases the mind. She is not thinking about her husband George on 'that mountain'. She is thinking about the next foot placement, the next hold, the path ahead, the top.

It is 8 June 1924, George and Irvine are on Everest. They are the only people in the highest camp in the world. They are thirsty. There is no moisture in the freezing high altitude air. Just as they are about to melt snow, George knocks the Una cooker and it skitters down over the scree. They will have to manage somehow because he cannot, he will not descend. Holding a stub of pencil between frosted fingers (one is definitely 'gone') George forms clumsy letters on a piece of crumpled paper – 'the game', he has said, 'is worth a finger'. But is it? What will today bring? He finishes with a determined flourish: 'Perfect weather for the job'.

In the Lake District, Ruth is still walking towards the summit of Great Gable. She reaches the ridge at Windy Gap. At the top of the mountain there is a copper plaque screwed into a vertical face in the summit outcrop has a list of the names of climbers who died in the war. Ruth is lucky. Her husband, George is not on that list.

On Everest, George and Irvine shoulder their rucksack frames each with two heavy oxygen cylinders. George breathes deeply through his mask and concentrates on putting one leather boot in front of the other. The nails in the sole bite. Another breath. Another step and on.

On Great Gable Ruth might imagine that if George was here he might have brought a rope to the dedication ceremony and insisted on going down via some challenging rock route. Ruth leans her legs forwards against the flat rock that rises like a solid table from the summit. From here she can see a crowd of people and still more emerging from the cloud.

Another step. Another breath. Plant the ice axe. Step. Breath. Axe.

Ruth can hear the odd cough, the crunch of stone under foot as someone shifts position. Arthur Wakefield is making a speech. He was on Everest with George in 1922. Wakefield is vehemently anti-German. Ruth knows that such resentment threatens the peace process. George is on Everest to get a 'label' for that peace. In the drizzly cloud on the summit of Great Gable in 1924, the bugler plays The Last Post.

As the last note of The Last Post is whipped away by the wind for the Remembrance Service in 2022, my husband and I stand on the summit of Great Gable. We are just two in a large crowd of 300 climbers who come here every year for this service. We face the copper war memorial plaque dedicated on 8 June 1924 and wait for two minutes of wind-buffeted silence.

## London and Cambridge 18–19 June 1924

Eleven days after the service on Great Gable, Ruth has just celebrated her thirty-third birthday and she is back at Herschel House. It is raining. The newspapers are full of the unseasonable weather and speculation about the washout Paris Olympics. The two most prominent athletes are runners Eric Liddell and Harold Abrahams who are to compete in the 100 metres.

In London, Arthur Hinks is at his office on Kensington Gore just south of Hyde Park when he receives a coded message: 'Mallory Irvine Nove Remainder Alcedo.' Hinks knows the code. 'Nove' means dead. 'Alcedo' means not dead. He takes out his pencil and under the message writes 'Killed in last engagement'. He composes a telegram to be sent to Cambridge the following day to honour *The Times* twenty-four hour MEC contracted news exclusive.

It is just after 8.00 pm in the evening of 19 June and still light. Ruth has just put the children to bed upstairs in Herschel House when there is a knock at the door. Ruth opens it to find a telegram boy. Almost immediately, a stringer for *The Times* arrives at the garden gate. Ruth knows that *The Times* has an exclusive news deal with the Everest expedition. There is obviously news. Is it good news? Ruth opens the envelope. Inside is a rectangular strip of paper with capital letters centred in the middle of the page:

Received here 7.30 pm
A 442 7.5 Kensington 0 40
MRS MALLORY HERSHEL HOUSE CAMBRIDGE

COMMITTEE DEEPLY REGRET RECEIVE BAD NEWS EVEREST EXPEDITION TODAY NORTON CABLES YOUR HUSBAND AND IRVINE KILLED LAST CLIMB REMAINDER RETURNED SAFE PRESIDENT AND COMMITTEE OFFER YOU AND FAMILY HEARTFELT SYMPATHY HAVE TELEGRAPHED GEORGES FATHER HINKS

# Chapter Twenty-Six

# 'If my soul could hold the hand of your soul'

'Climb if you will,' wrote Edward Whymper, 'but remember that courage and strength are nought without prudence, and that a momentary negligence may destroy the happiness of a lifetime. Do nothing in haste; look well to each step, and from the beginning think what may be the end.'

Edward Whymper,
*Scrambles Amongst the Alps*,
John Murray, UK, 1871

Friends arrive at Hershel House. Amongst them is David Pye. Ruth leaves the house. She walks. She just walks. The next morning she wakes the children and takes them into bed with her. She explains to them that their father is 'lost on Everest'. As Clare later recalled, they 'all cried together.'

David arrives again. Ruth wants to walk. Perhaps if she walks far enough she can walk away from herself. They walk all the afternoon along the Roman Road over the Gog Magog Hills. And the next. And the next. 'Thank heaven,' David told Geoffrey, 'the weather was perfect all the time; each day nature dressed herself more exquisitely than the last ... that somehow was a help.'

Ruth has already thought carefully about death: 'If we have a future life where there is no death it will be very nice', she told George on 20 July 1916.

I don't think I mind dying but I mind parting dreadfully, most especially from you. If my soul could hold the hand of your soul, and go together to the great new adventure of death, then I do not think I would fear it at all. But even if we died at the same moment, I expect we should each have to go alone. I could bear to leave [the children] I think, because [their life] is not my life, but my darling yours is.

George has been away for half their married life. Half of their relationship has been conducted through letters. Will the letters stop now? Where is the body? Where is the proof? Ruth tries to remain stoical as well-meaning friends drop in, but late at night in her room she unburdens herself to Geoffrey:

A lot of the time I feel numbed and quite unable to realise [it], there is only just a pain. But it is no use talking of it. It has only just happened and one has to go through with it.

Clare wakes up crying and is inconsolable. She has dreamt that her daddy is alive. Perhaps 'lost on Everest' is just that. Perhaps he will be found. Perhaps he just went down a different way and has found a tribe of interesting people, one day he will walk back in. Ruth picks up her copy of an anthology of poetry by Robert Bridges, *The Spirit of Man*. George took his copy to Everest. The title of the poem Ruth shares with Clare is *I Arise from Dreams of Thee*. It is by Percy Shelley. Ruth tells her daughter, that her father admired Shelley and that this poem was one of his favourites.

Ruth asks Mary Ann and David to spend three days helping her pack up Herschel House. She is leaving with the children for Westbrook until she can work out what she is going to do. Mary Ann is trying to come to terms with her own raw grief when she tells Geoffrey, on 30 June 1924, 'it is terrible to be with [Ruth] to see her beauty & her courage & her misery.'

* * *

## Pillar, Wasdale, Lake District – 2 June 2022

It is time to find those handholds – to hook my fingers into the clefts in the rock that Ruth used, to push the toes of my climbing boots into the footholds. The date is 2 June 2022. I am climbing with Mandy Glanville of the Pinnacle Club.

Immediately after George died, Ruth was so devastated that she had to fight a powerful sense that there was nothing left to live for. It was not something she shared widely. She quickly realised that she had no choice but to live for her children. In the first few hours and days, she made herself look up the rock to try to find a route up, to 'go through with it', to go through and out and into a future.

Mandy used to climb with Alison Hargreaves who she confirmed was an exceptional climber. Mandy is still a member of the Pinnacle Club. Mandy has suggested that of all the climbs on Ruth's Pinnacle Club application form, the best to start with is the New West climbing route on Pillar, which is a Lake District fell, and at 2,927 feet is the eighth-highest mountain in the Lake District. The fell takes its name from Pillar Rock, a prominent feature on the Ennerdale side, regarded as the birthplace of rock climbing in the Lake District. The rock overhangs Ennerdale Valley with a drop of 1,142 feet. Mandy confirms that we should approach the climb, as they would have, from the head of Wasdale where the river Mosedale falls towards Wasdale Head.

When we set out from Wasdale and take the climbers' path traverse to the start point of the climb, the early summer sun is shining. As I place my hands on the rock at the start of the New West route, hailstones bounce like glass grasshoppers off the grey granite surface. Mandy suggests that we reduce the risk and take an easier route. My stalwart co-conspirator Vanessa, our third, agrees. Both Vanessa and I have three nearly grown-up children. Wet rock is slimy and in June, hail melts. We climb Low Man, then High Man, the 'summit' of Pillar Rock, then we abseil down into Jordan's Gap. I think that we are done for the day, but the girls do not. We are going to climb Old West, the route Ruth climbed down.

I want the following to be completely plain so I offer the brief notes I took immediately after the climb:

Mandy set off up over a bit of rock so that quickly Vanessa and I couldn't see her. When she called 'Safe' as usual, we both looked at each other and giggled. Nervous laughter? Pillar is a very big rock hanging over a 1,000 foot drop. It's a kind of 'bank holiday corpses'-type rock.

Off I went for what I realised later was a Slab and Groove climb. I had to put the toes of my climbing shoes into holes and scramble crab-like over a smoothish piece of rock angled at about 30 degrees off the horizontal. When I had done that, I stood up and looked to see Mandy the other side of a large rock which protruded in an overhang. Without thinking first I said, 'How on earth did you get up there' – the bumper-sticker, cat-poster phrase of all imposter-climbing time.

Mandy patiently said that I needed to traverse around the corner and come up that way. Vanessa said later that she heard me and wondered what the hell was waiting for her if I really couldn't imagine how Mandy had got up something.

The second pitch meant putting one foot backwards onto a rock and pushing up in an upside down 'V'. I found myself waiting on a ledge. It was very quiet except for the sound of Mandy's metal climbing gear clanking. Some birds. No aircrafts, no cars, nothing. Incredibly still. There were midges. Hail and now midges. Really?

And then I sensed Ruth. Ruth had been here. It almost felt as if she *was* here. Since Pillar over hangs a sheer drop to the Ennerdale Valley, I knew academically that there was nothing else here but me and yet …

For the next 20 feet of the climb, I felt as if I was walking on the flat. I was on a familiar path that I knew so intimately I didn't even have to look where to put my hands or my feet. I just went up.

# Part IV

# After Everest

In the Pen-y-Pass scrapbook, which is held at the Alpine Club Archives, there is a picture of Ruth back outside the Pen-y-Pass Hotel in 1925. She is standing roughly where she stood back in 1919 at the survivors meet after the war when she was pushing George and his Studebaker down the hill. But instead of the Studebaker, there is Mary Ann. For me this is a picture of hope. It proves that whatever depths of sadness Ruth fell to after George's death, a year later, she was climbing again. Is it Ruth who has persuaded Mary Ann's husband Owen to lift his ban?

The picture is stuck onto the left hand side of a landscape page of Geoffrey's photograph album. On the opposite side of the page is a picture of some ladies with their backs to the photographer. It is as if Mary Ann and Ruth have wandered across the page, turned away from the photographer, clambered into the photograph and over the back wall of Welsh stone. The caption reads: 'the Pinnacle Club start out …' What did they start out for? In the middle of the page there is another photograph captioned: 'Tryfan. Summit'.

## Llanberis, Snowdonia – September 2022

At 10.00 am on 17 April 2022 my husband and I start out for 'Tryfan. Summit'. The sun is shining sharp shadows onto the mountain's sensational splintered profile. Tryfan has the back of a stegosaurus. I must look down if I don't want to trip, though I would rather look up at that back. As I am walking, it occurs to me that to a Lilliputian, the rocks on the path could be giant boulders. Height is relative not just to the next mountain but to each living thing. Perhaps this is how Ruth succeeded in viewing 'ordinary life' as the 'biggest experience'. She had a choice. We all have a choice over how we measure scale and perspective.

For the Pen-y-Pass climbers, the summit of Tryfan was a place to celebrate birthdays, feast days and a place to mourn lost friends – people with whom they had shared that summit in the past. It was and, perhaps is, a place of pilgrimage. In the background of the photograph of the summit in the Pen-y-Pass album, there are two large vertical flat-topped pillars known as Adam and Eve. The guidebook states that no one knows, or more importantly cares, which is which.

At the top of the page of thirteen photographs in the Pen-y-Pass album page titled 1925, there are two pictures of fathers and sons captioned: 'Maxwell & Son' and 'Popham & Son.' Is this how Geoffrey captioned them later, or was the phrase '… & Son' bandied around as a joke? There will never be a photograph of George and his son here.

As we are nearing the top of Tryfan in 2022, the cloud base becomes lower and mist begins pouring in over the pass. Pat Kelly died falling from a grassy gully on this very mountain a century ago. Despite all the tragedy, these hills are so beautiful and exhilarating. As I am enjoying the best scrambling I have ever done, part of me thinks: if experienced climbers can die in familiar mountains ten minutes from a busy main road, why not climb Everest?

Just as my husband and I are nearing the top of Tryfan, the mist thickens. We hear voices and stand aside to allow a group of three male climbers in their fifties pass on their way down. One with a long face observes jokingly to no one in particular, 'Who thought this would be a good idea?'

When he saw me climbing up after my husband he said: 'If you had any sense you'd sit down here and wait for him to come back!' And I think – if you only knew.

# Chapter Twenty-Seven

# 'What if'

Letters from Ruth Mallory,
Royal Geographical Society Archives, London

Mary Ann O'Malley's letters to Geoffrey Winthrop Young,
Royal Geographical Society Archives, London

Will Arnold-Forster and Ka Cox's letters to Ruth Mallory,
Magdelene College Archives,
Cambridge University, Cambridge

When Ruth is alone at night, she imagines George's last moment. She cannot help herself going back over the situation, replaying it and rewinding it to a point where George makes different choices, where she does too; the point at which his employer in Cambridge, Reverend Cranage decides not to release him from his new job at the Board of Extra-Mural Studies. Reversing the situation is natural. It is what George tried to do after the Sherpas died in the avalanche 'it seems almost impossible to believe,' George said back then in August 1922, 'that it has happened for ever [*sic*] and that I can do nothing to make good …'

Back then, Geoffrey warned George that 'to debate the "might-have-beens" is the road to madness …'

Ruth feels instinctively that whatever happened to George, whatever killed him, 'so easily might not' have happened at all. Noel Odell was the last person to see George. On 8 June 1924, Odell looked up from a ridge opposite and saw two dots at approximately 28,230 feet on the North Ridge. He checked his watch – 12.50 pm. The first dot ascended a rock obstacle, perhaps one of the three 'Steps' on the North Ridge, then after a while, the second dot joined it. From what he could see they were behind schedule but ascending – 'going strong for the top'. After a brief moment, the cloud blew in and obscured his view. The dots, he believed until the day he died, were George Mallory and Sandy Irvine.

What happened thereafter to the two tiny shapes ascending the North Ridge after the cloud hid them from sight? Did they continue on up scaling the heights? Or was the reality a small but fatal mistake, just a trip shortly after Odell last saw them? Ruth knows intellectually that whether the end was grand or prosaic, it has happened forever, 'and there is nothing I can do to make good'. But her brain has biological momentum. George is dead but away and there is no change to her immediate surroundings. Nothing has changed and yet everything has changed.

Ruth tries to adjust the circuits in her mind to a higher plane: a more spiritual and artistic level of imagining. She can visualise George ascending, but not him falling. If she focuses on the ascension, she can let herself believe that his crossing from this life into the next was metaphorically 'very beautiful'. But was it really beautiful? If her mind glances back to that moment in Snowdonia, she can remember the sensation of falling off a ledge – of snow, ice and a hurricane gale screaming over the ridge. That flash of adrenaline, the slowing up of time into increments, the sense of watching someone else falling – an almost out of body experience. Ruth writes to Geoffrey:

> Whether he got to the ~~lot~~ [crossed out and written 'top' in pencil] or did not, whether he lived or died makes no difference to my admiration for him, I think I have got the pain separate. There is so much of it and it will go on so long that I must do that.

In these letters, Ruth's voice is both faltering (writing 'lot' instead of 'top') and determined ('whether he lived or died makes no difference'). On 30 June 1924, Geoffrey explains to Ruth that he is consumed by 'a long numbness of pain, yet but a shadow of yours for indeed one cannot think of you separately … and the loss unutterable …' In her second, again undated, letter to Geoffrey after George's death, she corrects him:

> Of course you share George with me, the pain & the joy. I never owned him. I never even wanted to. We all had our own part of him. My part was tenderer and nearer than anyone else's but it was only my part. Geoffrey shall I keep my love fresh & pure & strong as it is now till I die?

But Ruth is starting to need reassurance not only about the fact that it might not have happened, but that George didn't mean it to happen.

> My dear Geoffrey,
>   I am very grateful to you for your long and thoughtful letter. I think I do understand it. You are quite right I know George did not mean to be killed, he meant not to be so hard that I did not a bit think he would be …

Why does Ruth feel that there was a question over whether he 'meant to be killed'? Although Geoffrey seems to have suggested that he does not think George meant to die, he will soon contradict this. Geoffrey will describe George's death as a kind of suicide, but not yet.

'I don't think I do feel that his death makes me the least more proud of him,' Ruth says carefully to Geoffrey in response to his implied question about whether it does. Kathleen, Geoffrey's sister-in-law, claims that her own husband's death was the best outcome in the circumstances. She is proud of him but proudest perhaps of the stoical self-sacrificing manner in which he died. Ruth is not Kathleen. Speaking to Geoffrey, Ruth clarifies:

> It is his life that I loved and love. I know so absolutely that he could not have failed in courage or self-sacrifice ... I am sending you the last letter I have had from George. You will find it very interesting. There will I think certainly be one more after this. I may get it tomorrow. You shall have the climbing part of it in due course.
>
> Oh Geoffrey. If only it hadn't happened. It so easily might not have,
> Yours
> Ruth Mallory

The letter that she is expecting is the letter she has been dreading ever since George signed up in the war. The letter from a dead man. Where is she when it arrives? David Pye tells Geoffrey that she is, temporarily he hopes, back at Westbrook. Is that where the RGS redirect her mail? Is she back on the bench in the yew alcove where she used to write to George during the war? Is she sitting there with her legs tucked up out of the rain when she opens that last envelope? Inside is a letter written in a tent at Camp I on 27 May 1924 before the final push. George needs Ruth to know that whatever happens, he has done himself proud. That the risks he took were not wrong ones, that the outcome is not the result of 'bad heroics'. It is like the light from a dead star:

> Darling, I wish you the best I can ... It is 50 to 1 against us, but we'll have a whack yet and do ourselves proud. Great love to you.

The telegram, the quickest way of transmitting news sent from Everest, had been a message not of light but of death. The posthumous notes that follow it are ones of hope. The irony is hard to bear.

Although Ruth does not know it, while she is trying to master this tragic end to her protracted months and years of waiting, Geoffrey and Mary Ann are forming the conclusion that George could not, or would not have turned back. There is a fine line between this and meaning to be killed. Mary Ann declares to Geoffrey:

> Of course you are right – it was George all over to have that one last try. I remember how he used to tighten himself up at a difficulty, & shove the thing through. It used to frighten me in Wales … It was so comic to hear George talk sagely of prudence & do you remember [she asks Geoffrey] his funny face of protest, [*sic*] if one told him so? But it is most bitter to think that as you say, there was no one to curb that lovely fearlessness, that eager courage & say: 'Not here – not now.'

Mary Ann and Geoffrey may be telling Ruth not to dwell on the 'might have beens', out of her hearing they are dwelling on the 'if onlys'. If only there had been someone to stop him and check his relentless 'frightening' urge to 'shove the thing through'.

Ruth realises that if George is to be the hero he had always wished to be, 'Galahad of Everest', she must be stoical and worthy of being the hero's wife. There is no suggestion of a posthumous 'Order of the Bath', as there had been for Captain Scott. Ruth will not become Lady Mallory. Amongst the pile of condolence letters Ruth received, there are two now in the Magdalene College Archives in Cambridge, that will be significant in her future.

One is from Will Arnold-Forster. Will tells Ruth that he agrees with Geoffrey, it is impossible to think of her and George separately, they were 'such a good unit – the Mallorys'. His wife, Ka Cox, writes on 11 July 1924:

> You are so gallant – always – so much the wife of George – But don't push your courage too far – come down to us [at Eagles' Nest, Cornwall] & rest.

The Arnold-Forsters know Ruth well enough to understand that she can force herself to appear to be gallant on the surface. But Ruth is still trying to piece together what happened as if since 'it so easily might not have', she can reverse it. The nearest Ruth can get is a letter that arrives from Odell:

> Dear Mrs Mallory, I was the last to see them on the mountain, & they seemed to be going so well that success seemed assured. Whether they actually reached the top must ever be a mystery, but I really think the odds are in favour of their having done so … From a mountaineering point of view they died a really glorious death, however it came about … We have

packed up what remains of your husband's kit, which you will eventually receive. All letters are also being returned to you ... Noel E. Odell.

A 'really glorious death ... however it came about ...' How did it come about?

\* \* \*

On 8 June 1924, just after midday, George and Sandy Irvine are ascending Everest by the North Ridge. They come to a rock pinnacle, possibly the First Step. One of them climbs it. The other joins them at the top. Shortly afterwards the clouds close in, the wind rises. It continues to rise.

The evidence for this is a typed sheet with eleven horizontal columns of figures and '-2- [II] Base Camp (Cont'd)' across the top. It records the barometric pressure on Everest on 8 June 1924 with a dramatic drop in pressure signalling a storm high up on the mountain.

The most experienced climbers who have climbed Everest by Mallory's route believe that it is unlikely that George would have attempted the Second Step with no belay and an inexperienced second man. As the weather worsened, he may have carried on ascending via the yellow rock band below the ridge route. This is where a hand-knitted mitten from the 1920s was found by Jake Norton in 2002.

## Chapter Twenty-Eight

# 'To turn back a third time, or to die?'

Dr Claude Wilson to Mary Ann O'Malley,
The University of Texas at Austin, USA

St Paul's Memorial Service, 17 October 1924,
pp.273–7, *Alpine Journal*: Volume 36, 1924

Condolence letters sent to Ruth Mallory,
Magdelene College Archives,
Cambridge University, Cambridge

It is a cold wet day on the 17 October 1924. Mourners make their way across London to arrive at St Paul's Cathedral just before noon. General Bruce and expedition and climbing leader Colonel 'Teddy' Norton are photographed at the foot of the cathedral steps with their top hats, black bow ties and umbrellas. Teddy is a distant relative of Ruth's through his grandfather the Alpinist Alfred Wills. On 4 June, four days before Mallory and Irvine disappeared, Teddy Norton and his partner Howard Somervell traversed below the ridge. Teddy achieving the new height record of 28,165 feet before turning back. 'Of all the truly miserable days I have spent at [Camp] III ,' he wrote in his diary on 8 June 1924,

> this is by far the worst. By now it appears almost inevitable that disaster has overtaken poor gallant Mallory & Irvine – 10 to 1 they have 'fallen off' high up.

For Teddy, George's fate is in the past, he 'fell off'. For Ruth he is caught in the unknowable present, still falling. A decade before Ruth's first thought on reading *Scrambles Amongst the Alps,* was for 'those left behind'. Now she is one of them but so are the expedition's survivors. On 2 July 1924, Ruth told Teddy that

> I have been and am so dreadfully sorry for you … I am glad you let no one try to go higher searching. It would have done no good & might so easily have ended in ~~pure~~ [crossed out] more disaster.

For as much as others attempt to ennoble it, it is a disaster in Ruth's eyes. '[Pure] disaster'.

St Paul's is full, with over 3,500 people in the congregation. The men from all three Everest expeditions have a block of seats near the front but Ruth and her family are all ushered to the choir stalls. Annie Leigh-Mallory, George's mother, takes her seat. To her, Ruth looks 'like a lily with its head hanging down'. Annie comments that the Irvines, sitting in the choir stalls across the aisle, are still in shock. They had no idea how dangerous it would be. Sandy Irvine was only 22 when he died. His mother lights a lantern and leaves it in the porch all night in case there should be some mistake, and her son is coming home.

The service begins with a hymn and Ruth stands. From her position in the front row of the choir, she can see King George V, the Prince of Wales, the Duke of York, the Duke of Connaught and Strathearn, and Prince Arthur of Connaught. Behind them are the members of the Alpine Club, the RGS and the MEC including Francis Younghusband, Arthur Hinks and Lord Curzon. Arthur Benson and George's non-climber university friends feel the service is pompous and nationalistic – the antithesis of George. But the world has inverted.

Standing in the choir, Ruth is at the foot of a chiselled limestone rock face. She is on the edge of a precipice looking 350 feet up at the vast stone dome of the cathedral. George has not left any financial provision for his family. Ruth will have to move back in with her father, not just temporarily while she finds her feet, but permanently. She does not have a choice. Nor does her father.

Thackeray Turner, standing in the choir stalls beside his daughter, has just been informed of the 'risk to the consequences' clause that George signed in the Mount Everest Committee contract. Mary Ann, almost family, received a condolence from Dr Claude Wilson on 20 July 1924 comparing Ruth's widowing with that of the wives of Antarctic explorers:

It's dreadful & recalls to me my cousin's [Dr Edward Wilson] fate, with Captain Scott in the Antarctic – His wife 'Oriana' ... is very proud of her lost 'Ted' ... & Ruth's George has gained immortal fame, & I almost envy him for his magnificent achievement ...

Back then, a decade ago, before the war, an equivalent memorial service was held for the five dead explorers of the Antarctic. Back then there was an outpouring of public cash to support the *Terra Nova* expedition's dependents, the widows and children. But now in 1924 the reaction is different. Apart from the mass widowing of the war, George had not left a final message like the plea found on Captain Scott's frozen corpse: 'For God's sake look after our people.'

As the service begins, Thackeray Turner rises to his feet for the first hymn. He has tried to protect himself against George's debt for a decade. The MEC contract effectively means that George assumed his father-in-law would not only pay off that debt, but provide for his family until the children became financially independent themselves. As the man of the house, Ruth's father has been approached by a publisher about his son-in-law's biography. To him, George's attitude to his family responsibilities might seem morally suspect but to the public, Mallory is a hero.

Marby, Ruth's older sister, is sitting near Ruth in the choir stall. She has made it clear that since their mother's death in 1907, she has been running Westbrook and she is not about to relinquish control. She has allocated Ruth rooms on the first floor, the 'Mallory Rooms'. It includes their old schoolroom, but Ruth's father will not allow her to continue her Montessori classes there. The first floor rooms mean that Ruth and her three young children can be out of the way. The hymn ends. The congregation sit with a sound like rumbling snow.

The Bishop of Chester begins his sermon: '*Ascensions in corde suo disposuit*: He has set ascents in his heart; or, as we should phrase it,' the bishop tells the congregation, 'He has set his heart on ascents.' Then he asks: 'Was it only the love of the high mountains that was set in hearts like these?'

From where she is standing in the choir stalls, Ruth can see 'that grim apostle' Francis Younghusband with his wife and daughter. 'Of the two alternatives', Francis Younghusband claimed:

> to turn back a third time, or to die, the latter was for Mallory probably the easier. The agony of the first would be more than he as a man, as a mountaineer, and as an artist, could endure.

What were those two alternatives, exactly? One, the 'love of the high mountains' and the other the love of family? Younghusband, a father himself, did not elaborate. To his mind, in the context of the British Empire, it was only the love of ascents that mattered.

The Mount Everest Committee concludes, on 27 June 1924 that George demonstrated supreme selfless: 'above all a subordination of his own private interests for the achievement of the common end.' Those disinterested 'private interests' were not shares, hobbies or leisure pursuits but his own flesh and blood. That the subordination involved signing away the Mount Everest Committee's financial responsibility for those 'private interests' – as George had done in his contract with them – was not, in the MEC's opinion, in conflict. It was in line with the general subordination to the all-powerful and all too dangerously ambiguous 'common end'.

From her exposed position on the ridge at the edge of the choir stalls with the stone chasm above her head, Ruth is being scrutinised by the entire congregation. Will she submit herself and her children to that 'common end' or will she lose her head? Like the strange desire to throw yourself off a precipice, will Ruth remain stoical and gallant or will she suddenly cry out and become hysterical? George Trevelyan writes on 6 July 1924, that 'it is terrible to think of what you have had to bear but we know your temper and quality and do not fear that you will fail.' Standing for the second hymn, Ruth sees George's former pupil Robert Graves who told Ruth on 22 June 1924

that you are a climber and can understand what he was after; and that anyhow you'll not have lost your head. So like George to choose the highest and most dangerous mountain in the world!

George's death is being framed as a kind of deliberate choice. There is a fine line between that and suicide, albeit of a self-sacrificial kind. For Ruth to question this interpretation, would be 'fail[ure]', it would be 'los[ing] her head'. After implying that George had not meant to be killed, even Geoffrey now claims in public that:

Difficult as it would have been for any mountaineer to turn back with the only difficulty past, to Mallory it would have been an impossibility ...

But a new and more terrible idea is taking hold. Montague Rendall, headmaster of Winchester College, told Ruth, on 25 June 1924, that 'I never forget how noble it was of you to let him go; his sacrifice is largely your sacrifice.' But is it hers or is it their children's sacrifice – Clare, Beridge and John's? It was George's choice but it was also Ruth's choice. The decision was made by Ruth when she said that she 'was willing' for him to return to Everest a third time. It was not the children's willingness, but hers. The children were not capable of choosing and yet they will have to live with the consequences. Does Ruth's mind glance to the child shot dead in Dublin? Does she sense an equivalence: the collateral damage of war, the collateral damage of Everest? She will not only have to live with the 'what ifs' and the 'if onlys', but as they grow older, she will have to answer the 'whys'. And yet is so easily might not have happened. She feels so sure of that fact. Was it a bad foot placement? A loose stone? A small slip?

*   *   *

On 8 June 1924, George and Irvine reach the slippery slabs on Everest sometime after midday. The slabs are covered in a thin layer of fresh snow. It would be easy to slip. It would be easy for the slip to become a fall. Irvine puts his ice axe down. Perhaps he does so in order to hold the rope between him and George with both hands. Because George is falling. Something hits his right elbow. The rope tightens suddenly with a jerk twisting painfully around his waist as he comes to a halt.

In 1933, Percy Wyn-Harris will find Irvine's ice axe with three nicks in the handle just before the First Step at 27,723 feet. It does not look as if it has been dropped, it looks more deliberate than that. It looks as if it has been placed.

# Chapter Twenty-Nine

# 'The Zennor Affair'

Mary Ann O'Malley's notes,
November 1925,
The University of Texas at Austin, USA

On page 5 of Mary Ann's notes, titled 'November 1925', she writes: 'He [David] began at once to talk about Ruth & the Zennor affair which worried him.' Just before this comment, Mary Ann writes that Ruth said that Mary Ann had 'made a dead set at David'. Mary Ann concludes that since Ruth 'is reliable', she must be right, she must have flirted with David. Unhappily married, she confesses that she sought affection as a starving man seeks bread. But the 'Zennor affair' does not refer to an extra marital affair, it does not refer to a love affair of any kind. The 'Zennor affair' is more dangerous. In the mass bereavement after the First World War, séance is such a common way of seeking closure that it has morphed into a high-risk form of entertainment.

Mary Ann is a keen 'tumbler pusher' herself. Unlike David, she is not worried about the 'Zennor affair'. Both of them have learned of it through Will Arnold-Forster's letter to Ruth. In the letter Will told Ruth that he chanced upon friends conducting a séance in Zennor, and though he declined to participate, he'd agreed to act as scribe. At the séance, Will wrote down a message from 'George'. The message was for 'Ruth'.

Evidence for the 'Zennor affair' no longer exists. I know that David Robertson, Ruth's son-in-law, burned the notes that Will Arnold-Forster took at the séances before submitting the Mallory papers to the Magdelene College Archives in Cambridge. But the impact it had on at least one life, is in my opinion, justification for looking into it now. To do this, I have visited Zennor and read reports in the local newspapers at the time, requoted on 4 May 1976 in *The St. Ives Times & Echo*. I have also drawn on conversations with Marianne Nevel, Val Arnold-Forster and Audrey Salkeld. The 'Zennor affair' required open mindedness from Ruth but it also required courage. It is perhaps, one of the most literally extraordinary episodes in Ruth's life.

\* \* \*

Ruth knows what George thinks of séance. At least she knew what he thought when he was alive back in 1917. They'd discussed séance in letters during the First World War. Ruth read *Raymond, or Life and Death: With Examples of the Evidence for Survival of Memory and Affection after Death* by Sir Oliver Lodge, published by Doran in 1916. Lodge, a respected physicist and member of the Royal Society, allegedly communicated with his dead son, Raymond, through a medium. Ruth sent the book to George and asked him for his opinion. George was sceptical: 'I expect you are quite right to doubt so much and that I am over credulous', Ruth told him on 7 August 1917.

> That's partly why I wanted you to read [*Raymond*] so much. I do not know anything at all about psychical research … Of course if the mediums are simply trying to do their sitters and don't really go into a trance it makes it different …

But after George's death, the 'Zennor affair' in Cornwall puts George's scepticism and Ruth's 'credulousness' to the test. She is in a precarious position again. She has a difficult decision to make. Will has invited her to Zennor to attend a séance, to dive into the hereafter. But he is not pushing her to do so. Ruth trusts him and his wife Ka. They are extremely sensible people. But she is frightened. Cornwall is the only place where Ruth ever confesses to being 'really frightened' in writing. Frightened for her own safety rather than George's.

## Cornwall – 2022

There is a sea cliff in Cornwall called 'Hell's Mouth' which, in the spirit of climbing Ruth's climbs, I would like to attempt. 'I would be happy to arrange some sea cliff climbing for you,' the Cornish climbing guide Matt George replies to my enquiry,

> but there's no climbing that any instructor will guide you on the area around Hell's Mouth. There are only a handful of recorded routes here, that possibly have never been repeated. The climbing here is extremely serious with absolutely dreadful rock quality. It really is climbing for only the most adventurous climbers with a great deal of experience in climbing loose rock.

A few weeks later, I am in Cornwall. I am standing at the top of the cliff that seems to overbite Hell's Mouth. Far beneath me the sea foam sucks around fang like rocks. There are Samaritan notices pinned to short wooden posts along the edge, yet there is so much beauty – the coconut scent of gorse, the cry of wheeling gulls and the wide blue Atlantic Ocean.

When Ruth stood at the bottom of this cliff looking up, she was 'really frightened'. Since this is not in her Pinnacle Club application form, I do not know whether she climbed it or not. She mentioned it in a letter to George remembering the time they came to climb 'Hell's Mouth' and the fact that she had been 'really frightened'. Generally Ruth regarded her fear as lack of courage. 'I hate having to question my courage,' Ruth told George, on 15 January 1917, during the war, 'I have been doing it more or less all my life and I have always had the fear that I was a bit of a coward.'

Looking at the routes up Hell's Mouth on the climbing guide map – routes now called 'Psychosis' and 'Paranoia' – I emphatically do not think Ruth was a coward. I leave them to 'the most adventurous climbers with a great deal of experience ...' and instead join Matt at Rinsey Head for a memorable day's top-roped climbing with my children in the sun-soaked Cornish riviera. My notes from the day say: 'K climbed Sancho VD; C climbed The Grove D "but much harder"; J climbed Williams Chimney HVS 70 feet.' Afterwards we finish with a Mallory-esque bathe in the sea. Whether or not Ruth followed George into Hell's Mouth, at least she could have bathed in the sea.

\* \* \*

In Godalming Station, Ruth steps up into the train carriage. She has a ticket for St Ives. Does her mind glance to the fear she felt once just north of her destination station on the sea cliffs at Hell's Mouth? She knows that no one is going to ask her literally or academically to go into 'Hell's Mouth'. The prospect of attending an occult meeting is a little 'frightening' but she has decided to take the risk – it may give her some answers.

On the long train journey west, Ruth can examine her own position on life after death. Ruth only learned that George was agnostic after his vicar father had conducted the church ceremony that married them. He always felt that heaven was not a good reason to behave well on earth. After her initial shock, Ruth came to regard George's reason for self-justifying good behaviour on earth as 'sublime'.

Although Ruth is a conventional Christian, her religion is slightly mystical. 'I am glad I never think of people as dead,' she told George on 21 October 1918, 'but always of them as more living than ever ...' For Ruth the dead lived and not just in a metaphorical sense.

Straight after Audrey Salkeld told me matter-of-factly and in passing that she, had seen Sandy Irvine's ghost in Zennor, she related a story about Ruth. One morning after staying with John Noel and his wife in London after George's death, Ruth told Noel that she had 'spent the night with George'. He said to her, 'You know that George is dead don't you?' But Ruth insisted that 'he came to me'. Although Ruth never describes George as a seeable 'ghost', in some sense, George is 'more living than ever' as far as she is concerned.

Séance is one thing, but in the mid-1920s, something more sinister is infiltrating St Ives. There is a new splinter group of occultists who style themselves as satanists. Ka, who was at Cambridge University a decade after 'The Beast', Crowley, thinks it is nonsense. The word 'paganism' was bandied about amongst Ka's fellow students including George Mallory – Virginia Woolf even nicknamed them the Neo Pagans. But Will, who recognises 'Neo Pagan' as his friend's 'Woolfish' witticism, is less amused, less able to dismiss Crowley's satanic cult.

Will now works with Gilbert Murray, the man to whom George had applied to for a job before his first expedition to Everest. Like Oliver Lodge, Murray is a respected public intellectual. Four years earlier in 1920, Murray published *Satanism and the World Order* with George Allen & Unwin. The threat, Murray insists, is insidious, toxic and very real. Will just wants Crowley's satanists out of his beloved county. When Ruth emerges from the train in St Ives station, wholesome Ka is waiting for her.

Will advises Ruth that when the Ouija board spelled 'George', who had a message for 'Ruth', he asked 'it': 'Did you reach the top?' The spirit answered that they had died of 'organic exhaustion'. The reason that he and Ka have asked Ruth down to Eagles' Nest is that 'George' finished: 'Tell Ruth to look after Frank. He is having a hard time.'

Ka and Will are both there with Ruth when a spirit is called up. The following notes are paraphrased: Ruth asks if 'George' can see them. 'He' says he can. 'Are you happy and busy?' asks Ruth. The spirit of 'George' assures her that he is. Ruth asks whether he reached the top and receives the same answer that Will noted in the previous séance. There is some further exchange and then the name 'Frank' appears. This is the same name that appeared in the previous séance that Will scribed for. The spirit of 'George' again 'dictates' that 'Frank' is in difficulty.

Ruth is so determined to be open about attending a séance that she writes to her mother-in law, Annie Leigh-Mallory the vicar's wife. In a letter that Audrey Salkeld has seen, Ruth relates the séance conversation with characteristic 'terrible honesty', as near verbatim as possible. She tells Annie that she can 'take it or leave it'. She asks if Annie knows of a friend or relative of George's called Frank because Ruth cannot think of one, especially not one who may need her help.

Ka is a magistrate specialising in child offenders. During the course of Ruth's visit, she asks Ruth what became of the Czech orphan boy she fostered,

Franz Knefel. Ruth informs Ka that, just after George left for Everest, Franz's biological father was widowed and married his housekeeper, Franz's biological mother. The moment Franz became retrospectively legitimised, he was invited to return to Vienna to be part of his biological family. Since he now had two parents living, the Kinderheim insisted. Franz helped George to pack his boxes for Everest in January 1924, as he had done in 1922 before Ruth said goodbye and put him on the boat train 'home'. He arrived safely in Vienna, that is all she knows. Ruth hopes he is happy.

Weeks after the 'Zennor affair', Ruth and her sister Marby, take the train to Vienna. Ruth and Marby have a complicated relationship. Ruth is acutely aware that with her children, three extra mouths to feed, the Mallory family require a disproportionate amount of the Westbrook resources. Perhaps Ruth has enlisted her childless spinster sister Marby with a view to balancing this out? As Marianne Nevel, Franz's widow related the story to me, Ruth arrives in Vienna and knocks on Mrs Knefel's front door. When she sees Franz, Ruth has her Montessori training to back up her intuition.

As Franz later recalled, Ruth invites Franz to accompany her home for a holiday. During the course of discussions, Ruth tells Franz's parents that a Powell relative of hers is opening a new school, Rendcomb College near Cirencester in Gloucestershire. Franz has impressed Ruth's father with his enthusiasm for woodwork. The new school has employed a craftsman from the Arts and Crafts to run the woodwork department. Ruth is sure that Franz's parents must realise what a chance this would be for their son. Marby tells Franz's parents that if they are amenable, she would like to pay for Franz to go to that school.

Later, when the train has left Vienna, Franz opens his suitcase. The letter he hands to Ruth is his most precious possession.

Anchor Line, T.S.S. *California*, 8 March 1924

My dear Franz,

    I never wrote to thank you for a very nice letter you wrote me in the Xmas holidays. I was so busy for a long time that I really didn't write any friendly letters till I came on board ship; but I hadn't forgotten you.

The letter is long and entertaining. 'Mr Mallory' tells Franz that there is 'plenty of dancing, the deck made gay with coloured lights and flags …'

Ruth hears George's voice, not in séance, but in reality as the train takes them north towards what Franz regards as his *'real'* home'. In the letter, George goes on to describe the journey to Everest across the plains of India to Darjeeling.

Up near Darjeeling we shall find pink & white magnolias in flower & also on many of the houses a lovely creeper Solanum jasminoides, which grows at Westbrook outside the drawing-room window – but at Darjeeling it grows bigger and flowers more abundantly ...

He talks of his fellow team members:

three of my companions for Mt Everest [are on board] [Sandy] Irvine, [Bentley] Beetham and [John de Vars] Hazard ... I particularly like Irvine who is splendidly built and rowed two years in the Oxford boat [Cambridge won 1922 and Oxford won 1923] ...

Franz never forgot the reception at Godalming Station. When Marianne told me this story on 18 January 2007, it was with a full heart. Franz remembered that Clare, Beridge and John were there on the platform. All of them had grown in the time he had been away but only Franz's clothes were obviously too small. The three children gave him

a very warm and affectionate welcome and on the way home [to Westbrook] took him straight to the tailor to have him measured for a new suit.

Franz was, as Clare remembered him, 'endlessly kind'. It is a two word biography, an epitaph, that Marianne, whom he later married, fully endorsed.

Perhaps Ruth is right. George is 'more living than ever'. It seems that he still has agency. Unless the situation is a complicated coincidence, the spirit of 'George' has affected significant change. It was after living at The Holt with Ruth and George that Franz and Mabel Barker's brother Patrick hoisted the flag of 'combined British and Austrian colours'. To all the adults who celebrate Franz's return to England, the combined nations flag is the simplest and most powerful image of an ideal, *the* ideal.

Franz is relieved to be back with Ruth. He spends the holidays at Westbrook and school terms at Rendcomb College where he trains with a Gimson and Barnsley-craftsman who recognises Franz's gifts. In 1934, Franz will become a British citizen and set up a furniture business 'Betula Co.', in London. But that is in the future. The 'Zennor affair' is significant. Marianne carefully stated that 'the Mallorys changed the course of [Franz's] life'.

But 'Frank' having a hard time, is not the only thing Ruth learned at the séance in Zennor. She also learned, from the spirit of 'George' that he had died of 'organic exhaustion'. How long did that take? What happened after Odell lost sight of the two dots behind the cloud that day on 8 June 1924.

*   *   *

It is some time after midday on 8 June 1924 on Everest and the wind is strengthening. George is trying to recover after his fall, a fall of no more than 10 or 20 feet. The rope around his waist is tight and painful. He cannot release it. Are his hands too frozen, his fingers too numb? Does he take his mask off? Does he jettison his oxygen cylinders? Every breath must be deep to suck the maximum oxygen out of the thin air, but his ribs are agony. Has he broken some?

He can gather in the rope. The end is frayed end. He felt it go slack. Is Sandy Irvine still alive on the other end, or was he dragged off the ridge by the weight of George's body. George is responsible for Irvine. Is he still up there or has he disappeared? Has he slid over the edge? If he has then he will certainly have fallen to his death on the glacier below. If he is still on the ridge, holding the other part of the 9-millimetre rope in his gloved hands, will he now start trying to climb down to George? Should he?

George's right sleeve is torn, his elbow is bleeding. He dabs the blood with his opposite sleeve. Can George hear Irvine's voice over the roar of the rising gale? Can George get enough breath to shout his name? Having established whether Irvine is alive or dead, George must make a decision. The choice is basic. He can either try to find a foothold to his right and move in the direction of the summit or he can feel for some purchase to his left and begin to try to make it back to their last camp, Camp VI. Which should he do? Which does he do?

Number 9 oxygen cylinder will be found by Eric R. Simonson in 1991 approximately 600 feet before the First Step at around 27,800 feet. It is one of the cylinders that George noted on the back of an envelope containing a letter from Stella Cobden-Sanderson.

# Chapter Thirty

# 'All Letters'

Noel Odell's letter to Ruth Mallory,
22 June 1924,
Magdelene College Archives,
Cambridge University, Cambridge

When I arrive at Westbrook in 2022, I am welcomed in by Justine. This house makes an impact on all who cross the threshold. Everyone I have interviewed about Ruth talks about Westbrook as the landscape in which they think of her still. The images come crowding in on me like anecdotal characters jostling for position.

I take one step in through the front door. I already know my way around this house. On the left of the vestibule is a lavatory. Apparently, this was the men's. When Thackeray Turner designed the house he positioned the ladies' lavatory on the servants' side of the house through the green baize door. Another few steps in and I enter a wide hall, with an elegant wooden staircase leading up to the left. The space is light and airy with plain light oak panelling on the walls. There is a fireplace at one end and an alcove at the other where I know there used to be an anthracite stove with shelves above it to display the family's hand-painted china vases.

To anyone else this might be just a hall. I imagine the family dancing. David Pye wrote that he taught the Mallory children Roger de Coverley right here in this hall in the Christmas holidays before George left for Everest in 1924. Clare, Beridge and even 3-year-old John danced with their parents, their grandfather and the Westbrook staff.

The high-ceilinged billiard room opens from the hall to the right of the front door. Beyond it there is a brick loggia out into the garden. It is similar to the one at The Holt but more than twice the size. In the early days of their acquaintance, George played billiards with old Thackeray Turner discussing politics as they smoked their pipes and chalked their cues.

I walk straight across the hall through a wide oak door into the drawing room on the right. Though they are not here now, I can imagine fifty 'educated ladies' seated for a League of Nations lecture. Afterwards they will have tea and cake. Ruth has just told the vicar's wife that, of course, they can host ten more; they will do so 'with joy'. Now she will have to communicate the joyful news to Prody and Rose in the kitchen as they try desperately to make war rations stretch for the legendary Westbrook tea.

The morning room leads off the hall to the left of the dining room. This is where Ruth used to sew with her mother, May. It is filled with light. There is a plaster work rose worked in tulips on the ceiling. That must have been made by her uncle Laurence. Looking out of the rectangular lead light windows, I can see a wide stone terrace. On the far side there is a low brick wall topped with flat Bargate stone slabs, quarried locally, and a large perfectly mown lawn stretching into the distance beyond. This is the wall along which Clare, in a white confection of a dress, walked as a 2-year-old child, her father offering her a gracious finger to ensure her safety as she balanced along the top.

Upstairs there are nine spacious bedrooms on two floors. Most were wallpapered with Morris & Co. paper. John's, in the attic, was papered in willow pattern. There was no plumbed 'newfangled' bathroom here when Thackeray Turner was alive, except on the servants' side. Only the large master bedroom has space for a hip bath that had to be filled by servants carrying hot water up the back stairs from the kitchen. To an extent, the house is an insight into the personality of an 'eccentric man', as Clare described her grandfather. All of the people who remembered him rolled their eyes at the thought of his multiple grandfather clocks and his interminable flute performances that they had to sit through 'without fidgeting'. This is the man who replaced George as the male presence in the Mallory lives. But the Mallory children were not perfect and long-suffering cut both ways.

Jocelin Winthrop Young, son of Geoffrey and Len, remembered visiting Westbrook when both Clare and John had temper tantrums. The placid Beridge appeared on this landing in the midst of slamming doors saying: 'This must be very difficult for you Joss'. Everyone loved Beridge. As young children, Paul Morgan, Ruth's nephew, and John dragged sheets across this wide landing ready to parachute out of the window. Ruth, discovering their intention, suggested starting instead from the low garden wall.

My priority is the rooms Marby allocated Ruth, the 'Mallory Rooms', the largest room on the first floor. I walk into a room that is square with a strip of windows overlooking the lawn. This is Ruth's old school room. Hilda Haig-Brown said everyone at Charterhouse hoped Ruth would restart her popular Montessori classes once she moved back to Westbrook in 1924. She did not. She stopped teaching altogether. Back on 31 August 1918, Ruth told George:

I get sick of Father's certainty on all subjects. It's so dull. I don't mind people laying down the law in words so long as they don't in their own minds too much.

But after George's death she no longer had The Holt to escape to and she was no longer financially independent enough to take a stand.

\* \* \*

On 6 November 1924, Ruth receives a delivery from Carter Paterson at Westbrook. Five suitcases and a brown paper parcel are unloaded from the back of a van. The last of George's effects, they are, presumably, taken up to Ruth's private rooms. The first thing that Ruth finds, as Carter Paterson's men set the boxes down, is an enormous pair of crepe rubber soled boots, unworn, in the parcel. She takes a sheet of writing paper and sits down, possibly at George's old desk, the Lupton designed oak desk that he had at The Holt. She writes a letter to the Mount Everest Committee telling them that since the boots are of no use to her, she will return them.

The suitcases are all locked. 'There were no keys with them,' the secretary at the MEC informs her, 'and it is thought that Mr Mallory had the keys with him when he was lost.'

… we presume that there will be among the papers the return half of his ticket to England. Perhaps if you find this you would kindly let the [Mount Everest] Committee have it.

(This from the MEC who has accepted no responsibility for his 'dependents'.) Ruth writes back directly to Hinks, an undated letter, stamped '29th November 1924' which reads:

Dear Mr Hinks,
I think this is the ticket you want. It is all I can find.
Yours sincerely,
Ruth Mallory

George is 'lost' the keys are 'lost', Ruth will have to wrench the locks open with a spanner. First she asks the MEC if she can keep the camera that George took to Everest. It was loaned by the MEC for expedition purposes but she would like it for John. All these MEC letters exist in 'carbon' copies at the RGS, but the document that interests me was archived on Everest.

This is a sensitive part of Ruth's biography, but it is important because of two things that happen next. The first became a cause of lasting regret and sadness for Ruth's children; the second caused Hinks consternation. In the suitcases are 'All [George's] letters', as Noel Odell wrote to her on 22 June that year.

On Sunday, 15 June, Norton had ordered all surplus supplies and equipment to be burned. Most biographers have assumed that George's letters were burned too. If Odell says 'All letters', Audrey Salkeld assured me, knowing Odell as she did, 'then that will mean "All letters".' Odell would not have edited 'All letters', in Audrey's opinion 'He was hopeless like that'. The implication of this dawns on us slowly.

In his careful 22 June letter to Ruth, Odell's handwriting is even, tight, small and regular. There are no crossings out, only a couple of unavoidable blotches because he was writing on a camp table in the Rongbuk Valley. Odell's script is that of a scientist, a man who valued accuracy over white lies or exaggeration. Did Ruth have a sense of danger? Did she suspect that she might come across something George would rather she did not know? I am in her safe space, the schoolroom and yet again there is that edge, the rope, the trust.

In the suitcases, Ruth finds many of her own letters to George. She wrote to George almost as much when he was away on Everest as she had during the First World War. Only one of Ruth's Everest-years letters will make it into the Mallory archive. It is the one she sent apologising to George for being 'cross and not nice' in what they did not realise would be their final days together back in 1924. Without her 'cross and not nice' letter to him written between 3–5 March, George's friends and future biographers might wonder at his reply when he told her that she should not worry about 'being an angel every day of your life'. If Ruth kept that letter, it would avoid misunderstanding.

What should she do with her other letters to him? During the First World War, on 7 January 1918, Ruth told George that 'I think nearly all [my letters to you] should be destroyed but I think a lot of yours should be kept as they will be interesting in after years.'

George protested. Ruth's letters to him were difficult to keep out of the mud of the trenches, but with or without her appalling spelling, they were 'like shafts of sunlight pouring in'. She promised that if he returned them to her in England, she would keep them. Now despite their intensely personal nature, their references to sex, to her periods, her body, her insecurities and to her heart – Ruth decides to honour her promise to George. She will not destroy her wartime letters to George. She never made the same commitment to him over her letters during the Everest years.

If Odell really returned 'All [George's] letters', did the suitcases contain correspondence from Stella Cobden-Sanderson and from fans like Marjorie

Holmes? These are letters to George, not to her. They are private as well as personal but if Ruth reads them, she will see a different side to the husband she thought she knew.

When very big things happen, I need to be outside. Inside will just not contain it. I wonder whether Ruth felt the same. I walk down the stairs and out of the front door with the garden map in my hand. I walk left over gravel and through a gate in a garden wall. I walk past the loggia, right under a pergola and arrive at the circular heart of the garden. In the middle is a large hexagonal pond, framed by curved flower beds. This is an exquisite garden, the soothing scent of lavender borders and roses everywhere.

I walk south up a pressed sand path. I am trying to find the place in the yew hedge where Ruth wrote to George. Gradually, I wind my way through curved grass paths, under pleached limes until I can smell the resin scent of yew. In Franz's photograph album, there is a photograph of a lady sitting on a circular table, perhaps a millstone, in a yew 'room' of clipped arches. She has her back to the camera. She is kneeling off to the right side looking down, perhaps reading.

*   *   *

In the letter from Stella to George found, perfectly preserved, in the pocket of his tweed jacket on Everest, Stella does not mention Ruth. Although Ruth never saw this letter, now in the Magdalene College Archives, she may have seen others. In that letter, the letter that Ruth never saw, Stella writes to George: in her looping hand she tells him: 'I think of you so often and try to imagine what you are doing. What is the weather doing, is it terribly hot?'

Stella remembers the year before when they first met in United States and the last days of George's lecture tour in New York. It was cold then as it is cold in London in the early spring 1924, now with the added chill of post-war recession preceding the Great Depression. But Stella must have seen the picture of George in his tropical suit in the Everest team photograph taken in Liverpool on the *California* which was published in the newspaper. Stella tries to imagine him in the heat now in early 1924 as he nears India. What is the weather doing out there in the Indian Ocean?

She talks politics like her famous suffragette mother Annie Cobden-Sanderson: 'London with strikes has been very exhausting and terrible for the wretched daily workers.' The London Underground workers have been on strike, resulting in congested roads and making walking (as she has just been doing through Hyde Park) the only real option. But despite the inconvenience, most people she's met seem to be in good spirits. 'It's amazing how good natured is an English crowd.'

Stella is full of entertaining gossip, of George Bernard Shaw theatre plays and politics and the Oxford and Cambridge boat race on the River Thames. She will not be going to Hammersmith to watch that race despite an invitation to join a party there. Nor will her mother. Hammersmith Bridge is the bridge over which her father threw the Doves Press metal type into the Thames. Too many awkward memories. But Stella is not given to despondency. She thinks she will catch the end of the season in the south of France to get out of the dark British winter.

Stella does not urge George to take care. She does not mention George's family, Ruth and the children, although of course, she knows exactly who Ruth is. She is the middle daughter of the Arts and Crafts' Turners of Godalming. Their parents were once very close. They still have many friends in common including the fine arts embroiderers the Craies. Stella is writing on note paper from the Forum Club at 6 Grosvenor Place because she has just spent an entire teatime shouting down old Mrs Craies's ear trumpet, with Mrs Craies shouting back. (Violet Meakin will go to work for the Craies when John Mallory starts boarding at Winchester College.)

Stella signs off:

I am longing to hear from you since your arrival
My love to you dear
Your affectionate
Stella.

Like Marjorie Holmes, Stella knows that she must mark all her letters: 'Personal'. He has told her that, after he leaves England she should address her letters to him to the 'Everest Expedition c/o British Trade agent, Jatung, Tibet.'

If Ruth finds other letters from Stella in those boxes, they would be in a similar vein – a similar sign off and no mention of Ruth or the children. Ruth might realise that in some ways, Stella has nothing to lose. In others, she must have realised that if George died, Stella Cobden-Sanderson would have to keep her grief entirely private.

George told Ruth that when the mail bag arrived at Base Camp on Everest, 'love flies in and settles in every tent'. But whose love? Ruth has lost agency, she is dependent upon her father's say so, but she has not completely lost control over her husband's life story. She has the bin, she has the bonfire. Something changes.

To the point that Ruth received the five suitcases, she had been going, as Mary Ann describes it to Geoffrey in letters now at the RGS: 'straight up hill, the only way'. But now she may not be so sure of the ground beneath her feet. What was George's relationship with Stella Cobden-Sanderson? Did Stella have anything to do with that 'difficult time' as George referred to it, following his return from the United States the previous year? Did he see her on his frequent trips to London? And was there just one 'Stella'? As he'd told her in his first letter after leaving earlier that year, Shelley only had one mistress, but what was George's relationship with his female fans? What a Pandora's box has Odell delivered with his promise to send Ruth 'All letters'?

As Ruth goes through the five cases, she must decide what to keep and what to destroy? How would she decide which truths about George to share and which to take to the grave lest the narrative unravel? The condolence letters from other women that survived selection by Ruth in 1924, are from Jelly, Ka and Mary Ann. Ruth keeps letters from people who effectively state that George had a one-way ticket, that he went to Everest 'to do or die', despite promising her to prioritise his return. Those letters are uncomfortable, terrible, yet Ruth makes herself pass these letters on for use in George's biography.

For Ruth to admit to reading letters from Stella and Marjorie, to knowing what others may already know, would destabilise the heroic legend. To do so would be, from her children's point of view, the ultimate selfishness. That is all they have left. Ruth could keep the letters, unburden herself to Mary Ann, David and Geoffrey, or she could destroy them. 'All letters' will never reach George's biographer. As all Everest historians know, all but one of Ruth's letters to George written after the First World War, will never reach an archive. This is what has made Ruth seem, to Robert MacFarlane, 'almost inaudible'. And yet perhaps the yawning archival gap speaks volumes?

In later life, Clare and John remembered that Ruth never spoke of George to them. She never tried to keep his memory alive. Was this her way of not giving into grief, or was it in reaction to what she discovered about George in the boxes she received on 6 November 1924? We will never know. All three children reacted similarly at the rare mention, by other people, of their father's name. Hilda Haig-Brown mentions that Clare talked about a surge of resentment every time his name came up 'that familiar feeling'. She was privately 'very bitter that their father had not made more of an effort to come back to them'. John's unequivocal advice for anyone climbing Everest, or climbing anything, was to leave a proper margin and to prioritise the return over the summit every single time. He and Clare both cited prioritising as the reason for their father's death, but was it? What happened up there on 8 June 1924?

*   *   *

It is late afternoon on 8 June 1924 on Everest. It is sometime since George's fall and he has begun moving towards Camp VI. He is cold, hypothermic. He is in pain. The screaming wind tears at his ripped clothing.

In 2006, Graham Hoyland who replicated the clothes that George was wearing on Everest, concluded that they were adequate if the weather remained good but dangerously inadequate if it did not. The barometric readings from Base Camp reveal that as Chris Bonington later told me: 'it must have been wild up there'.

It is difficult to climb with a rope cutting into the torso. It is difficult to get enough oxygen with no cylinders and broken ribs making the deep breaths required, painful. It is difficult to climb with a wounded right arm. And then … George falls again.

# Chapter Thirty-One

# Film Premiere

A typed copy of the letter that
Arthur Hinks sent John Noel,
the official expedition photographer,
dated 10 December 1924,
and addressed to Captain J.B.L. Noel,
Explorer Films Limited, 175 Piccadilly
Royal Geographical Society Archives, London

It is the evening of the premiere of John Noel's silent film *The Epic of Everest to Lhasa* – the official film of the 1924 expedition. Noel, who has invested a great deal of his own money into the enterprise, has planned a theatrical experience to rival Hollywood. He has brought seven Gyantse Tibetan holy men, 'lamas', back with him to London. Ruth is probably aware of the complaints against the patronising misrepresentation of Nigerian 'natives' at the (British) Empire Exhibition at Wembley earlier in the year. She may well have visited the Indian Pavilion, where a scale model of Everest made from white canvas attracted many visitors.

Ignoring the criticisms of Wembley, Noel has hired a set designer to provide context for the lamas. Before the screening, Ruth, the guest of honour, is given a tour behind the scenes. She walks into a dark Tibetan courtyard with a brightly painted backdrop of Himalayan peaks. She meets the monks with their cymbals, trumpets made from thighbones and drums crafted from human skulls. Those skulls have hit the headlines of the *Daily Sketch*: 'High Dignitaries of Tibetan Church ... to dance on Stage; Music from Skulls.'

Ruth must have been dismayed at the facile reporting of the *Weekly Dispatch*, issue 562, which identified the mountain itself as the 'leading lady' in 'man's passionate struggle to conquer the dreadful virgin of the snows'. As the widow of the conspicuously unknighted, 'Sir Galahad of Everest', Ruth may have consulted another leading lady, more familiar with celebrity.

In April 1924, when George was still alive, Jelly invited Ruth to her recent premiere of *Tzigane*, written for her by French composer Maurice Ravel. Now, she has welcomed Ruth to her home where her sister Adila is a practising psychic.

The Ouija board is often out in the d'Arányi household when they need advice from a deceased composer on how a piece of music should be played. Ruth knows that the d'Arányi sisters would not question Ruth's statement to Odell that she 'spent the night with George'. That they would not have hesitated at the Arnold-Forsters' invitation to Zennor.

Ruth does not want to be a leading lady, she does not seek limelight, but Noel insists that she must be included for the human story. Ruth has film star looks, she and George could sell the film, but Hinks is determined that Noel's moving picture film should be scientific rather than foregrounding particular people. Ruth eventually agrees to give Noel a quote that he can use for the final title. Does Noel realise that Ruth is known for her terrible honesty? Does he know that Ruth has recently read 'All letters' – the five boxes of George's effects sent by Odell from Everest?

The audience begin arriving. They emerge out of the London smog. To Noel's consternation, instead of leaving the smog outside, the smoky fog follows them into the theatre making it increasingly difficult to see the screen. The lights go down, the film begins.

First there are still shots of Everest. The smog hangs in front of the screen with black and white two-dimensional Tibetan clouds swirling behind. The film scrolls back in time to the journey across Tibet starting from the community at Phari Dzong. There are moving images of a woman smearing her child in butter, a wizened old man with a drum, and some Tibetan dancers. There is a man delousing a child and cracking the lice between his teeth.

It is three quarters of an hour before George finally makes an appearance during a gathering of the team in front of the tents at Base Camp. Towards the end of the film there is a sequence shot through a telescope. In the circular frame, three men set grey blankets on the snow in the form of a cross. It is a poignant moment. Everyone in the audience is aware that Ruth is present and that the blanket cross on the North Col was the expedition's pre-agreed sign for 'non-return'.

The final intertitle comes up. It focuses the audience's attention not on the noble enterprise but on the uncomfortable truth. In large white letters on a black screen it reads: Mrs Mallory regrets the whole enterprise.

Shortly afterwards on 10 December 1924, Arthur Hinks is in his office at the RGS dictating a letter to John Noel. He instructs Noel to cut the last title out of the film immediately lest it gives 'great offence to any friends of Mrs Mallory'. She is, Hinks assures Noel,

exceedingly proud of her husband's performance and would not like it suggested that she regrets the enterprise even though it involved his loss.

Noel argues that the title is a quote from Ruth, he does not want to cut it. Hinks insists. But Hinks does not erase Ruth's reaction entirely from the records. Hinks, like Machiavelli, is efficient. His secretary keeps and files a copy of every letter sent out from the RGS for the archive. Hinks has tried to erase Ruth's 'regret', not just for her husband's death but for the enterprise as a whole. Inadvertently, he has achieved the opposite. The archived 'carbon copy' of his 10 December letter means that his is the only record of this extraordinary incident that survives.

Hinks letter attempting to erase Ruth's reaction reveals her true feelings. She trusted John Noel, she trusted Hinks, she trusted George with her life, with her children, with judging whether the enterprise was worth the risk. It is not a rope but a long reel of 35 millimetre film on which there is a picture of George in the middle and a title quote from Ruth at the end. Noel is under contract. He cannot defy Hinks. The scissors come out. Ruth is cut off the end of the 1924 film, she is cut off the end of George's MEC rope. Hinks determines to make sure that Mrs Mallory will not be able to embarrass them again.

* * *

It is 8 June 1924. The wind is at hurricane strength and George is falling, his second fall. His arms are stretched above his head, clawing the rocky slope with his fingers. The scree and snow is still racing upwards past his eyes in a blur. His right boot hits something. There is a flash of pain through his lower leg. Finally he stops. He has hit his head badly. The injury is on his face, somewhere above his right eye. Instinctively, he bends his left leg at the knee and places it over his right where his foot is now at a right angle to the shin. At some point he rests his face against the mountain. Camp VI is only 900 feet away.

* * *

## Tibet – December 1924

Noel's Everest film could not have come at a worse time. The Tibetan government officials that Ruth saw in the auditorium at the premiere in London – the same officials that must have seen her final film title – send their review of *The Epic of Everest* back to their headquarters in Lhasa.

Three things happen in quick succession. The monastic orders in Tibet are appalled at the contemptuous irreverence shown for Tibetan Buddhism with the pre-performance 'carnival'. They declare that the seven Gyantse monks were never given permission to travel to England by their abbot. They are ordered home where they can expect severe punishment.

The Maharaja of Sikkim registers his extreme offence at the patronising and inaccurate portrayal of Tibetans delousing their children and subsequently eating the lice.

Permanent Undersecretary of State for India Sir Arthur Hirtzel wonders how one moving picture film can have brought them to the brink of an international incident. He orders a screening of the film for himself. Emerging from the dark room rubbing his eyes, he concludes that it was 'unspeakably boring' but that it could not cause 'more than that smile of kindly superiority which we generally assume when we see or hear of strange customs.'

Before the incendiary reaction to the film, Ruth had already registered her regret for the expedition in public. Ruth and George dreamt of a world where national borders would be unnecessary. In direct opposition to the Mallorys 'label' for peace, Everest becomes the catalyst for extreme nationalism. The border gates slam shut. The prime minister of Tibet issues a statement: 'For the future, we cannot give permission to go to Tibet'.

# Part V

# Life After George

After the Second World War, the Chinese Maoists were poised to take over Tibet. Tibet was unable to protect itself. The Communist Chinese invasion in 1950 led to years of turmoil that culminated in the complete overthrow of the Tibetan government, the self-imposed exile of the Dalai Lama and 100,000 Tibetans in 1959. Since that time, over 1 million Tibetans have been killed.

But for the purposes of this book, *Behind Everest* focuses on the immediate impact on the lives of individuals connected to climbers. The effect upon those at home starts with the mountain peak pushing up through the floorboards. As Ruth told George jokingly during their engagement when they were musing on how to furnish The Holt, 'chairs could just be boulders which would be cheap'. But the mountain continues to rise, pushing the boulders aside until it takes up most of the room. For some families, like the Mallorys, it will always be there.

## Parson's Nose, Snowdonia – 14 February 2023

We park in a layby on the road that runs through the Llanberis Pass. I follow Mark Reeves, my guide, over a stile to begin the hour and a half walk to the Parson's Nose. This is the climb that Ruth did at the beginning of this book. Back then in the Christmas holidays of 1914, Ruth had no children. She was roped between George and David as they climbed the Nose before heading on up to that ridge with the intention of continuing up to the summit of Snowdon. Mark has promised he is not going to push me off. (We only need to take the climbing research thing so far.)

As we walk up the narrow track, we discuss the psychology of climbing. Mark is an expert. I am drawn to the approach taken by professional mountaineer Ed Viesturs who states that if you enjoy the process of climbing, its less about the goal. Not getting to the summit, is not a failure, it is a 'non-success'. In *The Living Mountain*, published in 1977, mountaineer and poet Nan Shepherd, suggests that we must abandon the summit as the organising principle of mountains.

I have read a letter in which Ruth tells George that people who don't stick at things are 'feeble'. On some level she might have respected George for sticking at Everest. But Viesturs's strategy, the secret of his survival, is being able to turn back even 50 foot from the summit if it doesn't look good. Did Ruth believe that George could have regarded not getting to the summit as a 'non-success' that third time? Could he have turned back if it didn't look good or only if he 'gave out'?

Mark talks about 'the dark stuff' that motivates some climbers. He is not talking about Crowley-esque satanism but personal demons. Many climbers are motivated to push themselves to achieve something beyond the physical summit. Alison Hargreaves was one of these. She intended to be able to achieve financial independence as a mountaineer and mother, by climbing the three highest mountains in the world Mount Everest, K2 and Kangchenjunga, unaided – that is without Sherpa support or bottled oxygen. She was on track to achieve this when she reached the summit of Everest in this manner on 13 May 1995.

Mark and I discuss George and his complex need to be 'more tried' than he had been in the First World War. The most high profile mountaineer today is also an ex-soldier, Nirmal Purja. Purja is the first person to have climbed three 8,000 metre (26,246 feet) peaks – Kanchenjunga, Everest and Lhotse – without supplementary oxygen in less than nine days (5–16 May 2022). The last two were done in twenty-six hours.

Briefly Mark and I wonder what George and Ruth would make of climbers like Alison Hargreaves and Nirmal Purja? When they climbed Everest it was not an 'inaccessible peak'. Psychologically it is accessible because 6,664 people have climbed Everest several many times: the youngest to reach the summit is 13 and the oldest 80 years old. Physically it is accessible because Chinese climbers bolted a ladder to the Second Step in 1975 and each year, Sherpas lay fixed lines leading to the summit. There are also weather forecasts, radios, high-tech equipment etc. The third of Victorian climber Mummery's stages was that an inaccessible peak would become an 'easy day out for a lady': 779 women have climbed Everest to date. The first was Junko Tabei from Japan who summited on 16 May 1975. She preferred to be known as the thirty-sixth person to climb Everest rather than the first woman.

After an hour and half chatting and walking steadily up hill to the start of the Parson's Nose, I am hot. I am wearing a silk shirt and old tweed plus fours (my grandfather's) in an effort to climb as Ruth climbed it. When we start gearing up the foot of the climb, I tie my knot, then untie it. Mark says 'You did it right'. I tie it again. It doesn't look right. I untie it. 'That one was right too'. Suddenly my mind is blank. I can't remember how to belay.

I am thinking of Alison Hargreaves.

Anyone who went off to climb a mountain thinking that they wouldn't come back … its [*sic*] a very unfair thing to do especially with a young family.

I intend to come back. (Doesn't everyone?) At the bottom of the Parson's Nose, it starts to hail. Mark, who has checked the weather reports says 'This wasn't in the brochure'. I wonder if the Parson is trying to sneeze me off this mountain? A fanciful part of me wonders whether 'they', Ruth, George and David are saying: 'So you want to do it like we did it? Right. We'll give you our weather ...' But of course they aren't saying that and the hail stops and I tie my damn knot and put my hands in my pockets so that I can't untie it. ('Don't be so perfectly ridiculous'.)

We climb about four pitches until we get to a cleft (the place that 'the Parson' might have perched his spectacles), which we must climb down then back up the other side. It is the first time I have climbed with a rucksack on. Mark, a professional, has almost nothing in his pack and he has drunk all his water. Still an amateur, I have packed for all eventualities.

I have forgotten about being nervous until we have to ascend an open chimney pushing back onto one side and edging up the other side with our feet. At the top of the 'chimney' is what I think might be called a chock stone. Mark goes first. When he calls 'safe', I start. From somewhere above, he is keeping the rope between us taut in order to 'catch' me if I fall. But the taut rope must go around the chock stone and it wedges between it and the rock face. In order to release it, I must push my whole foot into a vertical crack and hold on with just the fingers of my right hand. With my rucksack on (water bottle sloshing) I must turn almost upside down to hook the rope out with my left hand.

Towards the top, the 'bridge' of the Nose becomes a ridge scramble. We reach the cairn at the top from which a wider ridge leads right around in a horseshoe before joining the flank of Snowdon. There is a dip in that horseshoe at Bwlch Glas. This is where George took his wife by the shoulders and 'forcibly pushed' her off the mountain.

On the day we are there, it is crystal clear. There is a bright blue sky with a stiff breeze blowing from the opposite direction to the howling gale of that winter's day of 1914. Beneath the dark grey ridge there is scree with big patches of snow. The surface of the steep slope becomes light green lower down, even in February. There is now a well-worn narrow path which starts vertically, with stone 'stairs' straight off the ridge nearest the summit of Snowdon. The path shallows out into 45 degrees off the horizontal as it crosses the 'precipice' beneath the scree and then switches back many times as it tracks down to Llyn Llydaw.

\* \* \*

Back at home, I look for published entries of Alison's diary, used as the source for David Rose and Ed Douglas's biography *Regions of the Heart: The Triumph and Tragedy of Alison Hargreaves*, published by Michael Joseph in 1999. There is a single quote that stands out for me: 'It eats away at me – wanting the children and wanting K2', she wrote. 'I feel like I'm pulled in two.'

I search online for Jim Ballard, Alison's husband widowed on 13 August 1995. There is a YouTube clip of him watching Tom, by then a teenager, bouldering in Spean Bridge, Scotland. Tom, a fine climber, like his mother, is all grace and focus, but watching him, Jim observes:

> When [you] transfer 'the game' to bigger peaks ... [it] goes from playing Russian Roulette with no or one bullet to playing Russian Roulette with quite a lot of bullets.

George Mallory also talked about climbing as a form of Russian Roulette in his unpublished essay 'Men and Mountains: The Gambler'. Ruth read all George's writing. She knew how George felt about risk. 'Great climbers have been caught – I admit it,' wrote George. 'But it has always been for one of two reasons: either, as in the early days of the mountains, they were ignorant, or else they were foolish in their gambling...' Unlike them, he believed that he did not take unnecessary risks. 'Condemn [those climbers] if you like,' he continued, 'but not us who don't do these things and don't get killed ...'

Finally I search for Alison's remaining child, Kate. In 1996 when I met Kate and her brother at BBC Books on publication of *One and Two Halves to K2*, she was approximately the age that Beridge Mallory was in 1924. Tom, who I also met back then, was 30 when he died on 24 February 2019 on one of the world's tallest mountains, Nanga Parbat in the west Himalayas. In her late twenties, Kate repeated the journey she had made as a child to K2, but this time to Tom's last mountain.

> I wanted to see what he had seen. To understand what went through his mind. To get a grasp of how he might have felt being here ... It's almost like Mum's cradling him ... & they are together forever now I wish I could be with them but I've still got Dad ... and Dad and I will pull together & hard as it is we know that they did what they wanted to do.
> *The Story of Tom Ballard: The Last Mountain*, BBC, 2021

Did Ruth ever feel like this? Did she want to see what George had seen? Did her children? Her grandchildren? What would she have made of John's son George Mallory II who successfully climbed Everest on 14 May 1995? George met Alison Hargreaves descending as he was ascending, a cross over moment perhaps. Recently, I asked my husband how he would feel if one of our three children climbed Everest. He said: 'I never want to be in that position.' Ruth would never meet her grandchildren but she encouraged them to embrace adventure, but not, it seems, to seek it at high altitudes.

# Chapter Thirty-Two

# A Body and an Ice Axe

Letter from Frank Smythe mentioned in
*Cornish Guardian*, 26 May 1938

Gilbert Murray,
*Satanism and the World Order*,
George Allen & Unwin, London, 1920

In spring 1933, Frank Smythe is sitting on a stool at Everest Base Camp looking through his telescope. He is a member of the fourth British Everest Expedition, the first to have been allowed into Tibet since the Everest film debacle of 1924. Smythe sees something that reflects the light differently. It is white but not snow white. It is lying on the scree at the foot of the North-East Ridge. He adjusts the focus taking care not to touch the metal eye piece with his bare skin. Staring through the lens, he thinks it might be a body. Frank realises that the news would create a sensation in the press if it were written about. Is he right? Is it a body? If it is, is it George Mallory or Sandy Irvine? He makes a detailed note of its position.

Percy Wyn-Harris, another member of the expedition, is at about 27,760 feet when he sees a wooden handled ice axe placed, as it seems, on a rock. He is 750 feet before the First Step. When he returns to Base Camp, he shows the axe to Frank Smythe and they plot its position on the map.

In 1924, when Frank Smythe was 24, he was nearly taken on the Mallory/Irvine expedition himself, but a man called John Hazard was taken instead. Frank has studied all the material and has met the survivors. He knows, from Noel Odell, that although most of them believe that George could not have turned back with the summit in sight, Ruth believes that he would have turned back, 'that he did not mean it to be so hard that he would be [killed]'. When Frank sees where Wyn-Harris found that ice axe, he can compare it to the position of the object he has seen through his telescope. Since the object, which might be a body, appears to be slightly nearer the final camp than the ice axe, if the body Frank saw is George's, Ruth would be right. But even if they keep it out of the press, is it fair to give her a hypothesis? It might not be a body. Even if it is, it might be Sandy Irvine's not George's. Frank Smythe swings the telescope away from the 'body'. He will keep quiet about that sighting. He does not want to cause 'a sensation'.

In Easter 1933, Ruth and her three children are walking back after a day's climbing. A 1926/1927 family photograph captures the three bare footed, straw hatted Mallory children in their cotton smocks having climbed a 10 foot high boulder while on summer holiday in Brittany, France. As John Mallory later put it, his mother made a conscious decision 'not to wrap us in cotton wool'. From the age of 8, they joined the children of the Winthrop Youngs, the Pyes and the Arnold-Forsters to begin 'proper' climbing at Pen-y-Pass.

Beyond climbing goals, Ruth's aim 'to educate the girls as well as the boys' is being realised. Her Powell relatives have paid for the girls to attend St Mary's Calne. Clare has a place to study history at Cambridge University. Beridge wants to follow her to study medicine. John is at his father's old school, Winchester College, with Kathleen (Scott) Young's second son, Wayland Kennet. Geoffrey Winthrop Young pronounces Clare and Beridge to be 'brilliant climbers' but for the moment he reserves judgement on 13-year-old John. Ruth, now in her early forties, returns with her children to the Pen-y-Pass Hotel after a good day's climbing.

She is handed a letter that has been forwarded from Westbrook. The letter informs her that an ice axe has been found by the First Step on the North Ridge of Everest. It has a wooden handle with three nicks in it. The writer wants to know whether George ever marked his things in this way. Ruth thinks not. There is no mention in the letter of Smythe's possible sighting of a body in the letter, but Ruth has moved on. She is less concerned with what happened than what is about to happen. There are new threats to her family and George is not here to help her negotiate them.

In 1933, the Nazi Party has taken hold in Germany. Although John is at school in England, Jocelin Winthrop Young and Mark Arnold-Forster have been studying at Schule Schloss Salem in Germany under the revolutionary headmaster Kurt Hahn. They have been brought back in a hurry. Will Arnold-Forster and Geoffrey Winthrop Young are appealing to the Labour coalition Prime Minister Ramsay MacDonald to offer Hahn asylum. Jocelin and Mark will become Hahn's first pupils when their parents help Kahn reestablish himself at Gordonstoun School in Elgin, Scotland in 1934. The school curriculum still closely resembles the prospectus that George, Ruth, David and the Winthrop Youngs' first devised back in the First World War years.

But in 1933, while Ruth and her Pen-y-Pass friends are attending the Easter meet, Hahn has just been taken prisoner by the Nazis. His life is in danger. In Wales, the post-climbing evening entertainment, the singing and country dancing, is replaced by urgent discussion. All of them have sons. (David Pye, who married later than the others, has baby Tristram. William will be born in 1938.) The memory of the last war is fresh, the risks, terrible, the danger, real. They must protect their children from having to fight and die because the peace process failed.

* * *

Five years later in 1938, Will Arnold-Forster, now an advisor to the National Peace Council and member of the Executive Committee of League of Nations, is on a ship bound for Canada for a meeting concerning Naval Disarmament. The League is crippled financially and politically by the fact that the United States has not joined up. Will and Gilbert Murray who is travelling with him aim to involve them in this side agreement on disarmament. Murray shares most of Will's views on peace keeping but unlike Will, he believes that satanism is a contributing factor to the threat to the world order. (The evidence for this part of Ruth's biography is found in the *Cornish Guardian*, conversations with Val Arnold-Forster, Audrey Salkeld and in a book by Gilbert Murray.)

In Zennor, on 25 May 1938, while Will was sailing west across the Atlantic, his wife Ka walks out of Eagles' Nest. She is heading up over the moor to visit Mrs Gerald Vaughan at Carn Cottage. Mrs Vaughan has a baby a few months old. She is convinced that the cottage has been cursed by satanists, specifically Aleister Crowley. Unconcerned by this, Ka reaches the cottage at dusk and goes inside. No one knows what to believe about what happened next.

> Sudden death of Mrs Arnold-Forster ... one of the best known women in Cornwall, and one who, with her husband Mr W.E. Arnold-Forster shared universal popularity. Her death came with complete suddenness in the most tragic circumstances. Except for a slight cold during the last few days she appeared to be perfectly well, and on Saturday afternoon was visiting some sick friends in one of the cottages on the Moor near her house when she was suddenly taken with a seizure ... One of the tragic features of the situation is that Mr Arnold-Forster is at present bound for Canada, his arrival there being due either on Monday or Tuesday ...
>
> *Cornish Guardian*

When Ruth hears the news she remembers that Ka had written to Ruth after George's death in 1924, 'if at any time in the coming years you or the children are troubled or ill – and want us telegraph and Will or I will come ...' It is so like Ka to put herself out for other people, no wonder she had gone to help

Mrs Vaughan and her child. Ruth, by now accustomed to her inverted world, speeds to Eagles' Nest. Ka is conscious when she is brought down from the cottage, but she dies two days later. As Val Arnold-Forster and Audrey Salkeld remembered it, Ruth was determined to counter rumours that 'Ka died in the haunted house with the *Bible* thrown across the room.'

Mark is at Gordonstoun when Kurt Hahn gives him the news that his mother is dead. Will receives a radioed message on board his ship. He is devastated but he cannot make the ship turn around.

The local community keep their distance. The best reassurance Ruth can offer Will on his return are facts. An author called Frank Baker, a friend of Ka's, claims that Ka had a heart problem she'd been keeping quiet about. Ka died of a heart attack – in Ruth's opinion there is no satanism and no blame.

By the time that Hugh Thackeray Turner dies on 11 December 1937, at the age of 84, the Turner portion of the Powell's inheritance has been long since used up. Ruth and Marby put the house on the market after holding Clare's wedding there in 1938. Many of those I interviewed attended that wedding. They remember Clare and the American Glenn Millikan, a fellow Cambridge student and climber, walking out of the church under an arch of ice axes held by their friends. (In a tragic repetition of history, Glenn would later die while climbing with Clare in Tennessee, leaving her with their three young children.)

Clare left Cambridge with a first-class degree in history and plans to become a lecturer when she and Glenn moved to the United States. Ruth, Beridge and John moved in with Ruth's cousin Eleanor 'Dorothea' Layton at her home in Northend, South Harting, near Petersfield.

Ruth was moving on. The Everest experience was behind her, and the children were becoming independent, living their lives. Beridge was at Cambridge University with plans (later realised) to become a paediatric doctor. Beridge often climbed at Pen-y-Pass with another American Cambridge student, David Robertson (whom she would later marry). John had just begun an engineering degree at his father's old Cambridge college, Magdalene. Although Ruth did not suspect it at the end of 1938, the tragic death of Ka marked the beginning of some of Ruth's happiest years.

# Chapter Thirty-Three

# Remarriage

Wandsworth Marriage Registry Book, 27 June 1939,
Wandsworth Borough Council Archives, London

Peter Gillman and Leni Gillman (interviewers)
Clare Millikan (née Mallory) (interviewee)

Following a short ceremony, Mrs Ruth Leigh-Mallory (widowed) and Lieutenant Commander Arnold-Forster (retired, widowed) sign the register at the Wandsworth Registry Office in London. It is 27 June 1939. Ruth's cousin Dorothea and Ruth's son John, sign their names as witnesses. Will is 53 and has been single for a year; Ruth is 48 and has been single for fifteen years. When Ruth writes her new address, Will advises the newest Mrs Arnold-Forster, that from now on she must put the apostrophe in Eagle's Nest, after the 's' – Eagles' Nest. He has been in touch with the council planning department over it. He is afraid that he is of a 'fastidious mind'.

John is on summer holiday from Cambridge and accompanies the newlyweds to Wandsworth Common for the honeymoon picnic. In one rare photograph, John and Will are lying on the grass as Ruth pours tea from a thermos. Ruth has a hole in the elbow of her jumper. Ruth realises that for John it is the end of an era. He was 3 when George died and does not remember his father. Now, at the age of 19, he has a step-father and a step-brother, Mark. John knows that his mother once turned down a proposal from a prep school headmaster near Godalming. To him she seems so self-sufficient, so self-contained that now, in 1939, John wonders why his mother feels the need to marry at all. Ruth answers John's question literally: 'I have fallen in love and been fallen in love with.'

Perhaps John also feels uneasy for the same reason that Ruth did when Leonard Huxley remarried after his wife's (Ruth's headmistress Julia Huxley) death. 'Doesn't it seem to you a very strange thing to do ...' Ruth asks George, on 5 August 1916, 'for a man to go with his second wife to the home he had lived in with his first wife and in which she had died?'

But this is different. Ruth is going there precisely because Ka died in the house. She wants to prove that there is nothing dangerous, nothing to fear at

Eagles' Nest. Surely, George and Ka would have wanted this. They would want Ruth and Will to look after each other. Ruth is no longer defined by being behind Everest, by being a widow, she is the wife of a public figure who has considerable influence in League affairs.

The end of Ruth as Mrs George Mallory, is also the end of an era for the Mount Everest Committee. The MEC met for the last time a fortnight before Ruth's marriage to Will. Arthur Hinks, resigns as secretary after twenty years devoted to the conquest of the mountain. But Ruth is no longer preoccupied with Everest. She is looking forward to the future. To swimming naked in the Atlantic with Will (also a naturist) and to being mistress of her own home, of her own life. She is looking forward to freedom and usefulness and she is nearer the goal of working for the League of Nations than ever before.

\* \* \*

To start with, Ruth was determined to try to fill Ka's very big shoes in the local community of Zennor. Ka was the secretary of the St Ives branch of the League of Nations. At the very least, Ruth will have to give League garden fetes. After moving back into Westbrook, although Thackeray Turner disapproved of Montessori, he allowed Ruth to accept Olave Baden-Powell's invitation to work for the newly formed Ranger Guides. Ruth has recently been promoted from lieutenant to captain of what she likes to think of as the Junior League of Nations. As Captain Ruth Arnold-Forster, she quickly becomes a respected county figure at League events.

When newly pregnant Clare comes home to Eagles' Nest, to visit her mother and new step-father, she thinks Ruth looks 'ten years younger'.

> she was physically in love with [Will] ... [She had] ... new colour in her face and sparkle in her eyes – staying down at Zennor – she looked very happy, she was happy ...

After years of enforced invisibility at Westbrook, Ruth is now active again. She is the chatelaine of the wind blasted Cornish castle and Clare observes the welcome change – she 'glowed'.

During the first few months of married life, Ruth and Will climb 'their' Snuff Box boulder in the garden. They scramble down the side of the valley and swim and sunbathe naked on the rocks that surround Zennor's secluded clear water cove. Will paints and draws. Seminal modern artists Ben Nicholson and Barbara Hepworth have moved to St Ives. Inspired by the artistic community, Ruth returns to her china painting and embroidering in the sunny morning room.

But Ruth wants to become more useful. Ka had employed Mr and Mrs Klisky do the gardening, cooking and housekeeping; Ruth does not want to challenge the status quo but asks Will whether she could become his secretary. She has a clear, childlike print which delights Will's publisher. She enjoys sitting in on League of Nations meetings.

But her secretarial career is short lived. Once, when they were alone, she asked Will: 'How do you spell really, is it "rely"?' They quickly agreed that since it completely changed the meaning, it might be dangerous for Ruth to continue. When Will invites his friend, Emperor of Ethiopia Haile Selassie, to stay at Eagles' Nest, Ruth comes into her own.

* * *

In 2022, Katharine, the owner of Eagles' Nest, takes me round the large airy house. At the time, it is in the last stages of refurbishment. Even walking around the builders' scaffolding and pots of paint, Eagles' Nest is spectacular. Ascending the main stairs, we walk left into a room with vast windows looking out over the Atlantic Ocean. This, Katharine confirms, is still known as 'the Emperor's Room'.

At the time that Haile Selassie first came to stay with Ruth and Will, he had been in exile since May 1935. The League of Nations had effectively sacrificed Ethiopia to Mussolini in its attempt to prevent another world war. In July 1936, Will led a controversial campaign against the decision, arguing that supporting weaker countries over stronger ones was precisely what the League was for. He arranged for Selassie to give a speech in defence of Ethiopia to the League council in Geneva and they became friends.

Selassie found staying at Eagles' Nest soothing. Walking around the garden, I notice alpine plants and small boulders so covered in dusty light green lichen that they look hairy. There are beautiful pine trees with what arborealists might describe as 'a horizontal habit', ideal for climbing. The air is sweet, the garden full of secret paths, 'rooms' and eddies with inviting benches cut into the hedging. Will set up a miniature train set when Mark was young. Val confirmed that Mark was the envy of children for miles around.

When Ruth meets Selassie, she recognises the guilty frustration that George felt before his headmaster released him to fight. Selassie's frustration is not just for himself but for a whole country. He, like George, feels his hearth 'an intolerable reproach'. He is safe whilst his subjects are in danger. Although Ruth empathises, she is practical. The Eagles' Nest loos refuse to flush to emperor standards, so she must see to the drains. Ruth has never been impressed with rank. Standing in the garden, she talks U-bends with the plumber and suggests that Selassie should try one of George's six routes up the Snuff Box boulder. Selassie is small, wiry and keen. By the time he leaves, there is a new route up one of the local sea cliffs named after him.

On 1 September 1939, two months after Ruth's marriage to Will, Germany invades Poland and war (Second World War) is declared. Ruth's step-son Mark immediately applies to transfer from the Merchant Navy (which he chose over a place at Cambridge to his father's dismay) to the Royal Navy. Geoffrey and Len's son Jocelin also signs up for the Royal Navy. Clare's husband, Glenn Millikan, telegrams E.D. Adrian, a climbing friend running the physiology department at Cambridge to ask whether he should return to Britain. He is told to 'Stay in America'. Shortly afterwards, Ruth's first grandchild, is born in New York. By this time Beridge has married David Robertson and moved to the United States too. Since 'unnecessary travel' is prohibited during wartime, Ruth cannot cross the Atlantic to see her daughters or meet her grandchildren.

With John still at Cambridge, Ruth has one remaining child in the country. To some her son and sons-in-law seem unfairly safe. Out of Ruth's earshot Geoffrey later concludes:

The majority of my kinsmen's and friends' sons are now safely pocketed in the Ministry of Information and other survival holes ... Those of us who hang on ... for the agony of that phone call that shall end real life for us, may be forgiven for a little grudge of the inequality with which the danger is being shared even among our kin and friends.

But Ruth knows well the agony of that telephone call, the telegram, the end of 'real life' that it may bring. She will not be selfless with John's life. There is no such thing as vicarious selflessness. She insists that John should finish his engineering degree. She keeps John safe through 1939, 1940 and even through summer 1941 when he is a 21-year-old fit young man, helping with the harvest at Tremedda Farm below Eagles' Nest. All the while her step-son, Mark, is in the Royal Navy collecting medals to tear his coat.

The evidence for this last section of Ruth's life comes from my conversations with Val Arnold-Forster, Marianne Nevel and Audrey Salkeld. Splicing various pieces together it seems that Will spent most of his time working for the Admiralty staying in the Arnold-Forster family flat in Wandsworth, London. Ruth visited occasionally to check on Franz. At one stage during the Second World War, Franz's business was taken over by the war office. He employed fifty people, about half of them women, and several Jewish refugee teenagers from Germany and Austria. One of his employees was the famous Russian born aviation pioneer Igor Sikorsky who, right there in Franz's workshop, was working up his ideas for rotor blades, for vertical lift for what would be the first helicopter.

When Will occasionally left his desk to come back to Ruth at Eagles' Nest, he reported that there was a renewed surge of anti-German feeling. From Cornwall, Ruth wrote to Franz. With his accent Franz was often called 'Fritz' even though he had become a British citizen. Ruth sent him George's tent, his climbing rope. She invited him to stay in Cornwall, but would he be safe? During the last war, writer D.H. Lawrence and his German wife, Freda lived in a cottage within sight of Eagles' Nest. They were accused of being spies and hounded out by the locals. Remembering George's spirit at the Zennor séance, Ruth helps Franz Knefel to Anglicise his name to Francis 'Frank' Nevel. On 14 September 1941, Ruth writes to him by his old name Franz: 'My dear, if later on things are better and you are able to get off a bit, do remember that we should love to have you here.'

Ruth walks through the rain to visit five outlying farms. 'I'm going to give them some First Aid classes,' she tells Franz. 'Chiefly because I think they are lonely and it will be nice for them. But it will take a bit of doing in bad weather.' Although there is electricity at the farm beneath the house, there is none at Eagles' Nest. (When Virginia Woolf stayed when Ka was alive, she complained that it was impossible to get warm even in bed.) By the summer of 1942, John joins the British Army Royal Engineers and, after training in Chester, he is posted abroad.

# Chapter Thirty-Four

# 1 June 1942

Sketch made by Will Arnold-Forster
kindly lent to the author
by Kate Arnold-Forster and Sam Arnold-Forster,
Arnold-Forster Archives,
Reading University Special Collections, Reading

Jochen Hemmleb, Larry A. Johnson
and Eric R. Simonson,
*Ghosts of Everest:*
*The Authorised Story of*
*the Search for Mallory & Irvine,*
MacMillan, London, 1999

Clare Millikan (née Mallory) (interviewee)
Peter Gillman (interviewer)

John Mallory (interviewee)
Kate Nicholson (interviewer)

The Second World War has been raging for over two years when Ruth is moved from Mount Vernon Hospital in West London to a convalescent home in Uxbridge, North London. From her bed, she can hear the air raid sirens. Ever since her days digging the heavy clay soil in the Herschel House garden, Ruth has suffered from back ache. When the pain returned in 1941, she thought it was 'the old trouble' again.

Geoffrey Keynes, George's climbing friend and John's godfather, is senior surgeon to the RAF, treating injured pilots. He makes an exception and take Ruth on as a private patient but is dismayed to find cancer of the colon. Keynes performs an operation to remove some of her intestine followed by what he calls 'a newer weapon', post-operative radium treatment. This involves inserting needles of radium under gas and oxygen anaesthesia. The needles have to stay in place for seven days. When Ruth finishes the radium treatment, she is very fragile. Will visits when he can. He is the boy with his finger in the dyke; he's spent two decades championing disarmament and now his work is unravelling.

* * *

Now Will sits at the foot end of Ruth's hospital bed with a sketchbook and pencil. He looks up at her. What does he see? Does he still see the girl to whom George first introduced him in 1914, the girl he'd told Will he'd 'found' in a field in Asolo? Does he see the matinee star from the double portrait photograph taken in Adrian Harding's studio in 1915? Does he see her as she was just after he married her in 1939 when she was glowing?

One of Will's exquisite pencil sketches in his daughter-in-law's possession, is of a lady whom the family believe is Ruth. It is unsigned, untitled and undated. If it is Ruth, she seems to be propped up on a big pillow with natural light falling on the right side of her now angular face. There is a sense of quietness, of peace. The left side of her face is rendered in cross hatched shadow. It is as if the artist is trying to read her, to fix her image in memory, time and space. The pencil hovers around the profile of her right cheek, her chin, her throat, her collar bones. Her wavy hair is worn down. She has a far-away look in her big eyes. The drawing is intimate, sympathetic and exquisite.

When Will leaves the hospital, perhaps with that sketch under his arm, Ruth can flick slowly through a scrapbook that Franz calls his 'family photograph album'. Franz visits often. His pictures of George are cut from newspapers. He does not have any photographs of his own of George in that album because back then in his early teens he didn't own a camera. He has pictures of Ruth's father, Hugh Thackeray Turner, reclining in a deck chair on the terrace at Westbrook, his neat white beard above his signature bow tie. He has pictures of himself on the terrace wall, legs crossed, with his arms around a white duck from Marby's small farm at Westbrook. He has photographs of John mid-air hurdling a rope high jump that they made on the grass tennis court, before Ruth's father pronounced the nets 'ugly' and planted an orchard instead. Most of the pictures seem to be taken in summer and they all have bare feet. Franz has pictures of the girls Clare and Beridge in summer dresses, long tanned limbs cartwheeling across a perfect lawn.

And Franz has three pictures of Ruth, expressive and full of action: here she is sitting on a rug with tea things all around her, pouring a bottle of milk into a jug for picnic tea; here she is part of a group trying to work out what is wrong with the camping kettle Beridge is holding; and finally, here she is – a full-length photograph. This is Ruth, half smiling, in a curiously conventional polka dot dress. She is walking briskly across the Westbrook lawn as if she is trying to reach whoever is taking the photograph before the shutter clicks.

Ruth dies on 1 June 1942. Her death is recorded in page 6 of the *St. Ives Times & Echo* on 5 June 1942:

We regret to record the death of Mrs. Ruth Arnold-Forster (wife of Mr W.E. Arnold-Forster of Eagles' Nest, Zennor) which took place at Northwood, London, on Monday.

Anne Keynes, Geoffrey Keynes's daughter-in-law, told me that everyone who knew Ruth was devastated, she had just found happiness again. The autopsy revealed no hint of cancer. Geoffrey Keynes couldn't put the anguish he felt into words. Instead in his autobiography *Gates of Memory* at the point where Ruth dies, he placed an illustration *The Doctor's Despair*, a drawing by Rowlandson of a surgeon, his face contorted by emotion as he looks down on the dead body of his patient.

## Everest, The Red Thread – 1 May 1999

On 1 May 1999, professional climber Conrad Anker is on Everest, just down from the First Step on Everest's North Ridge. The slope is treacherously steep. The air is frozen. He breathes from an oxygen bottle on his back. He is searching an area where, in 1933, Frank Smythe spotted what he thought was a body through his telescope from Base Camp.

As Anker is combing the slope, he spots something white as alabaster, sticking out of the ice. Anker checks in with the other climbers, other members of the search team. He uses a prearranged code phrase and then ceases communication.

The corpse in front of him is lying face down with the head up the slope. It is frozen and bleached by the sun. The body is at full stretch with the hands reaching up as if frozen in a position of self-arrest. It is as if the fall has happened only moments earlier and the climber is still trying to prevent himself from sliding further down the mountain.

The hands are ungloved. Strong sinewy fingers are sunk into the slope if still trying to find some secure hold. Much of the clothing has torn away in the wind. The back and left leg are exposed. The right leg is broken at a right angle just above the top of the climbing boot. The boot is an old leather boot with metal nails in the sole. Who is it? Is this the body of Sandy Irvine?

By now, the team have gathered around the body. Carefully, they separate the ragged layers of clothing on the torso. The first layer is a canvas outer garment. The next is a woollen jumper, a flannel shirt and finally cotton and silk underwear. One of the climbers crouching beside the body takes the back of the shirt collar between gloved fingers and carefully turns it over. There is a name tape sewn on: 'G. Mallory'.

At about 3.00 pm, after reading a burial service and covering the body in stones, the team put the artifacts that they have retrieved from the corpse's pockets, into Andy Politz's rucksack. It is time to return to Camp V. 'I was picking a route across this slope,' Politz said later, 'and every step of the way I was conscious that I have two kids and a wife back at home, and every step matters here.'

Amongst other effects in Politz's pack are several perfectly preserved letters. Some are from Mallory's brother Trafford and one from his sister Mary. On the envelope of one of the letters is a column of figures. These are later found to be oxygen cylinder readings. Inside the envelope is a letter from a correspondent unknown to the climbers.

Back in the camp they take out the envelopes and, carefully drawing the mystery letter out of the envelope, they examine the signature. At first they read it as 'Sweetie'. Was that the name Ruth called George by? Later they realise that the signature is actually, 'Stella'. Audrey Salkeld receives a message from Everest at her home in Cumbria, England. The message is marked 'Top Secret'.

Back on the mountain there are still many questions. There was no camera with the body. That camera – a Kodak Vest Pocket camera that George borrowed from Howard Somervell – might have contained undeveloped film with a summit shot.

## Pretoria, South Africa – 2007

The only two children left when George's body was found on Everest are John and Clare. (Dr Beridge Robertson died of brain cancer in 1953.) Clare suggests that the sale of the photographs might be used to raise money to 'clean up Everest'. The whole family are shocked by the amount of rubbish left by climbers on that once pristine mountain.

By the time I board the plane to Pretoria on 3 February 2007, only John is still alive. He and his late wife raised their family in South Africa. One of his daughters, Virginia (who the family claim is 'very like Ruth') has paved the way for this meeting.

On the way out to Pretoria in the plane, I have a chance to read an interview that Clare gave to the *Sunday Mirror* when she was 83. 'They were very much in love,' Clare told the reporter,

he told her before he set out that if he ever reached the top, he would leave the picture of her there. One of the first things I asked when I was told he had been found was what was in his pockets …

I know what was in those pockets. A watch with rust marks at 5.10 (whether morning or evening, of course, unknown), a tin of savoury meat lozenges, a brass altimeter, a pocketknife, a brightly coloured blue and red monogrammed handkerchief, string, Swan Vestas matches (still usable), more string, some letters and a pair of undamaged smoked glass sun goggles. But there was no photograph.

Clare's image of her mother's portrait, delicately balanced on the summit snow, is somehow perfect. It was one of the only times that Ruth mentioned George to her daughter after his death. Clare struggled with this: 'It would have helped us if my mother had been willing to talk more about our father.' When her husband died she deliberately talked about him to keep the memory alive for their children. And yet Ruth told Clare the photograph story.

When George received a similar portrait shot of Ruth during the First World War he wrote: 'Dearest one, I salute your image with kisses.' For a couple who spent half their married life apart, photographs held particular power. George must have asked Ruth for that photograph because on 19 April 1924, he confirmed that he had received pictures of the children, which 'I'm very glad to have, but you don't send one of yourself, naughty girl.' If the photograph she then sent out to George on Everest was returned in the five suitcases of effects – Ruth surely would not have told Clare that story.

\* \* \*

I arrive at John's house in Pretoria at a time of jacaranda blossom. The door is opened by a man with thick white hair and glasses. He is taller than I thought he would be – somewhere well over 6 foot with legs that merit his childhood nickname 'the leggy menace'. This is the son Ruth and George had longed for, born half an hour before his father returned from a climbing trip to the Alps on 21 August 1920. Now he is 86 years old, more than twice as old as his father was when he died on Everest aged 37.

When I show John the photograph of the dedication of the war memorial on Great Gable on 8 June 1924, he tells me that the person on the right is his mother, Ruth. Until then he and most Everest historians had assumed that she was with them on a beach holiday at Bacton, Norfolk. The Lake District memorial is often described as 'the world's greatest', since it is comprised, not just of that plaque on Great Gable but includes twelve Lake District summits. He has seen the Great Gable First World War memorial plaque himself, he thinks that Ruth took him there once. The 'tops' passed quickly into the care of the National Trust founded in 1895 and acquiring land and properties by the mid-1920s. John asks me if I have ever climbed in the Lake District as he has.

'Are you a climber?' I tell him about Cotopaxi but decide that, no, I am not. I hope to learn one day.

John asks me what I think happened to his father. Peter Gillman has kindly prepared me so that I know he asks all Everest research historians. I look up into the face of the man that I have come halfway round the world to meet. I tell him that we know that John's father fell twice because of the bruising. The bruising found round the waist of George's dead body would have taken between twenty minutes to one hour to form. It would only form if his blood was still circulating. After the first fall, it seems, from the position of the ice axe and the position of the body, that he was making his way not towards the summit but back to camp. George, John's father and Ruth's husband, was not in my opinion, ascending indefinitely. Ruth was right.

I start gathering the material John has given me to write this biography but he stops me and picks a vase off a side table, a sort of small chest of drawers. It is, he tells me, the 'hall table' from The Holt. For me it represents the turning point. The surface of that 'table' is the place where that letter, refusing Captain Farrar's invitation to join the expedition, lay awaiting the post box early in 1921. Ruth's phrase 'it so easily might not have' is just the flip side of 'it so easily might'. Sliding doors. Walking out of John's sliding glass doors into his garden, he sets the vase carefully on the wide bladed South African grass. 'That is one of hers'.

I have seen the sketches for this vase in Ruth's letters to George in the Magdalene College Archives in Cambridge. Crouching down to look at it, I see that it is now heavily repaired with ceramic glue. It has lived a whole life and somehow it makes me think of the fifteenth-century Japanese practice of Kintsugi meaning 'to join with gold' – an ancient philosophy that accepts and even celebrates flaws as part of life.  Ruth was, as her aunt Rosamond remarked to Mary Ann in 1914, 'Pure gold all through'. Turning the vase over in my hands I see carefully hand painted initials: 'CRLM'.

While I am looking at the vase, John tells me that although he now knows precisely where his father's body lies, he still does not know where his mother is buried. We are still standing there in the garden beside Ruth's vase when I give John page 6 of *The St. Ives Times & Echo* of 5 June 1942. On it is the death notice, announcing that Ruth's funeral service will take place in Zennor on Monday, 8 June 1942. It seems too much of a coincidence. Will Arnold-Forster was a man of fastidious precision. He must have chosen that date. A last act of true love for Ruth and of respect for his friend, George.

John and I have made our goodbyes and I am about to drive away when John remembers that he has something else to show me. We walk back into the house. He stands in front of a white painted wall on which he has hung three photographs.

John stands there in silence. He does not turn around. Still with his back to me he says: 'I would far rather have known my father, than grow up in the shadow of a legend.'

I look past him to the photographs. George Mallory, John's father, is on the right in his new lieutenant's uniform. Ruth, his mother, is on the left, looking out at me with clear focus. Between them, John has hung a picture of a mountain. Everest.

# Appendix I

# Ruth's Letter, 3–5 March 1924

Ruth's only surviving letter from the Everest years,
Magdelene College Archives,
Cambridge University, Cambridge

Herschel House
Cambridge

Tuesday 3rd

My dearest George,

I was very glad to find that the [SS] *California* did not sail after all till Saturday morning. I suppose it was because the weather was so stormy.

I am afraid I am going to do the one thing you told me not to. And use a ton of coke straight away. We are under thick snow here. Some fell on Saturday night but on Sunday night there was a heavy fall & yesterday was a glorious sunny day. The children played at making snowmen in the afternoon in the garden & had a lovely time. It was thawing most of the day & when I went to bed but it froze later in the night & was freezing hard this morning.

Blunt [the gardener/handyman] has again not come so I have rung up Mrs Salter & he is well so I have taken his address and written to him.

Nellie, the new cook, is so far very satisfactory. She seems very nice & cooks well.

Frances Wills is coming here tomorrow for five days. I shall enjoy that. We are both going to dine with the Cranages on Thursday before the lecture. So far I seem nearly as full of engagements as I was before you left. People are being most awfully kind and nice. Really I thing [*sic*] more friendly than they were at Godalming.

Mrs Cranage rang Vi up to find out when I was coming home [from Liverpool] that she might meet me with her car. Vi didn't know, but it was most awfully kind of her.

At Bletchley I got into the same carriage as John Christie. He was coming to Cambridge to stay with David [Pye] for the Greek play. So I saw him again in the evening.

I enjoyed seeing the Greek play quite a lot, the dresses were very good & the colour scheme pretty. As I did not understand it there did seem a lot of standing still and spouting at the audience. But I expect if I had understood it I should not have felt that so much.

I am so sorry you left your dressing gown behind. I am sending it to Bombay [today's Mumbai] & then addressed to Darjeeling in case it misses you.

Wednesday

I see that the *California* left Gibraltar on the 4th. So now you are in the Mediterranean. I hope it is warm and nice. I am getting rather worried about the garden. If the weather goes on being so cold I shall not possibly be able to get the necessary seed sowing done before I go away. If I can't do it I think I shall come back for a few days of solid gardening in April.

I hoped to do a lot of greenhouse seed sowing today but I can't get the seed boxes. The fish monger promised them but he has not sent them.

I went to the Quay Village performance last night. It was quite good and very swell arranged. There was no scenery so there were no long pauses as there so often are in amateure [*sic*] theatricals. I think the whole show was a great credit to Mrs Salter.

The young man we picked up at St Neots came round yesterday just as we were starting nursery tea so I asked him up and he was quite pleasant and jolly and evidently enjoyed seeing the children. Clare was in an appallingly talkative mood all day yesterday. Nothing would stop her tongue and at tea time she had her fling. I found her this morning before breakfast engaged in writing out thirteen times table. She has determined to write out and learn all the difficult ones up to 19 times she says.

Mrs Reade came to lunch yesterday I took her after lunch to see the new Sidney Sussex chapel & we met Mani Forbes there and then had a long talk about the chapel etc which Mrs Reade evidently enjoyed very much. I don't think I was very good company. My period had just come and I wasn't at all on the spot. I have just fallen down from ladder & all trying to get the climbing things into the loft. Luckily I did not hurt myself at all.

I have heard from Mr Raxworthy. My bank balance is overdrawn £823 and your £112 that is £935 in all. He suggests we sell of our £5000 Vickers 4% which would bring in £400 and £400 National War Bond for £420. If we get £2500 for The Holt we need only sell the Vicars [*sic*]. I think so I will tell him only to do that for the present.

Dearest one I do … you are happy and having a good voyage. I am keeping quite cheerful & happy but I do miss you a lot. I think I want you companionship even more than I used to. I know I have rather often been cross and not nice & I am very sorry but the bottom reason has nearly always been because I was unhappy at getting so little of you. I know its [*sic*] pretty stupid to spoil the times I do have you for those when I don't.

Very very much love to you my dear one,

Your loving

Ruth

# Appendix II

# Extract from Interview with Dorothea Pilley

Dorothea Pilley (1894–1986) – climber and founding member of the Pinnacle Club and author of *Climbing Days* (Harcourt Brace, 1935). Dorothea was married to climber and academic I.A. Richards. They had no children but Dorothea promoted women climbers especially in the next generation and is named as proposer on Clare Mallory's membership application form for the Pinnacle Club. The following letter, quoted from Dorothea's great nephew Dan Richards's *Climbing Days* (Faber and Faber, 2016) gives an insight into Harry Kelly's opinion of his wife Pat and to 'a woman's position in life'.

Letter to Dorothea Pilley from Harry Kelly (husband of the founder of the Pinnacle Club, Pat Kelly) following Pat's accidental death on Tryfan in April 1922.

Bramhall, Cheshire
May 2, 1922

Dear Pilley,

I should like to thank you for your letter of April 30th and what you say therein about Pat.

She was my wife but I think I am dispassionate enough in my judgements to be able to say without any bias that she was the finest woman I have ever met. We lived together almost the whole of the 24 hours of each day. She was always fresh & new. Courage, large-heartedness and love she had in plenty. I suppose I am only now realising what a part she played in my life. To her more than anyone else do I owe a sympathetic understanding of woman's position in life.

… Because of her all-embracing character and pure spirit, I am beginning to think that the mts. had a right in claiming her. All that one objects to now is the time – but this comes to us all – when we know not.

Believe me,
Yours sincerely,
H.M. Kelly

I am returning the letter you so kindly sent & hope the journal will fructify.
She had her heart set on it. May the P.C. [Pinnacle Club] prosper.

She was the means of its birth & she called it more than once, her child.
I should like to hear from you at one time or other

H.M.K.

# Appendix III

# Ruth's Remains and her Estate

Records show that Ruth's funeral was held in Zennor, Cornwall on 8 June 1942 but there are also records showing that her cremated remains are in Nightingale Cemetery, Waverley, Godalming. Perhaps Ruth's ashes were divided between her husbands? She left an estate of £6,427 (gross), £6,124 (net) – approximately £373,428 in today's money – with probate grated to her husband 'Lieutenant-Commander Arnold-Forster, Retired'.

# Appendix IV

# League of Nations

Letter to the author from Sir Christopher Greenwood, 15 January 2024 in response to a request for help in understanding Ruth and George Mallory's commitment to the League of Nations.

It is difficult to write about the League of Nations because it belongs to what Peter Laslett would have called 'a world we have lost'. [Laslett, Peter, *The World We Have Lost*, Methuen & Co. Ltd., 1965.] It has to be seen in the context not just of the carnage of World War One, which led so many to dream of an end to war, but also of the two Hague Peace Conferences (1899 and 1907) and the earlier Alabama arbitration between the US and the UK (arising out of the American Civil War) which gave rise to a really strong sentiment that diplomacy and international adjudication could remove the causes of war. The adjudication element was given concrete form in 1922 with the establishment of the Permanent Court of International Justice.

While the US never joined the League (which effectively crippled the League both financially and politically) it was a party to the Statute of the PCIJ and one of the judges from the US was Charles Evan Hughes, the (narrowly) unsuccessful candidate for the presidency in 1916 and later Chief Justice of the US Supreme Court.

Both the League and the PCIJ were remarkably effective for about ten years until the rise of Nazism. The PCIJ held its last hearing in December 1939 when the Second World war was already raging and its President (Judge Guerrero from El Salvador) made the following statement:

'In the last resort, recourse to international justice depends on the will of governments and on their readiness to submit for legal decision all which can and should be preserved from the arbitrament of violence. As for the Court, it means to accomplish to the full the duties incumbent upon it, and it will not weaken in that resolve.'

I have always found this very moving.

# Appendix V

# Abbreviations

| | |
|---|---|
| AC | Alpine Club |
| LAC | Ladies' Alpine Club |
| LON | League of Nations |
| LONU or LNU | League of Nations Union |
| MEC | Mount Everest Committee |
| NUWSS | National Union of Women's Suffrage Societies |
| RGS | Royal Geographical Society |

# Bibliography

**Photographs**
All copyright holders of the photographs contained in the plate section are credited in the image captions.

Photograph of Ruth and George included on the title page. (*Public domain*).

**Archives**
Archives used include:

Alpine Club Archives, London
Geoffrey Winthrop Young's Pen-y-Pass Photograph albums.
Geoffrey Winthrop Young kept four albums of photographic records of meets at Pen-y-Pass over the years; copies of which are kept in the Alpine Club Archives. In my opinion, the best written description of the Pen-y-Pass climbers meets from this time can be found in Chapter 1, 'From Genesis to Numbers', of *Snowdon Biography* by Geoffrey Winthrop Young and Geoffrey Sutton, and edited by Noyce, Wilfred, published by Dent & Sons in 1957.
Harry Ransom Center, The University of Texas at Austin
Ann Bridge (Mary Ann O'Malley) Papers 5C EW Box 19, Folder 8 and George Mallory Papers 5C EW Box 19, Folder 2.
Harold Porter's journal and minutes of Mount Everest Committee meetings.
Magdalene College Archives, University of Cambridge
(Group F Mallory Papers Files 1-VII, received January 1968 and March 1986 from John Mallory).
Pinnacle Club Archives, Pinnacle Club
Royal Geographical Society, London
The National Archives, Kew
Knefel, Frantisek Binowetz, Nationality and Naturalisation Certificate AZ4400, issued 15 June 1934.
Geoffrey Winthrop Young's Archives EE/3/5 RGS and G. Mallory Box 3 EE/3/1 RGS.
(See Notes on Sources after Preface.)

**Articles**
Anonymous, *Surrey Advertiser*, 'Death of a Lover of West Surrey: Mr H. Thackeray Turner: Champion of old buildings', Saturday, 18 December 1937
Author signed 'F.W.H.', Country Life, 24 July 1915, 'In the Garden, Mr Thackeray Turner's Garden at Westbrook, Surrey', pp.119–121.
Grindley L., The Life and Work of Hugh Thackeray Turner 1853–1937, AA Diploma in Conservation of Historic Buildings, Society for the Protection of Ancient Buildings, 1998
Jekyll, Gertrude and Weaver, L., 'Gardens for Small Country Houses', Chapter 4 'Westbrook Godalming', published by Country Life, George Newnes Limited, London and Charles Scribner, New York, USA, 1914.

Reeves, M., 'Llanberis Slate – The Full Tour', UK Climbing, 30 May 2011 (https://www.ukclimbing.com/articles/destinations/llanberis_slate_-_the_full_tour-3682)

Weaver, L., pp.92–7, 'Country Life, Country Homes, Gardens Old and New, Westbrook, Godalming: The residence of Mr Thackeray Turner', 20 January 1912

### Certificates and Obituaries

Clare Millikan's obituary, August/September, FCL Quakers newsletter, 2001
Girl Guiding Archives, 1919 and 1932
Ruth Arnold-Foster's will, 18 August 1939

### Correspondence and Interviews with Author

Arnold-Forster, Kate, March 2021
Bonington, Chris, 2007
Davis, Wade, 2021 to present
Evans, Denise (Pinnacle Club), 2022
Huxley, Andrew, December 2006
Gillman, Leni and Gillman, Peter, 2007 to present
Glanville, Mandy (Pinnacle Club), 2023
Gordon, Joanna, 2007
Greenwood, Sir Christopher, 2002
Haig-Brown, Hilda, December 2006
Kennet, Wayland (Kathleen Scott's second son), 2007
Keynes, Anne, 2007
Longridge, Stella, 2006
MacFarlane, Robert, 2007 to present
Moffat, Gwen (Pinnacle Club), 18 June 2022
Nevel, Marianne, 2007
Powter, Jeff, 2007
Pye, Tristram and Pye, William, 2007
Salkeld, Audrey, 2006

### Films

*Climbing Mount Everest*, Explorer Films Limited, 1922
  Film about Everest produced by John Baptist Lucius Noel.
*Elgar's Tenth Muse*, Berwick Universal Pictures
  A film by Paul Yules. The brief but intoxicating relationship between the ageing English composer, Sir Edward Elgar, and the young Hungarian violinist Jelly d'Aranyi. With James Fox as Sir Edward Elgar. Co-starring Selma Alispahić as Jelly d'Aranyi.
*Epic of Everest to Lhasa, The*, Explorer Films Limited, 1924
  John Baptist Lucius Noel's second film about Everest.
*Lost on Everest*, 2020
  A team of climbers set out to find Irvine and his climbing partner George Mallory. Directors Renan Ozturk and Drew Pulley.
*Finding Michael*, 2023
  Released on Disney+ in 2023. Directed by Tom Beard with Spencer Matthews, Bear Grylls and Nirmal Purja. Spencer Matthews goes to Everest to try to find his brother Michael who disappeared there twenty-three years earlier.
*Wildest Dream, The: Conquest of Everest*

Based on Peter and Leni Gillman's book *The Wildest Dream*. Released in the UK by Serengeti Entertainment in September 2010 as *The Wildest Dream*. Cast including Hugh Dancy as Andrew 'Sandy' Irvine, Ralph Fiennes as George Mallory and Natasha Richardson as Ruth Mallory.

**Online Films**

Climbing Mount Everest

https://player.bfi.org.uk/free/film/watch-climbing-mt-everest-1922-online

Mount Everest – Mallory and Irvine TV documentary

Includes interviews with John Baptist and Noel Odell: https://www.youtube.com/watch?v=YpMCG6Tgrlo

The Epic of Mount Everest (trailer only)

https://www2.bfi.org.uk/epic-everest

**Television Programmes**

*One And Two Halves to K2*, BBC

*The Pinnacle Club: The First 100 Years*, Pinnacle Club

*The Story of Tom Ballard: The Last Mountain*, BBC, 2021

*The World at War*, Thames Television, 1973

**Journals and Newspapers (a selection of)**

*Alpine Journal*

*Cornish Guardian*

*Daily Sketch*

*Pinnacle Club Journal*

*The Nation*

*The St. Ives Times & Echo*

Supplement to *The St. Ives Times & Echo*, 27 May 1938, p.3, 'Death of Mrs. Arnold-Forster, J.P.'

*The St. Ives Times & Echo*

Dated 5 June 1942, p.6, Death notice for Mrs Ruth Arnold-Forster

*The St. Ives Times & Echo*

Dated 12 and 19 October 1951, 'President of St Ives Labour Party [Mr W.E. Arnold-Forster] Dies' and 'Memorial Service Tribute to Mr. Arnold-Forster' respectively

*The Times*

**Websites (a selection of)**

https://magdalene.maxarchiveservices.co.uk/index.php/incoming_(Magdalene College Archives, University of Cambridge – Ruth Mallory Letters)

https://pinnacleclub.co.uk/_(Pinnacle Club)

htttps://www.artbiogs.co.uk/2/societies/womens-guild-arts (Women's Guild of Arts)

https://www.exploringsurreyspast.org.uk (Exploring Surrey Past – 'Mary Elizabeth Turner (1854–1907)

Embroiderer and supporter of women's suffrage by Miriam Farr, 'Julia Huxley, the campaign for women's suffrage and Prior's Field School' by Joanne Halford, Prior's Field School Archivist, and 'Christiana Jane Herringham (1852–1929) artist and Women's Suffrage campaigner' by Miriam Farr.)

https://www.frcc.co.uk/the-fell-and-rock-remembrance-round_(Fell & Rock Climbing Club)

Great Gable Memorial – There is a memorial service by FRCC First World War Memorial plaque on Remembrance Sunday on Great Gable every year. Memorial Round

(20 kilometres) and a Remembrance Round (37 kilometres). The names of the fallen are listed on the page 'We Remember'.
https://www.pc100.org/ (Pinnacle Club Centenary Project)

## Unpublished Sources
Dent, Catherine, 'The Ties That Bind: Virginia Woolf, Leslie Stephen, and Ancestral Mountains', University College London, London, 2021

Newton Dunn, Barbara, 'A Few Notes on the Turner Family'

Newton Dunn, Barbara, *An Impression of Ruth Leigh-Mallory in the 1930s*

Saunders, O.A., *David Pye: Biographical Memoirs, 1886–1960*

Stannard, Robin, Dissertation 'Hugh Thackeray Turner'

Steer, G.L. and Arnold-Forster, W., 'Abyssinia To-day', February 1939, Modern Records Centre, University of Warwick, reference: MSS. 15X/2/2/3

'A Family Memoir – T.W. Powell and M.E. Powell' and their ancestors compiled by two of their children, London, 1907

Arts and Crafts third exhibition catalogue 1890 (including an article by May Turner)

Excerpts from letters to George's sister Mary Brooke from her husband Ralph Brooke, 1917–1918

'From Uncle Charlie with his love to Marjorie, Ruth and Mildred', March 1907, Unpublished, handwritten sixteen page letter-biography of Mary 'May' Elizabeth Turner by Charles Marten Powell, her brother. (p.16 details Hugh Thackeray Turner's proposal to May on a Sunday evening in April at Piccard's Rough, a country seat near Guildford, Surrey, built for May's father Thomas Wilde Powell by architect Richard Norman Shaw in 1877.)

Interview with Clare Millikan (née Mallory) by Peter Gillman (unpublished transcript)

Letters from George's mother, Annie Leigh-Mallory to David Pye (strong objections to using George's letters in the biography, 1924)

Letters from Ruth Mallory to Franz Knefel, (Marianne Nevel, Private collection)

Old Rendcomb Newsletter, 20 May 1994 issue – editor W.J.D. White, p.11, tributes by Peter Wyon and David Haes

The Carthusian, October 1920, p.18 'Debating Society, 25 September 7.45 pm, 'That this House deplores the recent extension of our Imperial responsibilities.'

## Select Bibliography
Anhalzer, Jorge, Juan, *Guide for Mountain Climbers of Cotopaxi* publisher unknown), Ecuador, (date of publication unknown)

Andrews, Arthur Westlake and Pyatt, E.C., *Climbing Guide to Cornwall*, The Climbers' Club, UK, 1950

Alvarez, Al, *Feeding the Rat: Profile of a Climber*, Bloomsbury Publishing, London, 1988

Arnold-Forster, Mark, *The World at War (revised edition)*, Pimlico, UK, 2001

Baden-Powell, Olave, *Window on my Heart*, Hodder & Stoughton, London, 1973

Band, George, *Everest Exposed*, Harper Collins, London, 2005

Baden-Powell, Robert and Baden-Powell, Agnes, *How Girls Can Help to Build Up the Empire: The Handbook for Girl Guides*, (Girl Guides), Thomas Nelson and Sons, UK, 1912

Batten, Lindsey W., *The Single-Handed Mother*, George Allen & Unwin, London, 1939

Bonington, Chris, *I Chose to Climb*, Victor Gollancz, London, 1991 (first published 1966)

Bridge, Ann, *Facts and Fictions: Facts and Fictions: Some Literary Recollections*, Chatto & Windus, London, 1968

Bridge, Ann, *Moments of Knowing: Some Personal Experiences Beyond Normal Knowledge*, Hodder & Stoughton, London, 1970

Bridges, Robert, *The Spirit of Man*, Longmans, Green and Co., London, 1916

Clennett, Margaret, *Presumptuous Pinnacle Ladies: A Selection from the Early Journals of England's First Women's Rock Climbing Club*, Millrace, UK, 2009 (Article that appears on p.56, Chapter 6, 'Our Founder' is unattributed' but thought to be by Eleanor Winthrop Young.)

Clutton-Brock, Arthur, *The Cure for War*, Oxford University Press, Oxford, 1915

Clutton-Brock Arthur, *William Morris: His Work and Influence*, Williams and Norgate, London, 1914 (first published January 1914 and recently republished as an e-book, Parkstone International, New York, USA, 2015 and as hardback and paperback editions, Parkstone Press USA, Limited, USA, 2018)

Cobden-Sanderson, Stella, *A Letter from Stella: An Epilogue to the Publication of C–S The Master Craftsman*, Adagio Press, USA, 1968 (printed by Leonard F. Bahr during the early winter of 1970–1971 at his subterranean private press Adagio, 19972 Lochmoor Drive, Harper Woods, Michigan, 48225, USA. As usual, the type was set by hand and then printed one page at a time on a hand-fed C&P Craftsman. Author's limited edition copy is number 431.)

Cobden-Sanderson, Thomas, *The Journals of Thomas James Cobden-Sanderson 1879–1922*, Volumes I and II, Burt Franklin, New York, USA, 1926

Coffey, Maria, *Fragile Edge: Loss on Everest*, Arrow Books, London, 2003

Dalai Lama, *My Land and My People: Memoirs of the Dalai Lama of Tibet*, Potala Corporation, New York, USA, 1977

Davis, Wade, *Into the Silence: The Great War, Mallory and the Conquest of Everest*, Vintage Books, London, 2012 (first published by The Bodley Head, UK, 2011 and © Wade Davis)

Edwards, Elizabeth, *Women in Teacher Training Colleges, 1900–1960*, Routledge, Abingdon, 2000

Elliot, Margaret, *Prior's Field School: A Century Remembered, 1902–2002*, Prior's Field School Trust Limited, Guildford, 1988

Emmerson, Charles, *Crucible: The Long End of the Great War and the Birth of a New World, 1917–1924*, Vintage Books, London, 2020

Festing, Sally, *Gertrude Jekyll*, Penguin, London, 1991

Forster, E.M., *A Room with a View*, Edward Arnold, London, 1908

French, Patrick, *Younghusband: The Last Great Imperial Adventurer*, Flamingo, an imprint of Harper Collins, London, 1994

Fyffe, Allen and Peter, Iain, *The Handbook of Climbing*, Pelham Books, The Penguin Group, London, 1990

Gillman Peter and Gillman, Leni, *The Wildest Dream: George Mallory – The Biography of an Everest Hero*, Headline, London, 2000

Graves, Robert, *Goodbye to All That*, Jonathan Cape, UK, 1929

Green, Dudley, *Because It's There: The Life of George Mallory*, Tempus Publishing, UK, 2005

Grigor-Taylor, Barbara, *Everest by 'Those Who Were There': 1921, 1922, 1924*, Alpine Club, London, 2022

Haig-Brown, Hilda, various books in the Heritage Story Books series, Longmans, Green and Co., London

Hankinson, Alan, *Geoffrey Winthrop Young: Poet, Mountaineer, Educator*, Hodder & Stoughton, London, 1995

Hargreaves, Alison, *A Hard Day's Summer: Six Classic North Faces Solo*, Hodder & Stoughton, London, 1994

Hemmleb Jochen, Simonson, Eric R. and Hahn, Dave, *Detectives on Everest: The 2001 Mallory and Irvine Research Expedition*, The Mountaineers Books, Seattle, Washington, USA, 2002

Hemmleb, Jochen, *Ghosts of Everest: The Authorised Story of the Search for Mallory & Irvine*, MacMillan, London, 1999 (first published by The Mountaineers Books, Seattle, Washington, USA, 1999)

Hoyland, Graham, *Last Hours on Everest: The Gripping Story of Mallory & Irvine's Fatal Ascent*, William Collins, London, 2013

Hunt, John, *The Ascent of Everest*, Hodder & Stoughton, London, 1953

Janaway, John, *Godalming: A Short History*, Local Heritage Books, UK, 1983

Jones, Owen Glynne, *Rock Climbing in the English Lake District*, Longmans Green and Co., London, 1897

Keay, John, *The Great Arc: The Dramatic Tale of How India was Mapped and Everest was Named*, Harper Collins, London, 2001 (first published 2000)

Kelly H.M., *Pillar Rock and Neighbouring Climbs: A Climber's Guide*, Fell & Rock Club of the English Lake District (second in the series of FRCC guides started in 1922 which continue to this day)

Kent, Susan Kingsley, *Sex and Suffrage in Britain, 1860–1914*, Routledge, Abingdon, 1987 (first published by Princeton University Press, New Jersey, USA, 1987)

Keynes, Geoffrey, *The Gates of Memory*, Oxford University Press, Oxford, 1983 (first published by Clarendon Press, Oxford, 1981)

Lago, Mary, *Christiana Herringham and the Edwardian Art Scene*, Lund Humphries, UK, 1996

Laslett, Peter, *The World We Have Lost*, Methuen & Co. Ltd., London, 1965

Levi, Jan, *And Nobody Woke up Dead: The Life & Times of Mabel Barker –Climber & Educational Pioneer*, The Ernest Press, UK, 2006

Lister, Anna, Marsh, Jenny and Mason, Jan, *May Morris: Arts and Crafts Designer*, Thames & Hudson, UK, 2017

Lodge, Sir Oliver, *Raymond, or Life and Death: With Examples of the Evidence for Survival of Memory and Affection after Death*, Doran, 1916

MacFarlane, Robert, *Mountains of the Mind: A History of a Fascination*, Granta Books, UK, 2003

Mallory, George, *Boswell the Biography with a Portrait*, Smith, Elder & Co., UK, 1912 (Author's reference source: print on demand edition – printed in Great Britain by Amazon)

Mallory, George, Introduction by Gillman, Peter, *Climbing Everest: The Complete Writings of George Mallory*, Gibson Square Books, London, 2012 (first published 2010)

Maurois, André, *Ariel: The Life of Shelley*, (original publisher unknown – since reprinted by Kessinger Pub Co., USA), 1924

Morris, William, Preface for Arts and Crafts Essays by Members of the Arts and Crafts Exhibition Society, Rivington, Percival & Co, London, 1893 (p.134 'Book Binding' by T.J. Cobden-Sanderson; p.355 'Of Modern Embroidery' by Mary E. Turner)

Mort, Helen, A *Line Above the Sky: A Story of Mountains and Motherhood*, Ebury Press, an imprint of Ebury Publishing, Penguin Random House, London, 2022

Murray, Gilbert, *Satanism and the World Order*, George Allen & Unwin, London, 1920

Musson, Jeremy, 'Westbrook, Surrey, The Home of Mrs Francis Brown', *Country Life*, Future Plc, 16 July 1998

Nicholson, Virginia, *Singled Out: How Two Million Women Survived without Men after the First World War*, Viking Books, an imprint of Penguin, London, 2007

Noel, Sandra, foreword by Blessed, Brian, *Everest Pioneer: The Photographs of Captain John Noel*, The History Press, Cheltenham, 2003

Norgay, Jamling Tenzing, with Coburn, Broughton, *Touching my Father's Soul: A Sherpa's Journey to the Top of Everest*, Harper Collins, London, 2001

Norton E.F., *The Fight for Everest 1924*, Edward Arnold & Co., London, 1925 (also recently republished as a new edition with a foreword by Doug Scott CBE, Vertebrate Publishing, Sheffield, 2015)

Parker, Rozsika, *Subversive Stitch: Embroidery and the Making of the Feminine*, Bloomsbury Publishing, London, 2010

Peacock, Charlotte, *Into the Mountain: A Life of Nan Shepherd*, Galileo Publishers, Cambridge, 2017

Pedersen, Susan, *The Guardians: The League of Nations and the Crisis of Empire*, Oxford University Press, USA, 2015

Pilley Dorothy, *Climbing Days*, George Bell & Sons, UK, 1935

Pye, David, *George Leigh Mallory: A Memoir*, Oxford University Press, Oxford, 1927 (Author's reference source: edition with Foreword by Mallory II, George, Introduction by Pye, Tristram, Orchid Press, Bangkok, Thailand, 2002)

Quennell, Marjorie and Quennell, Charles Henry Bourne, *A History of Everyday Things in England, 1066–1499*, Batsford, UK, 1918 (Quennell, Marjorie and Quennell, Charles Henry Bourne, A History of Everyday Things in England series of three further history books for children written between 1918 and 1934)

Raverat, Gwen, *Period Piece: A Cambridge Childhood*, Faber and Faber, London, 1952

Richards, Dan, *Climbing Days*, Faber and Faber, London, 2016

Robertson, David, *George Mallory*, Faber and Faber, London, 1969

Rose, David and Douglas, Ed, *Regions of the Heart: The Triumph and Tragedy of Alison Hargreaves*, Michael Joseph, London, 1999

Salkeld, Audrey and Breashears, David, *Last Climb: The Legendary Everest Expeditions of George Mallory*, National Geographic Books, USA, 1999

Salkeld, Audrey, 'Kelly, (Martha) Emily (1873–1922)' *Oxford Dictionary of National Biography*, Oxford University Press, Oxford, 2004

Salkeld, Audrey and Holzel, Tom, Afterword by Winterson, Jeanette, *The Mystery of Mallory & Irvine*, The Mountaineers Books, Seattle, Washington, USA, 1986

Shepherd, Nan, Introduction by Macfarlane, Robert, *The Living Mountain*, Canongate Books, Edinburgh, 2014 (first published by Aberdeen University Press, Aberdeen, 1977)

Strachey, Lytton, *Eminent Victorians*, Chatto & Windus, London, 1918

Summers, Julie, *Fearless on Everest: The Quest for Sandy Irvine*, Weidenfeld & Nicolson, London, 2000

Symons, Alison, *Tremedda Days: A View of Zennor, 1900–1944*, Tabb House, UK, 1922

Thackeray-Turner, Hugh, *Notes on the Repair of Ancient Buildings*, Society for the Protection of Ancient Buildings, UK, 1903

Tosh, John, *A Man's Place: Masculinity and the Middle-Class Home in Victorian England*, Yale University Press, New Haven, Connecticut, USA, 2007

Unsworth, Walt, *Everest*, Oxford Illustrated Press Limited, Oxford, 1989

Wheeler, Sara, *Terra Incognita: Travels in Antarctica*, Jonathan Cape Limited, London, 1996

Whymper, Edward, *Scrambles Amongst the Alps*, John Murray, UK, 1871

Whymper, Edward, *Travels Amongst the Great Andes of the Equator*, John Murray, UK, 1892

Wilson, A.N., *After the Victorians: The Word Our Parents Knew*, Arrow Books, London, 2006

Winthrop Young Geoffrey, *Mountain Craft*, Methuen & Co. Ltd., London, 1920

Winthrop Young, Geoffrey and Sutton, Geoffrey, edited by Noyce, Wilfred, *Snowdon Biography*, Dent & Sons, UK, 1957

Winthrop Young, Geoffrey and Winthrop Young, Eleanor, *In Praise of Mountains*: An Anthology for Friends, Frederick Muller, UK, 1948

Woolf, Virginia, edited by Bell, Anne Olivier, *The Diary of Virginia Woolf: Volume 2 – 1920–1924*, Harvest Books, an imprint of Harcourt Brace Jovanovich, USA, 1978

Woolf, Virginia, *The Symbol*, London Review of Books, Volume 7, Number 11, (publisher unknown), 20 June 1985

Woolf, Virginia and Bell, Vanessa, edited by Dell, Marion and Whybrow, Marion, *Remembering St Ives*, Tabb House, UK, 2003

Younghusband, Francis, *The Epic of Mount Everest*, Edward Arnold & Co., London, 1926

# Index

## Notes

Ruth was christened Christiana Ruth Turner but, like many of those in the index, was known by her second name.

George Mallory, born on 18 June 1886 was given the Christian names George Herbert Leigh. It was not until 1914 that his father adopted by Royal Licence the surname of Leigh-Mallory. Generally, except for official documents like marriage certificates, George and Ruth used the surname Mallory rather than Leigh-Mallory but Trafford, George's younger brother, generally used the hyphenated surname. In the index those with the surname Mallory are found under 'M'. The letters GM are used in the index to indicate George Mallory.

Franz Knefel, born Frantisek Binowetz Knefel, changed his name to Francis 'Frank' Nevel during the Second World War so that when he married Marianne after the war, she became Marianne Nevel. They had five children. Franz is indexed under his original surname.

There are two Geoffreys, Geoffrey Winthrop Young and Geoffrey Keynes. In the index and the book, 'Geoffrey' refers to the former. The latter is always written with his surname.

Frank Smythe confirmed his initial 1933 suspicions in 1936 writing to Teddy Norton that he had seen what may have been a body but that: 'It's not to be written about as the press would make an unpleasant sensation.'

Some accounts say that it was John Noel to whom Ruth said that she had 'spent the night with George' after George's death in 1924, but John Mallory maintained it was Noel Odell.

Dear Reader,

We hope you have enjoyed this book, but why not share your views on social media? You can also follow our pages to see more about our other products: facebook.com/penandswordbooks or follow us on Twitter @penswordbooks

You can also view our products at www.pen-and-sword.co.uk (UK and ROW) or www.penandswordbooks.com (North America).

To keep up to date with our latest releases and online catalogues, please sign up to our newsletter at: www.pen-and-sword.co.uk/newsletter

If you would like a printed catalogue with our latest books, then please email: enquiries@pen-and-sword.co.uk or telephone: 01226 734555 (UK and ROW) or email: uspen-and-sword@casematepublishers.com or telephone: (610) 853-9131 (North America).

We respect your privacy and we will only use personal information to send you information about our products.

Thank you!